The 2011 Libyan Uprisings and the Struggle for the Post-Qadhafi Future

The 2011 Libyan Uprisings and the Struggle for the Post-Qadhafi Future

Edited by

Jason Pack

First published in 2013 by
PALGRAVE MACMILLAN®
in the United States—a division of St. Martin's Press LLC,
175 Fifth Avenue, New York, NY 10010.

Where this book is distributed in the UK, Europe and the rest of the world,
this is by Palgrave Macmillan, a division of Macmillan Publishers Limited,
registered in England, company number 785998, of Houndmills,
Basingstoke, Hampshire RG21 6XS.

Palgrave Macmillan is the global academic imprint of the above companies
and has companies and representatives throughout the world.

Palgrave® and Macmillan® are registered trademarks in the United States,
the United Kingdom, Europe and other countries.

ISBN: 978–1–137–30808–5

Library of Congress Cataloging-in-Publication Data is available from the
Library of Congress.

A catalogue record of the book is available from the British Library.

Design by Newgen Imaging Systems (P) Ltd., Chennai, India.

First edition: June 2013

10 9 8 7 6 5 4 3 2 1

CONTENTS

CONTRIBUTORS

Jason Pack, the editor of this volume, is a researcher of Middle Eastern History at the University of Cambridge and president of Libya-Analysis.com. He has spent the majority of the last decade living, working, and studying in Morocco, Libya, Egypt, Lebanon, Jordan, Iraq, Oman, and other Middle Eastern countries, as well as being a Fulbright Fellow in Syria in 2004–05. His articles have appeared in *The New York Times*, *The Wall Street Journal*, *Politico*, *The Spectator*, *The Guardian*, and *Foreign Policy*. Since 2008, he has worked in Tripoli, Washington, and London promoting academic, commercial, and diplomatic exchanges between Libya and the West. He has addressed the House of Commons about the struggle between Libya's new central government and the militias. He holds an MSt in Global and Imperial History from St Antony's College, Oxford University.

Lisa Anderson is president of the American University in Cairo (AUC). She is Dean Emerita of the School of International and Public Affairs at Columbia University. Among her many publications are *The State and Social Transformation in Tunisia and Libya, 1830–1980* (1986) and *Pursuing Truth, Exercising Power: Social Science and Public Policy in the Twenty-First Century* (2003). She has served on the board of Human Rights Watch and as president of the Middle East Studies Association (MESA). She is also a member of the Council on Foreign Relations (CFR).

George Joffé lectures and supervises on the international relations of the Middle East and North Africa at the Department of Politics and International Studies (POLIS) at the University of Cambridge. He is also a professorial fellow at King's College, London, and at the Royal United Services Institute (RUSI) in London. Previously he was the deputy director of the Royal Institute of International Affairs (Chatham House) in London. He is the author or editor of more than ten books including *Islamist Radicalisation in North Africa: Politics and Process* (2011); *North Africa: Nation, State and Region* (1993); and *Social & Economic Development of Libya* (1981).

Youssef Mohammed Sawani is the acting director for the Centre of Arab Unity Studies in Beirut and professor of Political Science at the University of Tripoli, Libya. He is the editor-in-chief of *Al-Mostaqbal Al-Arabi* and author of numerous scholarly publications in Arabic and English—his most recent include "The 'End of Pan-Arabism' Revisited: Reflections on the Arab Spring," *Contemporary Arab Affairs* 5(3), (2012) and *Revolution and Democratic Transition in the Arab World: A Road Map* (2012).

Ronald Bruce St John is an independent scholar who has served on the International Advisory Board of *The Journal of Libyan Studies* and The Atlantic Council Working Group on Libya. He is author of more than 15 books including *Libya: From Colony to Revolution*, second edition (2012); *Libya: Continuity and Change* (2011); *The Historical Dictionary of Libya*, fourth edition (2006); and *Libya and the United States: Two Centuries of Strife* (2002).

Richard Northern M.B.E. is the director of RN4 Consultancy, which advises businesses on the Middle East and Africa. He is also a senior consultant to International Hospitals Group, a British health-care company. For 35 years, he was a British diplomat. An Arabist by training, he served in Lebanon, Saudi Arabia, Italy, and Canada before being appointed Her Majesty's Ambassador to Libya from May 2010 to August 2011.

Wolfram Lacher has been a researcher at the German Institute for International and Security Affairs (*Stiftung Wissenschaft und Politik*, SWP) in Berlin since 2010. From 2007 to 2010, he worked in London as a North Africa analyst at Control Risks. He has studied Arabic and International Relations at Leipzig University, the *Institut National des Langues et Civilisations Orientales* in Paris, AUC, and the School of Oriental and African Studies in London (SOAS).

Henry Smith is a Middle East and North Africa analyst at Control Risks. He analyzes political and security developments, with a particular focus on North Africa. He has been traveling to Libya regularly since 2010. He studied Arabic and Middle Eastern politics at the University of York and SOAS.

James Brandon is an associate fellow at the International Centre for the Study of Radicalisation and Political Violence (ICSR) at King's College, London. Between 2008 and 2011, he was the director of Research and Communications at the Quilliam Foundation, a counterextremism think tank in London.

Noman Benotman is a former commander of the Libyan Islamic Fighting Group (LIFG). At al-Qaeda strategy meetings in Kandahar in 2000, Benotman warned the al-Qaeda leadership of their "total failure" to realize their aims and called on Osama bin Laden and Ayman al-Zawahiri to abandon violence. Soon after the 9/11 attacks, he distanced himself from al-Qaeda and later resigned from the LIFG. He is currently the president of the Quilliam Foundation. He is also a cofounder of the Libyan Human and Political Development Forum. In 2010, he was awarded honorary alumni status at the Near East and South Asia Center for Strategic Studies at the National Defense University in Washington, DC.

ACKNOWLEDGMENTS

Editing a book is a bit like assembling and leading a scientific expedition to chart an unexplored Antarctic mountain range. To make the team fit the task, each member needs to have his or her own unique expertise, experience, and capabilities, while also being personally driven to reach the common goal. The first questions for the editor are, therefore, not dissimilar to those of the expedition leader. First, the ideal route of approach must be selected given the topography. And then instead of deciding between bringing a seismic geologist or a cartographer, the volume editor chooses between an oil economist or a specialist on social media. Ideally, one would have both—and many other specialists as well. However, practical constraints and word limits make that impossible. Tough choices are inevitable.

Then there is the question of setting the pace that will assure that the team arrives at the mountaintop in unison. Some edited volumes allow large leeway for different kinds of contributions that do not necessarily engage directly with one another or attempt to form a coherent whole. My preference as a reader has always been for tightly edited and narrowly focused volumes, in which all the chapters contribute a different perspective but paint one cohesive picture. Dirk Vandewalle of Dartmouth College merits a special mention because his edited volume *Libya Since 1969: Qadhafi's Revolution Revisited*, published in 2008 by Palgrave Macmillan, is the inspiration of this work and will always remain the go-to reference for unlocking the dynamics of Qadhafi's détente with the West. Although I knew it would be impossible to match the elegance of Vandewalle's prose or the depth of his knowledge of Libya, I used his book as a template—attempting to adapt its structures and conventions to this volume's treatment of the events of 2011 and 2012.

I have been very fortunate to assemble a highly talented team with just the right range of skills and on-the-ground experience to flesh out a very particular thesis about the 2011 Libyan uprisings. They earned my immense respect for their patience in processing countless drafts of my edits and for producing insightful and original scholarship under grueling deadlines.

* * *

The process of editing a book inherently causes the editor to build up many debts of gratitude. It appears that the extent of debt accumulation is further compounded when it is the editor's first book. In fact, in my case, although the central principle that ties together this volume is my own, I have received much sage advice from many corners about the practicalities and conventions that govern the production of an academic edited volume. Due to space constraints, I can only thank a few of those people who have been very helpful and inspirational during the process.

Firstly, I'd like to thank Michael Dwyer of Hurst & Co. for his introduction to the fast-paced world of publishing and for his encouragement in March 2012 that my ideas were a sound and novel basis around which to organize a book. Next, I'd like to thank David Pollack and Mary Horan of the Washington Institute for Near East Policy, who in February 2012 published the Policy Focus report *In War's Wake: The Struggle for Post-Qadhafi Libya*, which I coauthored with Barak Barfi. Writing that report gave me the opportunity to flesh out many of the ideas from which this volume derives. David and Mary merit extra thanks for granting me the permission to use some excerpts from that report in this volume. Crucially, this volume would not have seen the light of day without Sara Doskow and Farideh Koohi-Kamali of Palgrave Macmillan who have been a constant pleasure to work with and have generously lent their expert advice about how to bring this volume to fruition.

I owe a large debt of gratitude to George Joffé for his constant support, his lightning-quick responses to my e-mails, and his many insights into the continuities of Libyan history. Sir Christopher Bayly and Philip Oliver—both of St Catharine's College, Cambridge— have been exceedingly generous with their time, experience, and wit. Many thanks to James Roslington for his efforts in suggesting ways to buttress the text with sound academic argumentation and clear flows of logic. Alison Pargeter and Alia Brahimi provided invaluable feedback about the role of the Islamists during the uprisings. Brian Whitaker, former Middle East editor at *The Guardian,* offered insightful comments about the role of Libya within the larger phenomenon of the Arab Spring. Michael Athanson, deputy map librarian and geo-spatial data specialist at the Bodleian Library at Oxford

University, was exceedingly gracious with his time and expertise in collaborating with me on preparing the maps for this volume. Jennifer Segal generously volunteered her artistic genius to synthesize several key aspects of the iconography of the new Libya. Her impressive cover artwork *Omar Mukhtar's Legacy and the 2011 Libyan Uprisings* is comprised of a pen and paper pointalist rendering of the Libyan national hero, set against a digitally illustrated map of the new Libya draped in the flag of the uprisings. Anja Wollenberg of Media in Cooperation and Transition (MICT) contributed much to refining my thinking about the novel features of post-Qadhafi media. Our article in the March 2013 edition of *The Journal of North African Studies*, Volume 18, Issue 2, "Rebels with a Pen: Observations on a Newly Emerging Media Landscape in Libya" is a useful overview for those interested in the evolution of the role of media in the new Libya.

Special acknowledgments are owed to Haley Cook for her vast expertise on contemporary Libya and her boundless generosity in sharing it. It is no exaggeration to say that she is possibly the most knowledgeable person about the day-to-day minutiae of the 2011 Libyan uprisings who was not physically there while the fighting was taking place. Our forthcoming "The July 2012 Libyan Elections: Appeasement, Localism, and the Struggle for the Post-Qadhafi Future" (Contemporary Arab Affairs Forthcoming) provides a comprehensive analysis of the lead-up to the elections, their conduct, and their implications for the constitutional process in Libya.

I'd also like to thank my former bosses at the U.S.-Libya Business Association, Chuck Dittrich, Bill Reinsch, and Ambassador David Mack, who guided me into the intricacies of how Washington formulates its policy toward Libya. They—along with Joshua Landis and my former professors David Richardson, David Edwards, and Martin Van Creveld—will remain trusted friends and inspirational mentors. Furthermore, this volume could not have been written without the constant sacrifices of my loving parents, Fred and Sandy, who have always gone the extra mile to help me surmount the obstacles in my path. Fred, in particular, has been an invaluable last-second proofreader and punctuation wizard.

* * *

Rarely do academics admit that they have learned a lot from and been inspired by diplomats. But the late US Ambassador to Libya J. Christopher Stevens was a role model of how foreign scholars, diplomats, and businesspeople should interact with Libya: in a culturally sensitive way seeking to forge connections with Libyans of all stripes and to understand the country on its own terms.

Chris Stevens was in Benghazi early on in the uprisings as special envoy to the National Transitional Council, and in this role he was America's eyes and ears on the ground. He forged meaningful personal relationships with the evolving rebel leadership, as well as with many other Libyans. He sought to help the Libyan people rebuild their nation. He believed that Western engagement in the 2011 Libyan uprisings was a moral and humanitarian necessity but that the uprisings must always be genuinely Libyan-led. All those who knew him deeply mourn his tragic passing—and in spite of the huge blow his death dealt to Libya's transition—we cling to his belief that the citizens and leadership of post-Qadhafi Libya can successfully tackle the country's internal divisions and the difficult inheritance of the Qadhafi years. Western policy makers, businessmen, and academics should not use Ambassador Stevens's assassination and the resulting fears about the security situation as an excuse to abandon Libya; they should embrace his legacy of active engagement. It is to Ambassador Stevens that this volume is dedicated.

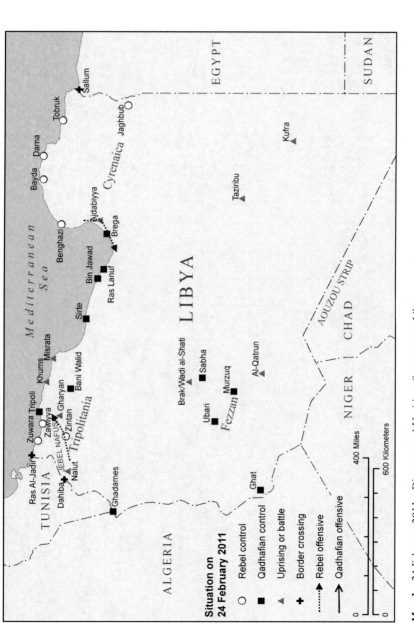

Map 1 24 February 2011—Disconnected Uprisings Sweep across Libya.

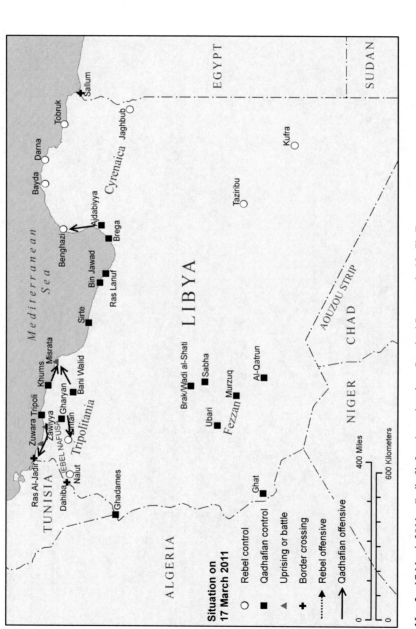

Map 2 17 March 2011—Qadhafi's Imminent Attack on Benghazi Prompts the No-Fly Zone.

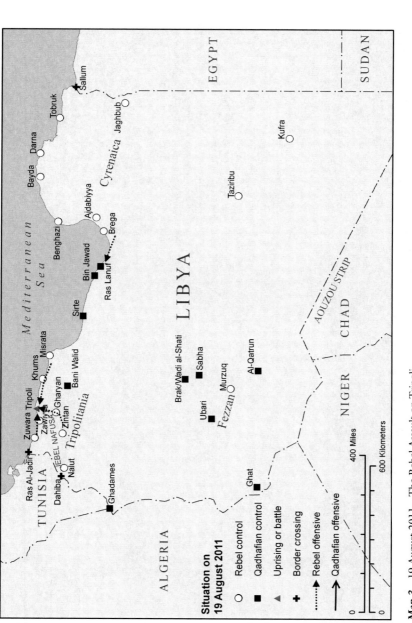

Map 3 19 August 2011—The Rebel Assault on Tripoli.

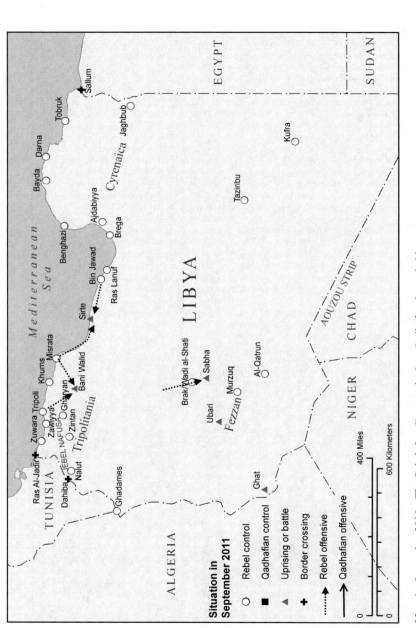

Map 4 September 2011—The Rebels Lay Siege to the Last Qadhafian Strongholds.

Introduction

THE CENTER AND THE PERIPHERY

Jason Pack

The political upheavals that began in Tunisia in December 2010 and then spread to other Arab countries exhibited certain features, which made them fairly unique. The extent to which they were bottom-up, leaderless, and devoid of an overarching ideology truly differentiates them from the French (1789), European (1848), Russian (1917), Iranian (1979), and Eastern European (1989) revolutions—with which they otherwise share certain similarities.

These unique features of the Arab Spring[1] movements were only possible because twenty-first-century communications technology allowed for spontaneous mass popular organization to occur without the mediation of "charismatic leaders," organizational hierarchies, or political parties. It also allowed regime brutality against unarmed civilians to be captured and instantaneously broadcast via social networks and satellite television across the world. Furthermore, it allowed the oppressed citizens of dictatorships to communicate in real time with their unseen allies in the Arab diaspora, the Gulf, interested Western governments, human rights groups, and media organizations.

This unprecedented ease of communication and the inability of even the most repressive regimes to fully hinder it allowed leaderless, ideology-free, and grassroots uprisings to overthrow some of the most entrenched authoritarian regimes in the world. As a result, in every Arab Spring country, it was very clear what the populace was rebelling *against* but highly unclear what they were rebelling *for*—or who could lead them after the successful toppling of the ancien régime. Consequently, this book prefers the term "uprisings" in place of "revolutions" when referring to all of the Arab Spring movements. Both terms imply a complete rejection of the old order and a spontaneous rebellion against it, but "revolution" tends to imply the creation of a new power structure buttressed by an alternative ideological framework, while "uprising" is a more ambivalent term, suggesting an upheaval that does not necessarily have clear goals or a defined leadership.[2]

* * *

Despite the novelty of the 2011 Arab uprisings, comparisons to other historical revolutions are instructive in categorizing their essential features. As in 1848 and 1989, each of the Arab uprisings was profoundly national despite happening in neighboring countries virtually sequentially, responding to similar social grievances, and espousing parallel aims. The existence of separatist movements in Yemen and Cyrenaica (eastern Libya) merely provide the exceptions which prove the rule.

More importantly, the lack of an overarching pan-Arab or pan-Islamic character to the Arab Spring movements crucially explains why even actors with supranational ideologies and organizations, such as different Islamist currents, did not tend to use their newfound positions of power after the upheaval to advocate for increased internationalism. The zeitgeist of the Arab Spring was "nation-focused," therefore, internationalist movements like the Muslim Brotherhood responded to it by largely abandoning their regional and supranational rhetoric to become deeply intertwined in the national political life of each country.[3] Moreover, the course of events in 2011 demonstrated that, by the start of the twenty-first century, political Arab Nationalism was long dead and that the nation-state had been progressively enshrined as the supreme forum for Arab politics since World War I.

This "national bias" was evident in Libya. As citizens of a highly artificial colonial amalgamation of three provinces (Tripolitania, Cyrenaica, and Fezzan) with markedly different histories and orientations, Libya's revolutionaries might have put forth primarily regional grievances. Thus, in the early days of the Libyan uprisings, it was unclear if one was witnessing an anti-Qadhafi Cyrenaican revolt, which had sympathizers and imitators in certain cities across western Libya, or a genuinely national movement. Yet it soon became clear that the vast majority of rebels sought to remake the Libyan nation-state—not to abandon it. Yes, the rebels preached the complete overthrow of the Qadhafi regime and the ensuing decentralization of power, but the notion of dismantling the Libyan state was anathema to most and stigmatized as treason. In short, although Libya witnessed a multiplicity of local uprisings, only a tiny fraction of the anti-Qadhafi partisans espoused either subnational (regional) or supranational solutions. The regionalists—dubbed federalists in the Libyan discourse—were initially so stigmatized for being a threat to national unity that all other competing political factions essentially closed ranks against them.[4] Furthermore, groups with a previously international agenda—like certain Islamists—chose to put forth a purely Libyan agenda so as to participate in the main currents of post-Qadhafi political life.

As in 1789, 1917, and 1979, the Arab uprisings initially exhibited a tendency to be supported by broad swaths of the population working together and transcending previous fissures, while only later did elements advocating for the most radical change inevitably flex their own muscles. We could term this "the Jacobin tendency." In Libya, this historical tendency can be seen as the marginalization of the "moderates" of the National Transitional Council, by the "Jacobins" of the local and regional militias in the wake of Qadhafi's ouster. In the early days of the uprisings, having served as a reformist technocrat under Qadhafi was not a disqualification for holding rebel leadership positions, yet increasingly after Qadhafi's fall, the diehard Jacobins—usually militiamen—set out to purge all state institutions and to control official rhetoric to force them to conform to their interpretation of the "ideals of the revolution."

As in 1789 and 1917, revolutions have a tendency to spawn geographically localized counterrevolutions. This could be termed "the Vendée phenomenon." Bani Walid, the hilltop center of the Warfalla tribe, embodied this principle. Although only a small proportion of its inhabitants were connected to high-ranking officials in the Qadhafi regime, the whole town became synonymous with opposition to the new Libyan authorities long after Qadhafi's death as his former loyalists or other persons persecuted by the new order flocked to the town. Although most of Bani Walid's antigovernment fighters were not actually pro-Qadhafi or seeking some sort of "restoration," they did harbor deep-seated grievances against the new order that had blocked their participation in national life. As of the beginning of 2013, Bani Walid had not yet been fully subdued and subsumed into the new order. Similarly to events in the Vendée in 1793, in Bani Walid local, ideological, religious, and tribal cleavages grafted on top of one another exacerbating previous societal fissures that lay underneath the surface of the ancien régime.

Lastly, as in 1789, 1917, 1979, and 1989, one explanation of the timing of the collapse of the ancien régimes was as a direct response to their attempts to open up their rigid economic and social systems and gradually grant their repressed people more freedom. Louis XVI attempted to reform France's tax collection and administrative bureaucracy; to create legitimacy for this action, he convened the

Estates General.⁵ Nicholas II was eventually toppled, not primarily by the proximal cause of the hardships of World War I, but rather because in 1905 he conceded to the protestors' demands for a Duma allowing a flourishing of political discourse and increasingly public signs of discontent.⁶ In Iran, the Shah's opening up of political space to dissenting voices throughout the 1970s as well as his concessions to Shi'i clerics and civil rights groups clearly facilitated his demise.⁷ Similarly, without perestroika and glasnost, the Soviet Union would likely have taken decades more to collapse.⁸ In each instance, the attempted reforms were deemed too gradual to alleviate concrete discontent, while simultaneously they undermined any ideological consistency or legitimacy that existed in the old order. Most critically, they fostered increased openness and political discussion, allowing for the uncontrolled spread of information, which in turn facilitated organization against the old order.

It should therefore be unsurprising that half-hearted attempts by Mubarak, Ben Ali, and Qadhafi to abandon the hegemonic domination of the public sphere by the regime and to replace older forms of "genuine" Arab Nationalist socialism with bits and pieces of Washington Consensus economic policies facilitated their overthrow. Although these *infitahs* (limited market-based reforms) may have brought more resources into the regime coffers, they emptied the old regimes of any vestige of ideological legitimacy or consistency while creating dangerous new avenues for the populace to access information. Into the ideological vacuum, markets facilitated the flow of not only goods but also new ideas and increased expectations.

In North Africa, each country progressively adopted the rhetoric and the trappings of free markets, human rights, and democracy, but did so in a way that perverted those ideals and actually changed little in the lives of the people. Yet in this process, genuine hopes for political reform, freedom of speech, and human dignity were raised. There was and could be no "Arab Spring" in the North Korea of Kim Jong-Il, the USSR of Stalin, or Qadhafi's Libya of the 1980s. Their repressions were simply too comprehensive and information about the true state of the country could not be obtained by a sufficient number of citizens.

This "glasnost" syndrome is crucial for the understanding of Libya. The reform processes and concomitant détente with the West from 2003 to 2010 spawned an influx of foreign capital, satellite dishes, the return of educated diaspora Libyans, and a vast rise in the standards of living among the urban middle classes. In their wake came an even greater rise in expectations, connections to the outside world, hopes for a better life for unemployed educated young men, and covert civil organizations. It also led to new forms of corruption and a rough-and-tumble "make hay while the sun shines" approach, especially among Qadhafi's children, which made a mockery of Qadhafi's ideology of the *Jamahiriyya* (massocracy) form of governance. Nowhere else in the Arab World was the discourse of human rights and market-based reforms more cynically bandied about as window dressing than in Libya, and nowhere else did the flirtation with the West, so dramatically showcase the brutality, incompetence, and opportunism of the state. Attempts to bring privatization and a modicum of transparency to the Qadhafian economy merely removed the veil revealing that the Libyan state was a kleptocracy administered by a dysfunctional and erratic family. Without Libya's turn to the West and the simultaneous pseudo-reform process, Muammar Qadhafi himself would likely have held on until his natural death.[9]

* * *

Among the Arab Spring movements, the 2011 Libyan uprisings stand alone for the extent of real change they inaugurated, for the role of outside powers in facilitating their success while not perverting their internal dynamics, and for the power amassed by spontaneous local and regional organizations based outside Tripoli and Benghazi. Only in Libya did the "periphery" conquer the "center."

The eight-month-long Libyan uprisings that began on 15 February 2011 (though popularly known as the 17 February revolution) and culminated in the 20 October capture of Sirte and the death of Muammar Qadhafi on the same day are best understood as waves of separate yet loosely connected anti-Qadhafi uprisings. They differed from the Arab Spring movements in Egypt and Tunisia by arising in and being dominated by the periphery.

The ancien régimes in Tunisia and Egypt possessed strong societal institutions, such as trade unions, national conscription army, civil society, *ulama*, and urban intelligentsias, while Qadhafi's Libya did not. In Egypt and Tunisia, these preexisting social institutions were galvanized by the popular uprisings of the youth and quickly swung over en masse to supporting the rebellion or at the very least refusing to oppose it. Analogous to the storming of the Bastille, which was facilitated by the desertion of the Parisian garrison of the French Guards,[10] the army's complicity in allowing the protestors to occupy symbolic locations in Tunis and Cairo quickly led to the collapse of the legitimacy of the ancien régimes. Faced with a bureaucracy and army no longer loyal to their autocrats, the Egyptian and Tunisian regimes were toppled by a swift decapitation at the center. In this way those uprisings were akin to a popular-led military coup and entirely dissimilar to a low-intensity civil war or asymmetrical insurgency, such as unfolded in Syria starting in 2011. In a manner similar to most successful military coups, especially relatively bloodless ones, the power of the Egyptian and Tunisian states were left largely intact. They remained vested in the central apparatus of governance and the preexisting institutions rather than in the people or in newly formed spontaneous organizations.

In Libya, the situation was the opposite. Qadhafi's ideology of a *Jamahiriyya* had prevented the formation of any national institutions. Furthermore, rather than the revolt beginning in the capital and the regime quickly fleeing as organized youth and civil society activists turned the bureaucracy and the army against it, the first uprising began in Benghazi[11] on 15 February 2011 and its success sparked disconnected uprisings in other Libyan towns, but mostly not in centers of regime power. Although Tripoli did revolt in force in response to Saif al-Islam Qadhafi's incendiary speech on 20 February, the regime quickly and brutally reasserted its authority and kept the population hostage.[12] For the next five months, the rebellion was sheltered away from the regime's power bases of Tripoli, Sabha, and Sirte. Meanwhile, on 27 February, elements of the rebel movement established an umbrella organization, the National Transitional Council (NTC), to serve as the "political face" of the multiple simultaneous uprisings and constitute a new "center" of power in Benghazi around which the nation's political life could be organized.

Between its creation and midsummer 2011, the NTC evolved into more than the mere political face of the revolution; it became the locus of power for a semisovereign government administering Cyrenaica, a territory larger than Germany but containing only around two million inhabitants. It was quickly hailed by international observers as remarkably effective in providing basic services, getting the banks running, and returning people to work. By midsummer, it succeeded in obtaining recognition from most of the world's countries as Libya's sovereign government, entitling it to claim ownership (although not immediate access) to $160 billion in frozen Libyan state assets abroad, to pump oil, and enter into business and diplomatic contacts on behalf of Libya.

Curiously, almost as soon as this alternative center was operational and acknowledged as the government of Libya by most of the world's countries, it quickly descended into internal bickering after the killing of the defense minister and general Abdul-Fattah Yunis on 28 July. It is difficult to overstate the importance of his assassination. The exact sequence of events that led to his murder and its precise implications for the rebels' nascent political life still remain murky. (Different perspectives are presented throughout this book, and Chapter 5 delves the deepest into the tribal and judicial implications of the episode.) His killing symbolized the radical nature of the revolutionary youth, spontaneous militiamen, and fringe Islamist activists, many of whom refused to be led by officials such as Yunis who had served in the Qadhafi regime. As a result of his murder and the ensuing recriminations, certain regional, tribal, and Islamist currents were put at odds with the NTC even though they fully supported its aim to topple Qadhafi. Many of them were to remain disaffected. Moreover, the inability of the NTC to pursue justice in a way that was satisfactory to aggrieved parties, through either a traditional tribal or a modern legal process, began to undermine the new Libya's justice system even before it was established.

Concurrently, throughout the summer, the NTC had become progressively militarily unimportant in the struggle to topple Qadhafi as a result of the delayed effects of the imposition of the NATO-led and UN- and Arab League–approved no-fly zone (NFZ). This is because the NFZ thwarted Qadhafi's attempt to retake eastern Libya in mid-March and rendered the battles along the coastal road connecting Ajdabiya to Sirte largely irrelevant to the success of the revolution (see maps 1, 2, and 3). The NATO air campaign and the 1,000 km separating Benghazi from Tripoli skewed the battles in favor of the defense.

Over the spring and early summer of 2012, the poorly disciplined rebel forces could hold onto territory with the help of air strikes, but they could not advance into Qadhafi-held territory. The unique military dynamic of the NFZ also allowed anti-Qadhafi rebels, not formally connected to the NTC, to exist inside Qadhafi territory without facing annihilation so long as they controlled whole towns that could be resupplied by sea, such as Misrata, or via the Tunisian border or Qatari helicopters, such as Zintan.

Without the NFZ, these pockets of resistance inside Qadhafi-held territory would have eventually been crushed by regime tanks and planes. Critically, with the NFZ in place anti-Qadhafi towns could survive entirely cut off from other rebel political and military structures. Therefore, from April to July, disparate local councils and militias spontaneously arose throughout the Libyan periphery to contest the regime on a city-by-city basis. Furthermore, as the rebels made territorial gains in August, local councils and militias also sprung up in these newly liberated areas, and the NTC struggled in its attempts to integrate these new local power structures into its own framework.

Rather than focusing on rebuilding infrastructure or creating a functioning bureaucracy, the militias tended to concern themselves with purging Libya of those who served under Qadhafi and attending to the pressing needs of militiamen and their home communities. These issues were and are highly popular with wide swaths of the Libyan population and conferred much legitimacy to militia attempts to subvert the NTC-led political process in order to attend to their members' needs. The NTC was thus largely unable to appeal over the heads of the militias directly to the Libyan people because throughout the transitional period it was too weak to launch infrastructure projects, create jobs, establish functioning institutions, or even establish sufficient demobilization or vocational training programs to get militiamen prepared for civilian employment. Additionally, it was woefully inept at public relations, while the militias, Islamists, and local councils frequently proved fairly savvy. In fact, when pressured, the NTC repeatedly caved in to militia, regionalist, and Islamist demands when they were expressed at gunpoint.[13] The only reason that the NTC was able to provide a modicum of security was that many militias agreed to rebrand themselves as part of the Defense Ministry's Libya Shield Force as they wished to secure the revolution against its enemies and, more cynically, had a vested interest in preventing rival militias from further entrenching themselves. Clearly, a legacy of the NTC's procedure for creating a new security infrastructure by coopting the militias has been deeply flawed institutions with unwieldy chains of command. Subsequently, the GNC has struggled to create genuinely national institutions and to rationalize the overlapping jurisdictions of the army, police, Supreme Security Council, and Libya Shield Forces; none of these flawed institutions have been able to prevent the new Libya from drifting towards chronic instablity.

However, despite its myriad practical failings, the NTC did succeed in establishing a legal and moral framework via which legitimacy to govern Libya would be contested. In this task—and the elections it held to create its successor body, the General National Congress—the NTC was remarkably effective. Surveying these dynamics, this book investigates the struggle among the many disparate actors (regionalists, Islamists, liberals, political elites, centralizing technocrats, and decentralizing militiamen) for dominance in post-Qadhafi Libya.

Understood in this fashion, one can conceptualize the NFZ as sustaining separate disconnected "uprisings" in the periphery in which each enclave operated without being part of an overarching military command-and-control structure. The existential threat faced by many enclaves necessitated the formation of novel spontaneous solidarity networks and political/military bodies laced with an intense esprit de corps. As soon as these communities liberated themselves (Zintan in April and Misrata in May), they entrusted political functions to the militias and local councils that sprouted from within. As far as the locals were concerned, it was the militias (i.e., the periphery) and not the NTC (the new center) that had liberated them.

*   *   *

The struggle between center and periphery in Libya unleashed by the 2011 uprisings recreated power relationships that had prevailed during the Ottoman era, when a weak center was forced to grapple with a recalcitrant periphery.[14] In the wake of the Ottoman reconquest of Tripoli from the semiautonomous Qaramanli dynasty in 1835, an Ottoman governor ruled in Tripoli for the rest of the nineteenth century. Local notables in Tripolitania's coastal towns paid homage to the governor but continued to hold power, while in the hinterland the Ottomans did not even possess symbolic authority as autonomous communities refused to pay taxes or let Istanbul interfere in their internecine tribal feuds.

Although the hinterland's distinct local power brokers united at times—first to oppose Ottoman attempts at centralization and later to fight the Italian colonization beginning in 1911—the animosities between various localities could not be patched over solely in the name of fighting an outside invader. The years 1919 to 1922 saw an intense Arab-Berber civil war in the Nafusa Mountains, where the Italians backed and manipulated the Berber side in a successful attempt to consolidate their control over Tripolitania.[15] Furthermore, tensions between the two provinces of Tripolitania and Cyrenaica meant that a unified anti-Italian jihad was impossible, and only the Sanussi Sufi order could coherently oppose the Italians. It could even be said that the jihad against the Italians exacerbated preexisting cleavages throughout Libyan society, especially those between urban and rural areas. In summation, European colonial rule (1911–1942) did little to centralize authority or create a functional bureaucracy—the exact opposite of its effect in Tunisia and Egypt. In fact, it further fragmented Libyan society and left an enormous power vacuum when the Italians were chased out by British tanks in World War II.

Since 1942 the Libyan periphery, consisting of nonurban tribesmen and urbanites with rural backgrounds, has continued to dominate the centers of power—under the British Military Administration and its Cyrenaican Sanussi clients (1942–1951), the Sanussi monarchy

(1951–1969), and Qadhafi's revolutionary regime (1969–2010). Under British influence during the British Military Administration and later the monarchy, tribally organized Cyrenaican elements backed by the Sanussi order shifted power from the Ottoman and Italian center of Tripoli to alternative centers such as Benghazi and Bayda. The wealthy and educated urban traders representing the Tripolitanian center progressively lost control, most noticeably as a result of siding with the Italian colonialists or backing Egyptian-inspired Arab Nationalism against the British and the Sanussis.[16] A similar dynamic played out after Qadhafi came to power in 1969. He relied on Maqarha and Qadhadhifa tribesmen from the remote marginalized areas of Sabha and Sirte. Although Qadhafi's regime deliberately avoided building institutions, it survived from 1969 to 2011 because it remained powerful enough to prevent the consolidation of rival power centers. Yet even at the height of his power, Qadhafi had to contend with occasional uprisings in the hinterlands. In short, an in-depth study of Libyan history over the past 150 years reveals a cyclical shift of power between the center and the periphery. Each time the periphery dislodges the center, it gradually constitutes a new center that is in turn dislodged.[17]

The 2011 Libyan uprisings witnessed two such cycles, as "peripheral" Benghazi temporarily conquered the center only to see itself quickly supplanted by new diffuse loci of power elsewhere. As former Oxford University geography professor Jean Gottmann postulated, "Peripheral location means [nominal] subordination to the center…A lack of resignation to such subordination would obviously lead to [continual] conflict and instability."[18] Like Afghanistan and Yemen, Libya may be yet another country in which the culture and history of peripheral actors do not allow them to accept a subordinate position, even to a center they largely accept as sovereign or legitimate. However, Libya might be the only example of an Arab oil country where the periphery remains dominant. Usually the requirement of the extractive industries necessitates a successful push toward centralization, bureaucratization, and nationwide infrastructure. Libya under the *Jamahiriyya* never quite achieved those, and post-Qadhafi Libya appears headed in the wrong direction as attempts to centralize authority are consistently rejected by certain sectors of the population. Furthermore, the landmark 6 February 2013 decision that the constitutional committee will be directly elected by the Libyan people abrogates the GNC's original mandate while facilitating the drafting of a permanent constitution which further devolves authority from the center towards the periphery.

Today, Libya has reverted from being a partially centralized dictatorship under Qadhafi (albeit one ruled by peripheral elements opposed to creating permanent institutions) back to its more traditional power structure, with a weak center having difficulty making inroads into a rebellious periphery. In post-Qadhafi Libya, local notables, tribal groups, and militias all vied to keep the NTC from extending its authority into their fiefdoms. This center-periphery analysis of the current situation is clearly in fitting with the claim of Professors Dirk Vandewalle and Lisa Anderson that Libya's twentieth-century history differed from other despotic Arab regimes in that it was uniquely "stateless."[19]

* * *

This volume examines Libya's politics from the Qadhafian past to the beginning of the post-Qadhafi future, seeking to flesh out the above thesis as well as to present an analytical history of the 2011 uprisings. Each chapter investigates a different thematic dimension of the uprisings and the transition. This approach brings the struggle for the post-Qadhafi future into clearer focus. The book concludes its treatment with the 7 July 2012 elections and the ensuing handover of formal authority from the unelected revolutionary National Transitional Council to the elected General National Congress (GNC) on 8 August 2012. This optic stresses that in the wake of the uprisings, the "transition period" to legitimate governance was characterized by a competition between formal, national, and legal authority—as represented by the NTC—and informal, local, and spontaneous authority—as represented by various armed bodies.

* * *

In Chapter 1, "Civil Activism and the Roots of the 2011 Uprisings," George Joffé examines the formal and informal governance structures of Qadhafi's *Jamahiriyya* regime, revealing how those very structures came over time to channel opposition activism. He demonstrates that the international sanctions of the 1990s witnessed the return of tribalism as a key pillar of support and legitimation for the Qadhafi regime, while the 2000s were marked by détente with the West and the growing "modernizing" influence of Saif al-Islam Qadhafi. Since the essential components of the "reforms" that Saif claimed to champion never materialized, the nucleus of Western-educated "reformers" he incubated transformed from a nexus of technocratic support for the regime into a crucial locus of antiregime civic activism.

Joffé also explains how Libya's unique *Jamahiriyya* system of governance effectively crippled the formation of independent organizational structures—except in very specific ways which drew upon preexisting social fissures. Furthermore, Libya's recent history progressively antagonized Cyrenaicans, Berbers, the educated, and Islamists, while Qadhafi's half-hearted attempts—alternately to placate and repress each of these groups—ultimately backfired, exposing the fact that the regime's repressive force had become "hollowed out." This, in turn, left the regime ill-prepared to confront a series of spontaneous uprisings which drew upon preexisting patterns of Cyrenaican resistance to Qadhafi, while also joining forces with "a transnational world of spontaneous communication."

In Chapter 2, "Dynamics of Continuity and Change," Youssef Sawani builds on Joffé's argumentation, highlighting how the "perpetual dynamics" of Libyan history—tribes, Islam, oil, and regionalism—were all at play in the uprisings and underlie the political parties, militias, civil society organizations, and local councils they created. As such, despite the revolutionary changes, post-Qadhafi Libya illustrates many striking continuities.

Seeking to present a comprehensive overview of the factors that shape Libya's post-Qadhafi future, Sawani details the origins of the National Transitional Council and its creation of a legal framework for a transition to elected constitutional governance. In so doing, he demonstrates how despite formulating "the rules of the game," those very rules left the NTC at a disadvantage as it was perceived as lacking both elected and "revolutionary legitimacy" and, hence, was unable to take bold actions to rein in the Jacobins (the militias) in the wake of Qadhafi's ouster.

Furthermore, Sawani demonstrates how Libya's fragmented history and the multiplicity of the uprisings facilitated the formation of myriad overlapping local and national organizations. He reflects on the results of the 7 July 2012 General National Congress elections, demonstrating how "the results mirrored not ideological divides but rather tribal and regional factors."[20] Sawani's analysis foregrounds the struggle between the center and the periphery for dominance in post-Qadhafi Libya.

In Chapter 3, "The Post-Qadhafi Economy," Ronald Bruce St John sketches the salient features of Libya's economy under the Sanussi monarchy and the Qadhafi regime, forecasting how it might develop in the wake of the uprisings. In so doing, he expands upon Sawani's identification of oil as a key "perpetual dynamic" of Libyan history, one which "constrains" the evolution of the relationship between the state and the Libyan people. He reveals how Qadhafi's legacy of subsidies, corruption, and a weak private sector is now decisively "constraining" the manner in which Libya's new central authorities handle economic matters.

Completing his broad brushstroke portrait of Libya's economy, St John adumbrates the challenges and opportunities the country now faces. The key hurdles remain a dysfunctional legal system, dilapidated infrastructure, culture of entitlement, underdeveloped private sector, lack of skilled personnel, and most crucially, the unpredictable security situation. Conversely, the country's unique strengths are its religious cohesion, moderate Islamic practices, and abundance of hydrocarbons and investment opportunities. Choosing to remain fundamentally balanced in his appraisal, St John concludes, "The post-Qadhafi era offers Libya a fresh opportunity to reject the *rentier* state pattern... Nonetheless, the hydrocarbon sector will remain the centerpiece of the economy for years to come and the new Libya will encounter the same problems the Qadhafi regime faced in achieving a major increase in oil and gas production."

In Chapter 4, "The Role of Outside Actors," Ambassador Richard Northern and Jason Pack present an insider's take on the international diplomacy surrounding—and intervention in—the uprisings. Deconstructing the motivations and actions of the major international players (France, the United Kingdom, the United States, Qatar, the United Arab Emirates, Italy, Sudan, and South Africa) reveals how each country's actions were conditioned by its own unique economic and diplomatic relationship with Qadhafi's Libya. Our approach also demonstrates how policy toward Libya was in many cases driven by resolute political leaders, who overrode the more cautious instincts of their diplomatic and military bureaucracies.

Unusually, the major Western and Arab powers were all in close alignment. The United Nations Security Council Resolution 1973 calling for prompt international humanitarian military intervention in the form of a no-fly zone was quickly drafted and passed, with ten favorable votes and five abstentions (Russia, China, Germany, Brazil, and India). The 2011 Libyan uprisings proved the ideal candidate for the implementation of the international legal paradigm termed "Responsibility to Protect." Thanks to Qadhafi's isolation and the real threat he posed to the safety of his own people, international public opinion and most world states regarded limited intervention as a humanitarian, diplomatic, economic, and geostrategic imperative. Such a perfect storm is unlikely to be repeated. Fortunately, it saved the rebel movement from certain annihilation by Qadhafi's counteroffensive in mid-March (see map 2). Unfortunately for the Syrian rebels in 2012–13, "never again would Putin succumb to humanitarian or popular pressure to grant UN-sanction to a Western-led attempt to remove a Russian ally."

The ensuing aerial intervention in the 2011 Libyan uprisings was unprecedented: it was sanctioned by the Arab League; it gradually morphed into the rebels' air force; and, despite lending decisive military support to the rebel cause, international actors mostly avoided meddling with evolving rebel political structures. When they (especially Qatar) were tempted to play favorites within the rebel camp, their actions usually backfired. As a result, we argue that the inability of Western powers in post-Qadhafi Libya to provide more decisive support and assistance to the Libyan central authorities to rein in the militias, build a functional administration, or combat the influence of extremist groups, must be understood as a consequence of their initial hesitancy to become intertwined in costly, unpopular, and open-ended nation-building activities. Western policy makers were acutely aware that overeager external involvement—even if well intentioned—might exacerbate domestic Libyan divisions and raise the specter that the humanitarian no-fly zone was merely the cover for a neocolonial enterprise.[21]

In Chapter 5, "The Rise of Tribal Politics," Wolfram Lacher explores how the uprisings led to a resurgence of "tribes" as social institutions, forums for debate, organizations of military mobilization, replacement governance structures, and axes of political conflict. Without reducing the uprisings to a tribal civil war, he argues that "tribal solidarities and rifts were important determinants of mobilization into revolutionary brigades, as well as polarization into opposing camps."

Lacher sets the stage by synthesizing the existing scholarship on North African tribes and the colonial legacy embodied in the term "tribe" arriving at a usable, yet very loose, definition of the tribe which is appropriate to the Libyan context. His definition is implicitly adopted in all the chapters of this book. With a firm grasp on the amorphous entity that is a Libyan tribe, Lacher shows how local communities rallied together around preexisting solidarity (*'asabiyya*) networks to govern and protect themselves as well as to fight for spoils and exact revenge, as the Libyan state crumbled around them. This process produced a range of novel institutions like the *majalis hukama'* (Councils of Notables) that sought to resolve disputes throughout tribal Cyrenaica but were hamstrung in their effectiveness because of the lack of an effective central authority with which to coordinate. Tragically, the tribal feuds unleashed by the uprisings, both those with an ethnic component such as Rijdalain-Zuwara and those between Arab communities on opposite sides of the civil war such as Mashashiya-Zintan or Bani Walid-Misrata, continued unabated into the post–civil war period. These feuds continue to present a primary axis of local politics that paradoxically inhibits the rise of a strong central authority and yet cannot be alleviated until that authority is capable of enforcing a reconciliation process upon the recalcitrant periphery. The most persistent of these feuds and the one in greatest need of reconciliation is that between "counter-revolutionary" Bani Walid and all of "revolutionary" Libya. Lacher meticulously details Bani Walid's internal politics, sketching the intricacies of the subtribal and generational resonances of internal Warfalla cleavages. As in the Vendée in 1793, familial, religious, and ideological cleavages all overlapped in a particular local context fueling the intensity of confrontation with the new order. It also ensured that the inability to integrate Bani Walid into the political structures of post-Qadhafi Libya would remain a stain on the new authorities' claim to be the legitimate sovereign over all Libya and all Libyans. In summation, Lacher's worm's-eye view of politics in the periphery complements the bird's-eye perspectives of earlier chapters, as both demonstrate different aspects of "a broader development that characterized the uprisings and their aftermath: the primacy of local interests and loyalties."

Chapter 6, "The South," by Henry Smith, builds on the foundation laid by Lacher. Smith examines how local uprisings and subsequent conflicts played out in Libya's Saharan interior, inhabited by the nomadic Tuareg and Tubu ethnic groups. Smith approaches his subject by demonstrating how both groups were marginalized and manipulated by Qadhafi—initially as part of his Arab Nationalist ideology and later as pawns in his quest for African hegemony. This sordid legacy of Qadhafi's repression and manipulation undergirded both widespread Tubu solidarity with the uprisings and those Tuareg elements who collaborated with the regime. Conducting case studies of Kufra, Sabha, and Ghadames, Smith shows "the role of the uprisings in briefly transcending old antagonisms" between Tubu and the Arab Zwai tribe in Kufra, between Tubu and certain Arab tribes in Sabha, and between the Ghadamsi Tuareg and the surrounding Arab population. Tragically, these new alliances proved short-lived as older patterns of communal antagonism resurfaced when the fight against Qadhafi ended.

Describing the situation in Sabha, Smith echoes Lacher's treatment of more violent developments in Bani Walid showing how even in areas thought to be "Vendéan strong holds of the counter-revolution," tribal and subtribal cleavages created local axes for conflict that bifurcated towns and neighborhoods in the new Libya. In this pioneering study of an underresearched area, Smith arrives at a sobering conclusion, "Libya's interim rulers had a rare opportunity in mid-2012 to engage Libya's diversity and attempt to reconcile inter-communal tensions. However, the weakness of the 'center' as seen in the state's lack of institutional capacity and the security forces' fragmentation hamstrung those who sought to seize the opportunity to connect Libya's diverse communities."

In Chapter 7, "The Islamists," Noman Benotman, Jason Pack, and James Brandon debunk the myth that a monolithic "Islamist" grouping played a coordinated role during the uprisings. We argue that "the multifaceted Islamist role transpired in more complex ways than is usually imagined, with sharp distinctions among the main *organized* Islamist groupings." To illustrate how the roots of each movement presaged the position it would occupy during the revolt, we retrace the history of Islamist opposition to Qadhafi. This treatment highlights the total failure of *Hizb Al-Tahrir*'s overt confrontation with the regime in the 1970s, the Muslim Brotherhood's inability to put down firm roots after its leadership was chased out of the country in the 1990s, the Salafists remarkable ability to gradually spread as a leaderless social movement, and the Libyan Islamic Fighting Group (LIFG)'s inability to topple the regime in a Cyrenaican guerilla war in the mid-1990s. Despite being in a position of weakness in the 2000s, the LIFG and the Brotherhood were given a second lease on life as the Qadhafi family pursued a reconciliation strategy toward them as part of its international repositioning relative to the post-9/11 "War on Terror."

These developments meant that Libyan Islamist movements were in disarray at the start of the 2011 uprisings and had accommodated themselves to the status quo. As a result, the fragmented LIFG haphazardly entered the revolutionary fold and the Salafists actively supported Qadhafi until deciding abruptly to switch sides after seeing which way the wind was blowing. Only the Brotherhood was fast out of the gates in grasping the significance of the uprisings and joining them in their early days.

Once eastern Libya was liberated, veteran LIFG members presided over the movement's ideological and structural transformation to allow it to benefit from the prevailing media, military, and fundraising opportunities afforded by the uprisings. Rebranding themselves as the Libyan Islamic Movement for Change (LIMC), these former LIFG fighters masqueraded as nationalists and patriots claiming that they were not only integral to the capture and administration of Tripoli but that they should also be entrusted with key national governance functions. Few Libyans were fooled by the bearded men in hastily tailored suits, and their close relationship with Qatar occasioned a backlash against them at the ballot box. Always more politically savvy, the Brotherhood mostly sat out the fighting, concentrating instead on grassroots social work and political mobilization. They achieved a respectable although far from dominant position in the GNC; the Salafists attempted to follow a similar grassroots strategy, albeit in a less organized and far more socially destructive way.

In the final analysis, despite all three major *organized* Islamist currents' fairly successful entrance into mainstream post-Qadhafi politics, it appears that the nebulous unorganized "freelance" jihadists—such as the Ansar al-Sharia movement blamed for the killing of the American Ambassador Christopher Stevens—are more likely to determine the country's future trajectory. As of the start of 2013, it is clear that freelance jihadists affiliated with Al-Qaeda have set up bases and training camps in Cyrenaica and Fezzan using them to launch attacks (e.g. at the In Amenas gas facility in Algeria), smuggle arms, and project their power into other ungoverned spaces like Mali.

If the Libyan center remains weak and the freelance jihadists—the most peripheral elements of the Libyan periphery—continue to play the role of spoiler, then Libya's future is likely to be one of progressive fragmentation. Without an improved security apparatus, even a very small number of committed jihadists lacking support from the general population will be able to derail the country's progress toward democracy and the rule of law. Although Libya's resource wealth, small population, and lack of sectarian fissures is enviable, it is also a double-edged sword making it more vulnerable to such blackmail than most postconflict countries. Libya's oil industry, infrastructural projects, and numerous foreign technicians are easy targets for jihadists (or the more prevalent non-Islamist local militias), while economic growth requires foreign direct investment and expertise, which can only be attracted if the security situation stabilizes.

In the Afterword, "Libya—A Journey from Extraordinary to Ordinary?" Lisa Anderson recounts Qadhafi's gruesome end as a metaphor for what Libyans currently face in surmounting the institutional—as well as psychological—legacy that they have inherited. Qadhafi's *Jamahiriyya* form of government was as extraordinary as the man himself; it was calculated to exacerbate local, regional, religious, and generational tensions beyond what most societies could bear. Despite this inheritance, Libyans display remarkable endurance and undying hope for a brighter future.

Expanding upon the concrete steps that Libyans must take to create an ordinary public life from scratch, Anderson displays the empathy and nuance with which outside observers must study Libya if they endeavor to understand it. Conventional democratic political practice cannot rise from the ashes of brutal tyranny as if it were a phoenix; it must gradually evolve after stability, security, and the rule of law have been enshrined. Anderson suggests paradoxically that the "local identities that were strengthened by the statelessness of the Qadhafi era and further fortified during the uprisings may yet prove to be building blocks for a novel experiment in the Arab world: government that is genuinely decentralized but still functional."

* * *

Attempting to assess the role of economics, outside actors, tribes, ethnic minorities, and Islamists in shaping Libya's future, this volume concludes that Libya cannot satisfactorily be governed in a "pre-modern" or "neo-Ottoman" fashion—with strong local leaders aloof from a weak central authority. Libya's wellsprings of intense local solidarity networks do, however, make such a situation possible on a human level. And sadly as of the beginning of 2013, events on the ground appeared to be headed in that direction. Once peripheral dominance becomes fully established, it would likely also be dangerously self-perpetuating. Yet, the imperatives of creating central infrastructural planning, a coordinated security apparatus, and a functional bureaucracy able to create jobs and push Libya's sclerotic state-driven economy into the twenty-first century are fundamentally incompatible with federalism (as advocated by certain Cyrenaican and Fezzani tribal leaders), the existence of semiautonomous militia-aligned city states (e.g., Misrata circa 2012) or whole areas of the country remaining outside the writ of the central government (e.g., Bani Walid and most of Libya's south).

Libya is likely to either go the way of Afghanistan without a Hamid Karzai figure, outside boots on the ground, or intense ethnic cleavages (i.e., dysfunctional anarchy with a well-intentioned, yet corrupt central government ineptly struggling to control the periphery) or of a more socially conservative, centralized, and democratic version of the UAE (i.e., sustainable development based on resource wealth, social peace, openness to outside influences, and a progressively more educated population governed by an elected technocratic state). Structurally, a middle ground appears an unlikely outcome. As the government of Prime Minister Ali Zidan began its tenure in November 2012, the jury was still out. Yet as the book went to press, the 6 February 2013 GNC decision (finally upheld by the April 2013 constitutional amendment) calling for the direct election of the constituent assembly illustrated that the GNC had definitively succumbed to populism—dissipating its own authority and emboldening the militias and federalists who frequently disrupt its sessions. These recent developments suggest that Libya could well fall into the Afghanistan trajectory: becoming an ungoverned space—perpetually in transition—where the periphery reigns supreme and informal power trumps formal institutions, paradoxically just as it did under Qadhafi.

The 2011 Libyan uprisings represent a sharp rupture with the Qadhafian past. This volume has focused on decoding the "big picture" political changes that the uprisings inaugurated. It has largely sidestepped cultural matters. Yet in that crucial domain, great transformations occurred as the creative energy of the Libyan people was unleashed and the proponents of freedom of expression became engaged in a struggle with a newly emerging "revolutionary" orthodoxy.

A cultural or social history of the uprisings still needs to be written—exploring the human dimensions of the "center" and the "periphery," of the "Jacobins" and the Western-educated technocrats, of everyday Misratans and Darnans who lost relatives, of the unemployed over-educated Facebook youth and the Salafists, of Berber nationalists and Cyrenaican separatists, of female NGO heads and medical doctors returned from the diaspora, and of militiamen who voluntarily turned in their arms returning to their day jobs and those who didn't, preferring to man check points, to block roads, to storm sessions of the GNC, and to inadvertently derail the country's progress.

Such a book would be filled with moving stories of sacrifice and of the undying hope for a better tomorrow that motivates most Libyans. It would explain that although Libya's postrevolutionary euphoria quickly turned to cynicism against the new central authorities, the memory of the 2011 Libyan uprisings remains a rallying cry of hope, empowerment, freedom, sacrifice, and shared purpose that motivates Libyans of all backgrounds toward increased civic engagement in building their shared future. Ultimately, it will be the culture and will of Libyans to put aside their differences, compromise, and work together—or lack of those virtues—that will determine the fate of the nation. To complement the political history we present to you now, we hope a corresponding social and cultural history of the 2011 uprisings will soon be written.

February 2013, London

NOTES

1. The term "Arab Spring" is frequently rejected by Arab authors as a Western construction that implies a teleological progression from dictatorship to democracy as from winter to spring to summer. Yet as the term derives from the analogy with the "Prague Spring" of 1968 and the 1848 Springtime of Nations, there is no reason the term should be seen as teleological, insulting, or should be shunned. George Joffé, "Algeria: Precursor to the Arab Spring," Lecture at St Antony's College, Oxford,

November 2, 2012. Nonetheless, this book has a slight preference for the more neutral and accurate term "the Arab uprisings."

2. For more on the evolution of the scholarly understanding of the term "revolution," see Jack Goldstone, "Towards a Fourth Generation of Revolutionary Theory," *Annual Review of Political Science* 4, (2001): 139–87. Goldstone critiques Theda Skocpol's classical (third-generation) definition of "revolution." In the process, he foregrounds the role of ideology as a legitimizing factor in revolutions.

3. The trend away from internationalism is certainly not irrevocable. A new pragmatic Islamist internationalism could easily surface to fill the ideological vacuum left by the Arab Spring, but its precise tenets have yet to be articulated.

4. Only the failure of the post-Qadhafi regime to quickly bring security and material benefits to eastern Libya, coupled with the 6 February 2013 decision to allow direct election of the Constitutional Assembly, have allowed the federalists to regain prominence.

5. William Doyle, *The French Revolution: A Very Short Introduction* (London: Oxford University Press, 2001), 32–36.

6. Robert D. Warth, *Nicholas II, The Life and Reign of Russia's Last Monarch* (New York: Greenwood Press, 1997).

7. Nikkie Keddie, *Modern Iran: Roots and Results of Revolution*, (New Haven: Yale University Press, 2003).

8. Scott Shane, *Dismantling Utopia: How Information Ended the Soviet Union* (Chicago: Ivan R. Dee, 1994).

9. Many popular accounts of the Libyan revolution have attempted to blame Western nations and multinational corporations for participating in the "rehabilitation" of the Qadhafi regime. This case is made most coherently and poignantly in Ethan Chorin, *Exit Gaddafi: The Hidden History of the Libyan Revolution* (Croydon: Saqi, 2012). Although Chorin acknowledges that an "unintended consequence" of Western policy was giving the Libyan people the tools to overthrow Gaddafi, he maligns Western actors as motivated by greed and frequently "played" by Qadhafi to boost his prestige and leverage. Chorin's argument neglects that many Western nations (especially the United States and the United Kingdom) were deeply ambivalent about the Qadhafi regime and understood that its song and dance of economic reforms was not accompanied by a genuine opening of public or commercial space, let alone an improvement in the lives of everyday Libyans. This ambivalence allowed for Western diplomats and businesses to strengthen the nascent Libyan private sector, foster covert civil organizations, and cultivate those few individuals within the Qadhafian bureaucracy who advocated for real change, while simultaneously pursuing "engagement" with the regime. Crucially, the détente between the West and Libya allowed Western diplomats, researchers, consultants, and corporations an insider's perspective from which to become truly acquainted with the main actors in Libya. The acquisition of detailed personal knowledge and contacts was essential for the West's role in the

2011 uprisings. In short, a balanced appraisal of the role of the West in the years 2003–2010 in helping or hindering the Libyan people's actualization of their aspirations has yet to be written, but were it to be, it would likely conclude that Western engagement with Qadhafi should be vindicated both morally and strategically as a policy choice. Conversely, in the view of this author, the events of the last five years in Iran have shown the manifest failure of the opposite policy of consistent nonengagement diplomatically followed by nonsupport for the Green Revolution. For a more detailed analysis of Chorin's argument in *Exit Gaddafi* and how it misrepresents the motivations for and consequences of Western engagement in Qadhafi's Libya from 2003–2010 please see Jason Pack "Engagement in Libya Was and Remains the Right Answer," *The Spectator*, January 31, 2013, http://blogs.spectator.co.uk/books/2013/01/engagement-in-libya-was-and-remains-the-right-answer/

10. Doyle, *The French Revolution*, 42.

11. Benghazi was the traditional locus of opposition to Qadhafi. The town had been favored by the monarchy of King Idriss al-Sanussi before Qadhafi came to power, and remained associated with social, tribal, and religious currents associated with the monarchy. It was there on 17 February 2006 that protests had broken out in response to an Italian minister's wearing a tee-shirt bearing the Danish anti-Muhammad cartoons. After Mubarak was forced from power in Egypt on 25 January 2011, Libyan Facebook activists began planning a "day of rage" for the five-year anniversary of the cartoon uprising. The regime became aware of this online organizing and attempted to nip it in the bud by arresting Fathi Terbel. Terbel had achieved prominence inside Libya from 2006 onward for representing some of the families of the victims of the Abu Salim massacre in their lawsuits for redress from the regime, and for conducting a weekly protest in front of the Benghazi courthouse. He achieved international fame when his arrest on 15 February 2011 provided the key first spark that would have Benghazi free from Qadhafi within days, and most of the country up in arms within a week.

12. For a detailed, readable, and informed blow-by-blow account of the events of the early days of the uprisings, consult Chorin, *Exit Gaddafi*, 187–208.

13. Haley Cook and Jason Pack, "The July 2012 Libyan Elections: Appeasement, Localism, and the Struggle for the Post-Qadhafi Future" (Contemporary Arab Affairs Forthcoming).

14. Jason Pack and Barak Barfi "In War's Wake: The Struggle for Post-Qadhafi Libya," *Washington Institute for Near East Policy*, February 2012, 1 and 6–7, http://www.washingtoninstitute.org/policy-analysis/view/in-wars-wake-the-struggle-for-post-qadhafi-libya. The following section explaining the historical grounding of the center and periphery paradigm constitutes a modified extended excerpt of this work, from which the analytical framework of this introduction derives.

15. Angelo del Boca, trans. Antony Shugaar, *Mohamed Fekini and the Fight to Free Libya* (New York: Palgrave Macmillan, 2011).

16. Anna Baldinetti, *The Origins of the Libyan Nation: Colonial Legacy, Exile and the Emergence of a New Nation-State* (Abingdon: Routledge, 2010).

17. Both this cyclical pattern and the role of nonurban groups in catalyzing it are remarkably similar to that detailed by Ibn Khaldun in his fourteenth-century *Prolegomena*. Fascinatingly, Libya appears to be the modern Arab state in which Ibn Khaldun's theories remain most relevant.

18. Jean Gottmann, ed., *Center and Periphery: Spatial Variation in Politics* (London: Sage, 1980).

19. For a thorough treatment of this idea, see Dirk Vandewalle, *Libya since Independence: Oil and State-Building* (London: I. B. Tauris, 1998); Dirk Vandewalle, *A History of Modern Libya* (Cambridge University Press, 2006); and Lisa Anderson, *The State and Social Transformation in Tunisia and Libya* (Princeton: Princeton University Press, 1986).

20. For a more detailed treatment of how the local dimension was paramount in the GNC elections, consult Haley Cook and Jason Pack, "The July 2012 Libyan Elections: Appeasement, Localism, and the Struggle for the Post-Qadhafi Future." This article also expands on Sawani's argument in Chapter 2 that despite the absence of widespread violence, the elections themselves constituted a field of divisive social contestation which reinforced various local, tribal, and religious cleavages in Libyan society. Moreover, the article demonstrates that although the National Transitional Council's policy of appeasement may arguably have saved the elections from sabotage by regional tensions, it exerted a profound unintended influence on Libya's future constitution: it set the precedent which allowed the GNC to abrogate its own mandate to appoint the constitutional drafting committee of sixty on 6 February 2013.

21. In fact, as the security situation in post-Qadhafi Libya progressively deteriorated throughout 2012 many Libyan politicians and Western commentators accused the major Western powers of abandoning Libya. For a succinct argument advocating for increased American involvement in building coherent Libya security and governance institutions consult, Jason Pack and Karim Mezran, "The Importance of Stabilizing Libya," *The Politico*, February 15, 2013, http://www.politico.com/story/2013/02/the-importanceof-stabilizing-libya-87680.html; and Jason Pack, Noman Benotman, and Haley Cook, "Libya Needs International Assistance, Not Drone Attacks," *The Hill*, February 15, 2013, http://thehill.com/blogs/congress-blog/foreign-policy/283475-libya-needs-international-assistance-not-drone-attacks.

1

CIVIL ACTIVISM AND THE ROOTS OF THE 2011 UPRISINGS

George Joffé

One of the most surprising aspects of the recent uprisings in Libya was the apparently spontaneous emergence of organized political activity inside a state where, for four decades, formal political action outside the repressive confines of Muammar Qadhafi's *Jamahiriyya* (massocracy) system had simply not existed. In fact, the imposition of the *Jamahiriyya* so fragmented Libyan society that even informal structures, such as Libya's complex tribal system or institutions linked to Islam, no longer appeared to provide a basis for political coherence. At the same time, however, in the wake of the crisis between Libya and the West, which began in the late 1980s, the innate contradictions within the Libyan state—given the repression inherent in the *Jamahiriyya's* illusion of "direct democracy"—together with issues of succession and reconciliation with the outside world, began to generate opportunities for precursors to social movements to emerge. These were to seize their moment in early 2011 and provide the momentum needed to destroy the Qadhafi regime. This chapter seeks to uncover the ways in which this occurred after first setting the scene by discussing the political system that Muammar Qadhafi put in place after the "Great September Revolution" in 1969.

THE JAMAHIRIYYA

Superficially, modern Libya under the *Jamahiriyya* system would appear to have been an idiosyncratic authoritarian state, ruled by a charismatic, mercurial, and unpredictable leader, Muammar Qadhafi, who brought the contemporary state into being through a military coup on 1 September 1969. The Great September Revolution ushered in a state initially based on Nasserist Arab Nationalism which, within five years, reformulated itself as a *Jamahiriyya*, in which sovereignty was said to reside in the Libyan people who exercised full authority over the "stateless state" through direct popular democracy. This new Libyan state was "stateless" in the sense that its sources of legitimacy and authority were both dispersed throughout society by the principles of direct democratic action by the population over all aspects of administrative and political behavior and incarnated in the person of its leader, despite the fact that he occupied no formal function within it. This meant that impartial institutions—accountable to a legitimate sovereign authority, itself constitutionally accountable—did not exist but were simply figments of a personalized and unaccountable political imagination.[1] Its economic functioning was predicated on the modernization of Libyan society as a result of its increasing integration into and exposure to the global economy as the new state became an oil producer. This was a process that had begun under the Sanussi Monarchy that had preceded the Qadhafi regime but which, because its own power base had depended on the tribal society of rural Cyrenaica, had been incapable of retaining the support of the new social strata that had emerged from the modernization of Libya's expanding urban society, particularly in Tripolitania.

A crucial element in the modernization process, alongside the proliferation of new institutions, such as trade unions and other civil society organizations, had been the dramatic growth in education. This progress depended on teachers brought in from Egypt and led to the popularization of the ideology of Arab Nationalism,[2] which in turn provided an alternative to the narrowly based religious tribalism of the monarchy.

The revolution that occurred in 1969 thus initially enjoyed massive popular support. Buoyed up by oil revenues, it enabled the new regime to experiment with its political initiatives in the first few years. Thus, as the single-party system associated with Arab Nationalism failed to retain popular support, it was gradually replaced, between 1973 and 1979, by a "popular committee" system of direct populist control. However, by 1975, as oil revenues unexpectedly declined as oil prices weakened, political opposition to the new regime began to emerge, culminating in an unsuccessful coup from within the regime seeking to end Qadhafi's ideologically driven foreign and domestic policies. Two years later, 22 of the officers involved were executed, thus rupturing the integrity of the Union of Free Officers, which had carried through the 1969 revolution, and setting the regime at odds with the Libyan armed forces. Over the next five years, the regime became gradually more intolerant and increasingly personalized around the figure of Colonel Qadhafi and his small clique, the *rijal al-khayma* (Men of the Tent) drawn from the remnants of the Revolutionary Command Council which had presided over Libya's brief experiment with Nasserist Arab Nationalism after 1969 and the Union of Free Officers who had helped him mastermind the original coup which had brought him to power.

At the same time, the economy was also subjected to revolutionary measures of allegedly populist control through the popular committee system, designed to eliminate the private sector, which caused an outflow of Libya's commercial elite.[3] By 1984, the process was essentially complete, and Libya had become *gleichgeschaltet*[4] in that the allegedly populist control of political and economic life masked a profoundly intolerant, autocratic, and proto-fascist corporate system which exercised its hegemony over the economy as well. Although, on the surface, there continued to be a plethora of civil society organizations in operation, now they were all brought under rigid central control, as freedom of expression, too, was effectively suppressed, not only as a crime but also as a heresy, in the supposedly perfect system of direct popular democracy that Colonel Qadhafi had now espoused. The baleful consequences of this on the daily life of Libyans are excellently captured by Hisham Matar in his novel *In the Country of Men*.

This new system of direct popular democracy was supposed to be articulated through the Basic People's Congresses (BPCs) through which the views of the population on local, national, and international policy matters were to be expressed and through which it, in theory, controlled the "popular committees" responsible for translating policy into action in the political, economic, and social spheres. Their views, incidentally, were in practice expressed through mandated delegates from the BPCs at regional congresses and then in the General People's Congress (GPC) which acted as Libya's parliament. It, in turn, elected the members of the General Popular Committee, Libya's equivalent of a ministerial cabinet, which in theory formulated policy in accordance with the principles passed on to it by the GPC. This policy was then transmitted through the bureaucracy to the popular committees created by and accountable to the BPCs, thus completing the bottom-up, top-down pattern of the circulation of power that was thoroughly unique to Libya. This pattern was also, in practice, extremely time-consuming, and since in reality it ran counter to the personalized centralism of the *Jamahiriyya* system, it soon lost the initial support that it had enjoyed. By the start of the new century, fewer than 10 percent of the population actually exercised their supposed democratic authority over the Libyan body politic.[5]

The ideological and intellectual foundations of this novel political construct were expressed in *The Green Book*[6]—Colonel Qadhafi's political testament and vehicle for his Third Universal Theory, which he proclaimed was an alternative vision to both Communism and Capitalism.[7] Rejecting the monopoly of both capital and labor as explicatory drivers, Colonel Qadhafi argued instead that human society and the polities emerging from it were driven by nationalism and religion. His vision of nationalism was not territorially based but rather ethnic, cultural, and implicitly religious. Indeed, the Libyan leader viewed the essence of religion as strict monotheism, of which Islam was the ultimate and purest expression.[8] As important, he believed, was the innate unicity inside the Islamic corpus. He viewed the split between Sunni and Shi'i Islam as a kind of "false consciousness." As had been the case under the Fatimid dynasty in North Africa, he argued, the two traditions were really mirror images of each other, and he called for Libya to be the center of a second *dawla Fatimiyya* (Fatimid State) as a focus of the historical integrated Arab homeland that formed the core of his political vision, despite—or perhaps because of—his endorsement of a united Africa at the end of the twentieth century.[9]

The Colonel's concept of a new universal theory first emerged in June 1973, just two months after the "people's authority," the guiding principle behind the direct popular democracy that characterized the *Jamahiriyya*, was proclaimed. As Ronald Bruce St John has pointed out, it marked "the end of the ideological beginning" of postrevolutionary Libya.[10] Such ideas formed the basis of the formal Libyan political experience and the practice of the Libyan stateless state. Since, in the Colonel's eyes, it represented, in essence, the ideal solution to the problem of representation, dissent from such an ideal, even in the form of oppositional political movements or currents, would be a kind of heresy that inherently called for the elimination of such dissenters.[11]

In reality, of course, the Libyan state did not operate in accordance with its proclaimed ideal as defined so far in this chapter. In practice, after 1973, Colonel Qadhafi, although he had no formal role within the state, controlled all aspects of Libyan policy, delegating its execution to trusted colleagues.[12] This intense personalization of the policy process meant that it was inevitably arbitrary in nature and practice, for the Colonel relied on a small circle of advisers, the *rijal al-khayma*, which had administered the new revolutionary state in the first five years of its existence after the Sanussi Monarchy had been overthrown. Other agents were drawn from the Colonel's own immediate and, on occasion, extended family. The formal administrative structure of the Libyan state thus merely served as a vehicle for executing the policies that emerged from this informal central core—effectively a court around the "Guide of the Revolution."

Needless to say, the Libyan people themselves soon tired of the institutional paraphernalia of the "stateless state" through which they were supposed to practice direct popular democracy. It has been estimated that less than 10 percent of them ever bothered to participate in the BPCs. Mabroka Al-Werfalli established that, in Benghazi, participation in the congresses fell from a high of 70 percent in 1989, having been between 60 and 70 percent in preceding years, to a low of 10 percent in 1997.[13] The Qadhafi regime had realized early on that the BPC system might produce results it did not want, so it created a new institution in 1979 designed to galvanize both the original revolution and the political system to which it had given birth: the Revolutionary Committees Movement (*harakat al-lijnat al-thawra*).[14] This movement, unlike the Libyan state and its institutions, came directly under the control of Colonel Qadhafi and his close collaborators and remained so until the end of the Qadhafi regime.[15] In addition to its role as a mechanism for threatening the population through repression and its use of arbitrary "people's tribunals," it also served as an institution for galvanizing the political system. Its militants, as a result, were inserted into the formal political system as agitators, both to activate the system and to ensure that its outcomes corresponded with the intentions of the leadership.[16]

The most important feature of this new initiative was the nature of its militant cadres. Ostensibly they represented the idealism of Qadhafi's Libya—comprising revolutionary youth, the product of the enthusiasm that greeted the early years of the revolution, carefully nurtured by the leadership. Originally, the committees had no formal authority, emerging as "self-proclaimed zealots" in response to the colonel's call. From the very start, one of their roles was to highlight "recalcitrant behavior" on the part of members of the BPCs. As early as 1 March 1979, the Revolutionary Committees Movement were given formal authority by Colonel Qadhafi, to whom they reported directly, to organize elections for the popular committees which acted as the executive arms of the BPCs.[17]

Revolutionary commitment, however, was only one dimension of the membership of the Revolutionary Committees Movement. The other reflected an instinctive awareness within the Qadhafi regime that its natural support base lay within the constituency that had always spontaneously offered it unstinting support: its own tribal background. Colonel Qadhafi himself, quite apart from his revolutionary partners in the Union of Free Officers, had always looked to his relatives for support and had also tended to rely on more distant kin to ensure the survival of the regime. Indeed, despite the early revolutionary enthusiasm of modernized urban elites—which soon waned—and that of the mass of the population, as long as it enjoyed the economic benefits of the revolution, real power in Libya was, in essence, an expression of tribal solidarity (*'asabiyya*). This explained why, over time, the Revolutionary Committees Movement and the security services have all been controlled by and, to a significant degree, populated with members of Colonel Qadhafi's own tribe and the small number of tribes associated with it.

Tribalism, in short, was the third, informal, level of power in Libya—after the "people's authority" and the Revolutionary Committees Movement—and provided the underlying glue that held the regime together. Historically, tribes had been the informal and spontaneous form of political organization on which Libyan society had been based. The Cyrenaican tribes, in particular, had constituted the backbone of support for the Sanussi Order and the Monarchy, which was created from it at Independence in 1951.[18] In a sense, the 1969 coup had also been a reversal of this monarcho-tribal order, placing the Sirtican tribes, which had been formerly subservient to the Cyrenaican tribes and from which Colonel Qadhafi himself came, in the political driver's seat instead. (The phenomenon of inversion of tribal hierarchies pervades Libyan history. It will be discussed further in Chapters 5 and 6, where it will be shown how the 2011 uprisings completed a "full cycle" of tribal inversion representing a return to *certain* tribal patterns prevalent during the monarchy.)

Over time, the tribe from which an individual came became an important indicator of the degree to which, whatever his formal political or administrative position might have been, he had access to real power. This equation had prevailed under the monarchy and its successor, the *Jamahiriyya*, and will probably continue into the post-Qadhafi period as well. Similarly, for those who did not have the appropriate tribal background, the degree to which they could become clients of those who did, determined their own personal freedom of political action. Alliance patterns, then, became a second line of support within the political system in which the Revolutionary Committees Movement and the security services were the key components.

Even the electoral mechanism became subservient to tribalism as a fascinating account of elections in Ajdabiyya, on the coast of the Gulf of Sirte, made clear.[19] And, as Mansour Omar El-Kikhia had pointed out, "A large number of candidates run and are elected along tribal affiliation, and bloody battles between tribes have taken place over land or political posts."[20] It is quite clear that, even in the general electoral process, theoretically outside the issue of direct regime control of the national political process, tribalism reasserted itself, despite regime attempts to control it. Indeed, such attempts were really part of an initiative by the Qadhafi regime to harness tribalism in Libya to serve its own purposes. This was the dominant factor in understanding how power was articulated and manipulated in Qadhafi's Libya and harkened back to historical forms of social and tribal organization discussed at greater length in Chapters 2 and 5.

Conversely, of course, the regime itself sought tribal allies and used tribalism as a further means of controlling the political system and of isolating dissidence. Thus, in the 1970s, the Qadhafi regime deliberately removed tribal institutions from its political and administrative processes, confining them to the social sphere instead: administrative boundaries were deliberately drawn to break up tribal unities; and, new "modernizing administrators" without local tribal affiliations were brought in to replace the traditional shaykhs.[21] By the late 1980s, the treatment of the tribes had been reversed as the system of "modernizing administrators" failed to achieve the objectives set for it by the regime. Suddenly, the leadership began to court tribal leaders, in part to assure itself of their support in the wake of the American bombing raids on Tripoli and Benghazi in April 1986. It was also anxious to recruit tribal leaders to identify and counter opposition to the regime.

As part of this process, it persuaded tribal leaders to sign, on behalf of their tribes, a certificate of allegiance (*wathiqat 'ahd wa mubya'a*) to the regime—a kind of parallel to the traditional *bay'a*.[22] Once this had been done, the tribe then was made responsible for the loyalty of its members. Conversely, tribes gained a degree of autonomous action within formal political activities and, as Amal Obeidi reports, even student elections in urban Benghazi essentially became tribal contests, and the tribes regained the role they had lost in the 1970s as autonomous political agents. This relationship was formalized in 1993 with the creation of a new institution within the political fabric, the so-called Popular Social Leadership (*al-qiyadat al-sha'abiyya al-ijtima'iyya*). This brought the tribal leaderships into formal municipality-based institutions under a state-appointed coordinator, chosen from among their number. The coordinators, in turn, formed a committee in their own right under a national coordinator.[23] In theory, of course, the objective was to use the tribal leaderships as both coercive instruments to maintain tribal loyalty to the regime and as a means of demonstrating that loyalty to the wider world. Of course, the reverse could also be true: namely, that tribal leaderships could also acquire autonomy when the interests of their own tribal clientele were affected, as was to occur in 1993 in Bani Walid.

This new institution really highlighted the tribal revenge upon the regime. Rather than being excluded as they were in the 1970s, the tribes were now incorporated as political players in the 1990s, with the regime acknowledging their role in granting it legitimacy. In addition, while the regime had always relied on its own client tribes for support within the revolutionary and security institutions it had created, now all the tribes, whether associated with its own client tribes or not, formed part of the consensual political umbrella over the regime. In other words, the relationship between the tribes and the regime was an experiment in alliance politics, with the regime seeking to build bridges with as many tribes as possible and not alienating those tribes that kept their distance—in a modern replicate of the traditional *saff*[24] relationship. As important was the fact that traditional tribal leaders were also rehabilitated as political agents in their own right.

This, however, created a powerful tension within the political system based on tribalism, which continued to persist up to 2011, as tribal leaderships had acquired a degree of autonomy from the revolutionary leadership of the state. Indeed, in 1993, when faced with the failed Bani Walid coup, in which a group of disaffected army officers drawn from the Qadhadhifa and Warfalla tribes had planned to assassinate the Libyan leader, the leadership tried to mobilize the tribal system it had created in dealing with the aftermath.[25] In 1995, having obliged tribal leaders to sign "certificates of honor" (*wathiqat al-sharaf*) in which they took responsibility for the actions of tribal members, it then used this to try to force the leadership of the Warfalla tribe to execute tribal members involved in the coup, in a demonstration of loyalty to the regime. The Warfalla tribal leadership refused to comply with the result that the regime itself had to take responsibility for the executions! Given the fact that the Warfalla were one of the tribal pillars of the regime, this independence on the part of its leadership was unwelcome, to say the least. In a similar way, after the American bombing raids in 1986 on Tripoli and Benghazi, the revolutionary leadership of the state sought to ensure the loyalty of the Cyrenaican tribes, traditionally hostile to the regime because of their marginalization after the 1969 revolution because they had originally supported the Sanussi Monarchy.

Perhaps the best indication of the importance of Libya's tribes in the structure of the idiosyncratic Libyan state was the fact that, in October 2009, when Colonel Qadhafi was anxious to find some formal position for his son Saif al-Islam, he proposed that he should occupy the position of coordinator for the Popular Social Leadership (PSL). The fact that Saif al-Islam never took up his father's offer was another matter, reflecting his awareness that acceptance would have made him a creature of the regime, rather than a power center in his own right, as he then sought to be. However, the offer was a statement both about the position that Saif al-Islam occupied in the emerging power structure in Libya and of the significance of the tribes in defining the location of power within the state.

Apart from a few honorary organizations that were tolerated, such as an association bringing together former members of the Union of Free Officers, which had led the 1969 revolution, the tribes and the Revolutionary Committees Movement were, perhaps, the only bodies in Libya under the Qadhafi regime that enjoyed agency and institutional autonomy, at least up until the end of the 1990s. Beyond that, as was pointed out earlier, the regime retained rigid control over all other purportedly autonomous organizations throughout the country. However, this picture began to change due to the social developments at the end of the twentieth century and the political changes after the suspension of United Nations sanctions in 1999, which had previously been imposed against Libya in 1992 as a result of the Lockerbie affair. It is these changes that may, perhaps, enable us to explain the pattern of events that led to the collapse of the Qadhafi regime in 2011, and the chaotic situation that immediately followed its demise.

Political Fragmentation and the Advent of Dissidence

By 1999, Libya was a very different place from the one in which the 1969 revolution had taken place. On the one hand, the initial enthusiasm that had greeted that revolution had long since been dissipated by the autocratic and personalized political system that had emerged from it. The embryonic civil society that had begun to take shape under the monarchy had been atomized, and civil and civic freedoms had been suppressed.[26] The economy, despite the normative decentralization proclaimed by the regime, had in fact been placed under central control. Even though initial measures of political liberalization emerged after 1987, with the removal of restrictions of foreign travel, the liberation of political prisoners, and a human rights charter, little really changed. Attempts made to liberalize the economy faced the combined opposition of the leadership and the Revolutionary Committees Movement.[27] At the same time, the Libyan regime began to make half-hearted attempts to persuade Libyan exiles abroad to return and revitalize the economy.[28] Those who did return began to construct a private sector economy with reluctant regime acquiescence and implicitly, thereby, became another potential pole of resistance to the regime's hegemonic control.

On the other hand, Libyan society had been profoundly changed. There had been massive urbanization with 77 percent of the country's inhabitants living in urban settlements, and the two conurbations of Benghazi and Tripoli and their satellite towns housing 51 percent of the total population. Education had burgeoned as a result, alongside massive improvements in housing and health care, particularly in the early years of the Qadhafi regime. By 2004, there were 1.7 million students in Libya's 5.9 million-strong population, with over 200,000 in the tertiary sector and a further 70,000 at technical and vocational centers.[29] This figure compared with 13,418 students in higher education in 1975, when Libya had only two universities—Al-Fatah in Tripoli and Qar Yunis in Benghazi. By 2004, the number of universities had risen to nine and there were also 84 technical and vocational centers.

Many Libyans had also received tertiary education abroad with state support, although detailed statistics are not available. By 1978, for instance, there were more than 3,000 students in the United States and about the same number in Britain.[30] Their presence there, however, depended on political whim; in 1985, for instance, all students abroad had their government grants terminated, and they were forced to return suddenly to Libya where some faced trial and summary execution before revolutionary tribunals for alleged treason.[31] At the same time, Britain broke off diplomatic relations and, a year later, the United States imposed sanctions on Libya, which were reinforced in 1992 by the United Nations as well. The result was that, by 2002, there were only 33 Libyan students in full-time education in the United States. After full diplomatic relations were restored, the number of Libyans studying abroad rapidly rose, with the official provision of 7,000 scholarships for students in the United States and a further 3,000 in Britain. In reality, other constraints prevented so many individuals studying abroad and, at the start of 2011, there were estimated to have been 1,000 Libyan students in the United States, 8,000 in Britain, and a further 600 in Australia.[32]

The significance of this emphasis on education was that, despite the suffocating conformity imposed by the Libyan regime through its exclusive control of the media alongside the security services and the Revolutionary Committees Movement, its educational policies created a meritocratic professional community with experience of the wider world and of the political alternatives it could offer. That, in itself, would become an implicit challenge to the Qadhafi regime after the United Nations sanctions on the regime, imposed as a result of the Lockerbie affair in 1992, were suspended in 1999. This informal and potentially dissident community—largely because of its exclusion from the regime and the growing corruption that surrounded it—meshed in with other interlinked developments that were to give that challenge form and substance in the decade leading up to regime collapse in 2011.

The Role of Saif al-Islam

The growing influence exerted by Saif al-Islam, Colonel Qadhafi's second son, over the Libyan public scene posed an indirect challenge to his father's *Jamahiriyya* system. In fact, during the first decade of the twenty-first century, all of the Qadhafi children began to become involved in Libyan public affairs in one way or another, their roles often underlining the intense personalization and corruption of the regime around the immediate family of its founder and, correspondingly, the profound fragmentation of Libyan society by it. Saif al-Islam himself, after his education at Al-Fatah University in Tripoli, went to study in Vienna, where he came under the influence of Shukri Ghanem, the then head of the research division of the OPEC secretariat. He later undertook graduate study at the London School of Economics in Political Science.[33] In Libya itself, he was placed in charge of the Al-Qadhafi Charitable Foundation, which he was able to use as a platform for his expanding political and economic interests.

One of the outcomes of Saif al-Islam's exposure to the wider world and his Western education was his realization that Libya would have to change if it was to cope with globalization and increased commercial and cultural contact with the outside world as a result of the end of its isolation over the Lockerbie affair. Another outcome, incidentally, was a growing and extremely profitable role for Saif as interlocutor for companies wishing to do business in Libya. This was done both through the Al-Qadhafi Charitable Foundation and through the One-Nine group of companies that he controlled. Under the influence of, initially, Shukri Ghanem and, later, of the group of international academics and businessmen that he associated with his foundation, he began to propose a formalization of the Libyan political system and the removal of its arbitrary and repressive characteristics, as represented by the Revolutionary Committees Movement. Interestingly enough, his father seems to have tolerated his implicit critique of the ideology of the regime, as well as his suggestions for modifying its practices, although he was repeatedly reined in and the practical consequences of his initiatives did not amount to very much. In the final analysis, of course, he reverted to total support for his father when the Qadhafi regime faced defeat in 2011.[34]

The important consequence, for our purposes, was that Saif al-Islam's public positions, in this respect at least, provided an outlet for a new generation of Libyans, the beneficiaries of the regime's educational policies who were anxious to exploit the apparent opportunities created both by the hesitant liberalizing initiatives undertaken by the regime in the late 1990s and by Saif al-Islam's initiatives in the following decade. Quite apart from initiating a degree of public debate on political issues, he also, through his commercial interests, created newspapers and television channels that offered alternatives to the stultifying media run by the Libyan state or by the Revolutionary Committees Movement. Even though they were eventually closed down in 2010, while they were in operation they provided vehicles through which hints of political and social alternatives emerged into the public domain. The successful opposition to them came from the Revolutionary Committees' leadership (which also resisted moves to liberalize the economy under Shukri Ghanem as prime minister between 2003 and 2006) and ultimately from Muammar Qadhafi himself.

Nevertheless, Saif al-Islam was able to create a nucleus of support within the University of Qar Yunis in Benghazi and within the Al-Qadhafi Charitable Foundation, where issues of constitutional change and political and economic liberalization were discussed by a group of "intellectuals and academics" according to Zahi Mogherbi, who was himself a leading member of the group.[35] Their projects and discussions took more tangible form when the Economic Development Board (EDB), which was headed by a reformer, Mahmoud Jibril (later to be the first premier appointed by the National Transitional Council), commissioned a formal report on what Libya should become by 2025. Indeed, their activities, which were widely known inside Libya, began to create the impression that an autonomous space for political action could be created and permanent change in the repressive political system was on the way.

Direct challenge, however, continued to be an extremely hazardous undertaking, as the experiences of Fathi al-Jahmi were to show. Indeed, the mere fact of voicing the most generalized criticism of the regime was sufficient to ensure imprisonment and punishment. In October 2002, Fathi al-Jahmi, a deputy in the GPC, voiced criticism of the regime's policies and was immediately thrown into prison, where he was severely ill-treated. He was eventually released at the start of 2004 as a result of American pressure, and voiced his criticisms again. Although he was in theory protected by the official American interest in him, his family was put under severe physical pressure to force him to be silent. He was first confined to his home under a form of house arrest and subsequently taken back to prison where he remained despite appeals by his family to the US government. In prison, he faced a possible death sentence, according to *Human Rights Watch*, as he had been charged under Articles 166, 167, and 206 of the penal code—trying to overthrow the government, insulting Colonel Qadhafi, contacting foreign officials (an American diplomat in Tripoli), and establishing an organization proscribed by law. His health deteriorated as he was denied medical treatment, despite the fact that he was suffering from diabetes. Eventually, when he fell into a coma, he was hurriedly removed to a clinic in Jordan, where he subsequently died in mid-2009.[36] In other words, individuals could still easily be persecuted for the most mundane comments and, without powerful protectors, were open to extreme ill-treatment.

Direct Challenges to the Regime

Yet, despite this casual and incompetent brutality, the first decade of the twenty-first century did show signs of a political thaw. Indeed, the second factor that was to permanently change the political environment began slightly earlier, in the late 1990s. This was a series of direct challenges to the hegemonic power of the regime, to which it reacted with attempts to find compromise, rather than outright repression—in some cases because of the influence of Saif al-Islam. The challenges were of various kinds, but all of them contributed toward an impression of the fragmentation of the power of the state; of its unity of repressive purpose being partially "hollowed out" and of it being forced to share the public sphere with other emerging autonomous centers of action. Two of them were direct challenges to the state itself and three more opened up an autonomous sphere of political action that was, in the final analysis, to create the opportunities for the events of 2011 that led to the regime's collapse.

The Issue of Tribalism

The first of the direct challenges involved the vexing role of tribalism inside Libya. The ways in which the regime's initial attempts to destroy tribal loyalties eventually gave way to an attempt to co-opt tribal power as a means of reinforcing regime control have been discussed in some detail above. One of the ironies in this was that although tribalism as an underlying structure to the Libyan social system was marginalized by the processes of modernization and urbanization that dominated the early years of the Qadhafi regime, its conscious adoption of tribal paradigms later on revived the role of the tribal ethos. This process, combined with the way in which an atomized society was produced by regime policies, made the recreation of collective identities all the more natural. It also gave tribal leaders a degree of unintended autonomy from central control, despite the creation of the PSL committee which was meant to restore the authority of the regime.

The dangers inherent in this approach were revealed by the refusal of the Warfalla leadership to take responsibility for punishing the leaders of the abortive 1993 Bani Walid coup. The incident marked the beginning of the alienation of the Warfalla from the regime, an alienation that was reinforced by the deliberate persecution subsequently of those factions of the tribe that had kinship connections with the coup leaders. A similar alienation occurred in the factions of the Qadhadhifa which had been connected to coup members, again because of regime victimization.[37] Ironically enough, such incidents only underlined the implicit weakness of the regime, rather than its strength. The autonomy its retribalization policies had imparted to the tribes resulted in the Warfalla leadership and many tribal factions refusing to actively support the regime once the civil war broke out in 2011. Furthermore, there were two other examples indicating that the regime was gradually losing control: the attitudes of the Cyrenaican tribes to the regime; and, the attitude of the regime to the *Amazigh* (Berber) tribes of the Jabal Nafusa.

The dominant *Sa'adi* Cyrenaican tribes maintained a traditional hostility toward the regime, largely because of their loss of influence in the state with the downfall of the Sanussi Monarchy, for which they had provided crucial support. In addition, these tribes, nine in number, had traditionally dominated the other *murabtin* (tributary) tribes of Cyrenaica and the Sirte basin, including the Qadhadhifa, Colonel Qadhafi's own tribe.[38] In one sense, therefore, as mentioned above the 1969 revolution also represented an inversion of the traditional tribal system, with the *murabtin* tribes now dominating the social and political system, which was bitterly resented by the *Sa'adi* tribes— even though Colonel Qadhafi's second wife and the mother of all but one of his sons came from one of them, the Bara'asa.[39] Cyrenaicans consequently believed that the regime discriminated against them, particularly in terms of the distribution of economic resources. It remains difficult to prove to what extent these grievances were real or imagined. Nevertheless, there was a constant sense of alienation of eastern Libya from the rest of the country.

A much more egregious case of tribal discrimination concerned the *Amazigh* (Berber) tribes of Libya, located in the Jabal Nafusa or in oases such as Awjila. From its inception, the Qadhafi regime evinced considerable hostility to these groups, primarily because of their declared separate ethnicities, in the sense of being culturally and linguistically different from the majority Arab population of Libya. Their sense of separateness was heightened by the fact that these *Amazigh* communities were predominantly Ibadhi in terms of religious practices and thus distinct, once again, from the majority population. Manifestations of *Amazighté* were repressed, *Amazigh* names were banned and activists were persecuted and imprisoned. Since *imazighen* (Berbers) had traditionally been prominent in the Libyan armed forces, they subsequently suffered discrimination in terms of employment and preferment, which added to their alienation from the regime as well. The regime even went to the extreme of settling Arab tribes on *Amazigh* lands in an attempt to dilute their sense of cultural and linguistic homogeneity. Libya eventually found itself pilloried in the United Nations Committee for the Elimination of Racial Discrimination. This international awareness of Libyan discrimination eventually forced Colonel Qadhafi to engage with *Amazigh* representatives and, in 2005 and 2006 a series of meetings took place, which seemed to indicate that the regime would moderate its attitudes. With Saif al-Islam's enthusiastic support, the ban on the use of *Amazigh* names was abandoned.

In 2007, however, the Qadhafi regime reasserted its rejection of the *Amazigh* identity as a separate cultural component of the Libyan population. Regarding their "separateness" as merely a consequence of colonialism, the regime once again asserted its belief that Libya was a homogenous Muslim Arabic society in culture, language, and belief. Although the regime later recoiled from the international condemnation at its reaffirmed attitudes by allowing some *Amazigh* cultural events to take place in late 2007, *Amazigh* activists found themselves under renewed assault and repression. It was a development that the regime was much later to rue when, in mid-2011, it was Jabal Nafusa that became one of the centers of effective violent antiregime resistance which directly led to the collapse of Tripoli and, subsequently, to the destruction of the regime itself.[40] (Issues surrounding *Amazigh* identity as a locus for opposition to the Qadhafi regime and later tensions within the post-Qadhafi state are discussed in greater detail on numerous occasions throughout this volume. For the most comprehensive treatment, consult Chapter 5.)

Interestingly enough, the regime was quite inconsistent over its attitudes to Libya's other non-Arab communities, particularly the Tuareg and the Tubu from Tibesti. The Tubu, it is true, did face discrimination in some of the southern oasis centers in which they were located, such as Kufra and Sabha, but this had much more to do with competition with other, neighboring desert communities for access to scarce resources as small communities of the normally transhumant Tubu became sedentarized in Libya itself.[41] The Tubu, incidentally, had been instrumental in Libya's claim on the Aouzou Strip along its border with Chad and, from the 1970s up to the 1990s, Libya had been an overt supporter of FROLINAT, the Chadian independence movement based on the Tubu, even engaging militarily in Chad on two occasions.

The Tuareg were quite a different matter. Although the Tuareg, who are nomadic and spread throughout the Central Sahara and in the Sahelian countries of Mali and Niger, are also of *Amazigh* origins, the Qadhafi regime did not treat them with the same hostility as it displayed to the sedentary populations of Jabal Nafusa, partly, no doubt, because the indigenous Libyan Tuareg community, centered around Ghat, was relatively small. Instead it used the larger community as a vehicle of its foreign policy, in order to assert its control over the Sahara, much to Algerian displeasure. In 2007, the Qadhafi regime attempted to mediate in a Tuareg rebellion in Mali, only to be brusquely warned off by Algeria, which considered issues of Saharan and Sahelian security to fall within its own sphere of influence. Nonetheless, the regime had pretensions to be, in some sense, the tribal hegemon over the Saharan regions and began to recruit Tuareg as mercenaries. Eventually, they were used as support troops (estimated at 5,000-strong)[42] for the internal security forces of the regime during the civil war in 2011, thus earning massive popular hatred for their behavior. In the aftermath of the collapse of the regime, most of them have returned to northern Mali and Niger where they have contributed to regional instability, including a rebellion in Mali.[43] (For a more detailed treatment of the Tubu and Toureg communities under

Qadhafi, as well as their position in Libyan society in the wake of the 2011 uprisings, please consult Chapter 6.)

Tribalism, in short, was not only the third level of the regime's support base, as suggested above; it was also an indication of regime weakness, particularly after the regime abandoned its initial attempt to dismantle tribal influences and co-opted them instead. This allowed traditional enmities, dating back to the monarchy and even earlier, between Cyrenaica and Tripolitania to reemerge, alongside the new confrontation between Cyrenaican tribes and those of the Sirte basin, traditionally subservient but now dominant in the Revolutionary Committees Movement and the security services. It also sharpened traditional tensions between Arab and non-Arab tribes in Cyrenaica which were also to threaten the integrity of the post-Qadhafi state. Perhaps most important, in the atomized, fragmented society that the Qadhafi regime had created in Libya, tribal identity and tribal ethos acquired new prominence within the informal identity politics of the state. This was an issue that was to come to the fore during the uprisings as tribal and local origins dictated political loyalties and military allegiances, frustrating attempts at reasserting central authority after the Qadhafi regime had collapsed.

THE RELIGIOUS DIMENSION

Interestingly enough, despite the fact that Colonel Qadhafi himself was an observant Muslim and his vision of the ideal state owed much to Islam, his regime managed to antagonize Libya's religious hierarchy and much of the population very early on.[44] Between 1973 and 1977, the regime brought religion under its control, removing control of the *waqf* and mosques from the *ulama* and redefining religious and legal practice.[45] In doing so, of course, the regime antagonized a significant portion of the population who were pious, observant Muslims who resented radical change, which they considered heterodox, being visited upon traditional religious institutions, even if a major reason for the regime's actions was to destroy the institutional base upon which its predecessor, the Sanussi Monarchy, had depended. Yet religious institutions were, in essence, the sole remaining platform through which resistance to the regime's policies could be voiced since the formal political arena had been closed down. Thus, religious figures, such as Shaykh Muhammad al-Bishti of Tripoli, became focal points of popular resistance, particularly by the youth, to the regime until they were repressed—in Shaykh al-Bishti's case, he suddenly disappeared in 1980.[46]

As such organized resistance was decapitated, and an antiphonal interaction developed as scattered popular protest and clandestine organization engendered regime repression. Scattered protest could be easily dealt with by the police and security forces, but clandestine organization was another, much more serious matter in the regime's eyes. The result was that peaceable movements, such as the Muslim Brotherhood, known in Libya as the *Hizb Islami*, or as the *Jama'a al-Islamiyya al-Libiyya*, suffered repeated repression on the basis of Law 71 of 1972 as subversive organizations or as "heretics" (*zandaqa*), given the state-ordained changes in Islamic practice. Over the years, many were executed in public, and thousands of others were swept into prison. With the limited liberalization in Libya at the beginning of the twenty-first century, the attitude toward the Brotherhood softened slightly—of the 152 individuals arrested for involvement in Islamic organizations in 2002 facing long prison sentences, only two faced death sentences. However, after an intervention by the al-Qadhafi Charitable Foundation, they were eventually released in 2006 on the thirtieth anniversary of the proclamation of the "People's Authority"— the founding act of the *Jamahiriyya*.

Attitudes toward more extreme movements were not so indulgent, however. Quite apart from a series of individual attempts between 1996 and 1998 to assassinate the Libyan leader, in the latter part of the decade the regime faced a concerted threat from an extremist Islamist *salafi-jihadi* organization, the Libyan Islamic Fighting Group (LIFG) (*Jam'at Islamiyyah al-Mutaqatilah*). This first emerged in Libya in June 1995 and resurfaced periodically for several years thereafter, mainly in the major towns of the *Jabal al-Akhdar* (Green Mountain) region—Benghazi and Derna in particular. It had been created in the 1980s in Afghanistan by young Libyan recruits to the jihadist cause against the Soviet presence there, although the movement that they created had nothing to do with the global jihadist vision later espoused by al-Qaeda. Its concerns were strictly national, for its sole target was the Qadhafi regime, which it saw as impious.[47]

The movement was subjected to repeated military repression in Libya, after it had been uncovered, involving sweeps through the *Jabal al-Akhdar* and reprisals in Cyrenaican towns.[48] Although originally it was not fully clear whether it was a genuine Islamist opposition to the Qadhafi regime or simply a tribal opposition to the regime using an Islamist rhetoric, it soon became clear that Islamic radicalism had appeared on the Libyan scene. By then, however, the savage response by the security forces appeared to have worked, so that the rigid security in the Derna and Benghazi regions was eased at the end of 1997. Indeed, despite the regime's official hard-line policy toward its Islamist opponents, there were rumors that in 2000 the regime told groups abroad, as well as the LIFG, that their members would be allowed to return, provided they made a public recantation—something which, even if they had been marginalized by the security forces, they were then not prepared to do. They began, in response, a campaign of assassination of officials in Cyrenaica but that, too, was quickly curbed. After a ferocious campaign of repression and the arrest of its militants abroad, who were subsequently returned to Libya, over 190 members of the group were imprisoned, thus effectively dismembering it.[49]

Over the following two decades, the Libyan authorities, at the instigation of Saif al-Islam together with former LIFG members who had already recanted, persuaded the group in prison to renounce its previous jihadist ideology and to compile a recantation. As a result, the majority were released from prison in 2008 and 2009, with the balance being released, ironically enough, in January 2011 so that violent jihadism ceased to be a threat to the regime, although the danger of its revival always remained. Yet, even if the threat of organized violence had abated, the convictions of former jihadists over the illegitimacy of the regime remained, thus providing an implicit focus for resistance to it, should the right conditions arise. Indeed, this occurred after February 2011, although the jihadi option was never readopted, with the activists gathering around figures such as Abdul-Hakim Bilhajj, who had recanted his extremist past to become a leading figure in the resistance to the Qadhafi regime, and Ali Sallabi, who had mediated the recantation process, instead. In the same way, the leniency shown to moderate Islamists also meant that their analysis of the regime implicitly underlined its inherent illegitimacy for pious Muslims, and Libyan sympathizers of the Muslim Brotherhood abroad, from 2003 onward, were quite vocal in their distrust of the regime in Libya, organizing protests, particularly in Europe, to underline this. (For more on the growth of Islamist organizations in opposition to the Qadhafi regime and their role in both the 2011 uprisings and the struggle for power in post-Qadhafi Libya, please consult Chapter 7.)

SPECIFIC CRISES

Religious opposition to the Qadhafi regime, whether moderate or extremist, thus added to tribal opposition in creating a fundamental, if latent, hostility to the regime. Both, furthermore, combined with the secular critiques of the intellectual elite, particularly in Cyrenaica, which had been given the opportunity to voice its views by the limited and hesitant liberalization of the first decade of the twenty-first century, to undermine the regime's autocratic hegemony over public space. Yet, quite apart from these generic factors, there were three specific issues that underlined the growing political weakness of the regime, despite its continued reliance on repression. All three crises, furthermore, heightened the sense of alienation in Cyrenaica, in particular, and, given the fact that the political liberalization engendered by the timid initiatives of Saif, had progressed furthest there, groups emerged, in Benghazi in particular, which were prepared to exploit the opportunities that these issues were to offer.

The first of these incidents occurred in 1996 when, on the orders of the regime's security chief, Abdullah al-Senussi, prison guards at Abu Salim prison in Tripoli, where political prisoners were housed, violently suppressed a prison riot with 1,300 deaths, many of them natives of Cyrenaica. After many years, and in the face of angry demonstrations from the families of the victims, the regime eventually admitted what had happened and promised compensation to the families of the victims, although none was ever paid. The fact that the families of the victims had eventually dared to demonstrate about their loss indicated the potential weakness of the regime because of its unpopularity, and its acknowledgment of what had happened confirmed this impression. The demonstrations also brought to the fore a group of courageous lawyers who were prepared to challenge the regime, despite the personal danger involved.

At about the same time, a scandal erupted in Benghazi over the infection of 413 children with HIV/AIDS in the main general hospital in Benghazi. The actual cause of the infection was the appalling hygiene standards at the hospital.[50] However, the regime tried to blame a Palestinian doctor and five Bulgarian nurses—Bulgaria has long supplied medical staff to Libya, but they are frequently disliked by their Libyan patients who accuse them of racism. In the end, the regime eventually had to agree to their release and repatriation to Bulgaria, under pressure from the European Union, rather than executing them as it had intended in order to appease the anger in Benghazi over the incident. The families in Benghazi, however, continued to believe in their guilt, and their release added to the generalized unpopularity of the regime as well as showing that, despite all its bombast, it was vulnerable to external pressure and, therefore, could be challenged. Once again, those who had been prepared to give public voice to the angry families seemed to have acquired a degree of immunity from repression through their boldness.

Finally, in 2006, public anger at the antics of an Italian cabinet minister on satellite television led to a riot outside the Italian consulate in Benghazi—satellite television from Italy can be easily accessed in Libya. The minister had provocatively revealed a T-shirt emblazoned with a series of cartoons produced in Denmark the previous year lampooning Islam and the Prophet Muhammad. The reaction in Benghazi revealed both the depth of Islamist sentiment in the city and the sense of impunity that had developed in Cyrenaica toward the regime. The police in the city reacted, and in the ensuing melee at least ten people were killed. This, in turn, led to further resentment and demands for compensation, which further reinforced the individual lawyers who were already representing families concerned over the prison massacre and the HIV/AIDS scandal. Their protests were reinforced by the fact that the Qadhafi regime suspended the interior minister because of the police overreaction.[51]

In short, by the end of the first decade of the twenty-first century, a series of developments in Libya, particularly in Cyrenaica, had combined to both overcome the social atomization and fragmentation induced by the Qadhafi regime and create the impression that the regime itself had been "hollowed out." In other words, public perceptions were such that there was a generalized feeling that its repressive grip had weakened; underlying social structures had reasserted themselves, and potential new political elites had begun to emerge. The interesting point here is that, unlike the situation in other autocratic states in North Africa and the Middle East, Libya, given its intensely personalized and idiosyncratic political system, had never created what Daniel Brumberg has described as a "liberalized autocracy."

He defined this, in the Arab world, as, "...a set of interdependent institutional, economic, ideological, social, and geostrategic factors [which] has created an adaptable ecology of repression, control and partial openness."[52] Such strategies of "state-managed political liberalization," he argued, were used by Arab governments to avoid "the challenges of democratization," and enabled external powers, such as the United States and the European Union, to persuade themselves that genuine liberalization would ultimately be possible.[53] Such an approach would have been quite impossible for the Qadhafi regime to adopt, given its commitment to the concept of the *Jamahiriyya*, whatever its need for rapprochement with the West or the pressure applied to it by the group around Saif al-Islam. As a result, the new openness in Libya was never to be enshrined in an incipient social movement, as proved to be the case elsewhere,[54] but was to be represented by individuals who, accurately judging the implicit weakness of the regime, were prepared to confront it over specific issues.

In essence, in Libya there were never any organized movements, as was the case elsewhere in North Africa, which, despite strict regime supervision, could, nonetheless articulate limited dissent and which, once the opportunity arose—as, for example, in Sidi Bu Zid in Tunisia in mid-December 2010—could frame inchoate populist resentment at regime repression into a coherent program of contesting the regime itself. Instead, there were only individuals who would attempt this, often with no organized support and facing the concentrated wrath of the authorities, rendering them vulnerable to isolation and repression. And it was only when a fully autocratic regime, as in Libya, miscalculated by threatening the population itself, that their individual sacrifices could become emblematic of populist resentment and drive forward mass resistance.

THE CONSEQUENCES

All these factors were to come to a head in the latter part of February 2011 and were to introduce the events and organizations that, together with the aerial intervention of NATO forces in pursuance of United Nations Security Council resolution 1973, were to culminate in the destruction of the Qadhafi regime in late October of that year. Indeed, the pattern of events that occurred is a fascinating testimony to both the persistence and the spontaneous reformulation of informal social structures despite decades of repression intended to eradicate them. They also demonstrate how mutable and flexible such structures can be in adapting to changing and hostile social and political environments. After all, the Qadhafi regime came to power in a world of holistic anti-imperialist ideologies, of which it was one, and was to disappear in another totally different world characterized by globalized communications and the revived hegemony of the imperiums it itself had been designed to replace. It is hardly surprising, then, that Western powers felt able to turn so readily on a regime which they had previously been so willing to embrace, while the Qadhafi regime never really understood its own vulnerability within an integrated world of satellite television and information technology.[55] Organized resistance was only part of the challenge; with that, no doubt, the regime could have coped—what it could not do was to respond effectively to a virtual transnational world of spontaneous communication.

Thus, the events that set off the crisis were in part a youthful response to events in neighboring Tunisia and Egypt which had seen the collapse of the Ben Ali and Mubarak regimes and in part a product of improvements in communications technology (as discussed in the Introduction). An Internet message proposing Libya's own "Day of Rage" on 17 February seems to have attracted considerable attention among Internet-literate youth, especially in Benghazi. The date had been specifically chosen to commemorate the anniversary of the 2006 cartoon riots and the deaths which had occurred then, but it was also associated with the ongoing protests by the representatives of the families whose relatives had died in the 1996 prison massacre. And, in an implicit rebuke to Colonel Qadhafi himself, the veteran Cyrenaican leader Omar al-Mukhtar, who had been executed for leading the resistance to Italy in the 1920s, was chosen as its symbol.[56] (Mukhtar is depicted on this book's cover in a tribute to the manner in which he appeared in revolutionary street art, tee-shirts, and bumper stickers.)

Two days before the planned protests, the regime attempted to decapitate the potential for demonstrations by arresting two well-known protesters, the lawyer representing the victims of the 1996 prison massacre, Fathi Terbil, and a well-known writer, Idris al-Mismari. That, in turn, engendered demonstrations on the two following days in which the security forces killed protestors whose subsequent funerals became occasions for further clashes and deaths, until on 17 and 18 February part of the army which garrisoned the city rebelled under the leadership of Abdul-Fattah Yunis, Libya's interior minister and a Cyrenaican by origin who had defected from the regime. Proregime elements in the city were either killed or chased out. The potential of the informal social structures that had been created during the previous decade then came to the fore as, through an initiative led by Mustafa Abdul-Jalil, himself also a Cyrenaican and Libya's former minister of justice, an impromptu group, composed of tribal leaders, lawyers, professionals, and university teachers, emerged within nine days of the outbreak of the demonstrations to create what was to become, some days later, the National Transitional Council.

It is an interesting speculation as to whether such a body could have emerged so quickly had there not been the slow molding of informal social structures over the previous decade in the ways described above. Similarly, it seems to have been no accident that this should have occurred in Cyrenaica first—although Tripolitania was to experience simultaneous uprisings in Misrata and Zawiya which eventually succeeded at a massive cost, but which lacked the spontaneous social organization that appeared so quickly in Benghazi. Ironically, as the uprisings spread in the months that followed, much of the population, suddenly confronted with the problems attendant on the collapse of a centralized administration, spontaneously turned to the only form of political organization that they had known, the local congresses and popular committees, to provide the local organization that they needed to ensure communal life.[57] But the success of the regime in eradicating all vestiges of civil society was demonstrated in the way that the actual resistance to the Qadhafi regime eventually organized itself as a series of autonomous militias which refused to recognize the overarching authority of the National Transitional Council or any other grouping, while the tensions between them were increasingly articulated along tribal and regional lines. In other words, both its own demise and the difficulty that new institutions have faced in emerging from the chaos of its defeat are a testament to its success in creating its perfected vision of the "stateless" state.

As a result of all these factors, Libya today, in the aftermath of the collapse of the Qadhafi regime, is a sociological curate's egg, which reflects the complexity of its historical construction against the background of a regime determined to eradicate any competitors to the political and social ideals it had set for itself. Tribal ethos and religious belief survived its onslaughts while the regime's own policies of modernization created a new cosmopolitan elite, aware of alternative political models and anxious to develop them, should the occasion arise. And that is, in effect, what happened, both because of the regime's own egregious repression and through its hesitant attempts at political liberalization, attempts that, in the end, dictated both its own demise and the structures, ideas, and aspirations that would replace it!

NOTES

1. Moncef Djaziri, "Creating a New State: Libya's Political Institutions," in *Qadhafi's Libya: 1969 to 1994*, edited by Dirk Vandewalle (New York: St. Martin's Press, 1995), 188.
2. Zahi Mogherbi, "Social Change, Regime Performance and the Radicalisation of Politics: The Case of Libya," in *Islamist Radicalization in North Africa: Politics and Process*, edited by George Joffé (London: Routledge, 2011), 33–34.
3. Ibid., 38–40.
4. The term means "coordinated" and is specifically used to describe the process by which the National Socialist (Nazi) Party took control of Germany in the 1930s as it fashioned a "fascist-style" corporate state of the kind developed in Italy under Mussolini. See Karl Dietrich Bracher, "Stages of Totalitarian 'Integration' (*Gleichschaltung*): The Consolidation

of National Socialist Rule in 1933 and 1934," in *Republic to Reich: The Making of the Nazi Revolution; Ten Essays,* edited by Hajo Holborn (New York: Pantheon Books, 1972), 109–28.

5. See Mabroka El-Werfalli, *Political Alienation in Libya: Assessing Citizens' Political Attitude and Behaviour* (Reading: Ithaca Press, 2011), 105–21; Amal Obeidi, *Political Culture in Libya* (Richmond: Curzon Press, 2001), 156–67.

6. The ideology expounded in the Green Book is further elaborated by Colonel Qadhafi's pronouncements which have been collected in annual volumes as *al-Sijill al-Qawmi.* Specifically religious discourses are available as *Khutab wa-Ahadith al-Qa'id al-Diniyya.* A very early (and now rare) source for them is to be found in Meredith O. Ansell and Ibrahim Massaud al-Arif, *The Libyan Revolution: A Sourcebook of Legal and Historical Documents* (Harrow: The Oleander Press, 1972).

7. Ronald Bruce St John, *Libya: From Colony to Independence* (Oxford: Oneworld, 2008), 157–59.

8. An excellent source for Colonel Qadhafi's essential ideological attitudes is François Burgat, "Qadhafi's Ideological Framework," in *Qadhafi's Libya,* edited by Vandewalle, 49–51.

9. Antonino Pellitteri, "*Al-Dawla al-Fatimiyya*: Politics, History and the Reinterpretation of Islam," *Journal of North African Studies* 16, no. 2 (June 2011): 261–71.

10. St John, *Libya,* 159.

11. Law 71 of 1972 was quite explicit in this respect, providing the capital penalty for political dissenters. The law actually condemned any form of group activity based on a political ideology that challenged the principles of the "al-Fateh revolution," and Article 3 of the law provided the death sentence for joining or supporting any group prohibited by law. This law was backed up by a series of provisions in the Penal Code: Article 206 (Law 48 of 1976) provided for the death penalty for membership of a proscribed organization, Article 208 banned forming or joining an international organization, Article 178 provided life imprisonment for disseminating information that "tarnished" Libya's reputation abroad, and Article 207 provided for the death sentence for any challenge to the basic principles of the Libyan state or for any attempt to overthrow it.

12. George Joffé and Emmanuela Paoletti, *Libya's Foreign Policy: Drivers and Objectives,* Mediterranean Papers Series 2010 (Washington, DC: German Marshall Fund of the United States, 2010) http://www.gmfus. org/archives/libyas-foreign-policy-drivers-and-objectives/; Joffé and Paoletti, "The Foreign Policy Process in Libya," *Journal of North African Studies* 16, no. 2 (June 2011), 183–214.

13. Indeed, participation in the BPCs seemed to have been an activity undertaken only by a small minority, much along the lines of participation in party activity in single-party or multiparty regimes, although the Libyan system was explicitly not party based. See Obeidi, *Political Culture,* 164; al-Werfalli, *Political Alienation,* 54.

14. There was also a desire to counter traces of tribalism that manifested themselves in the actual operations of the BPCs, as Omar El-Fathaly and Monte Palmer noted, "The deliberations of the basic people's congresses continue to reflect vestiges of tribalism, deference to social status and a tendency to use new-found popular powers to settle old parochial scores" (Omar El-Fathaly and Monte Palmer, *Political Development and Social Change in Libya* [Lexington, MA: Lexington Books, 1980], 213).

15. Hans-Peter Mattes regards this as the beginning of the bifurcation of the Libyan state into: (1) an institutional sector, where the Qadhafian leadership had no formal control, that being the duty of the "people's authority"; and (2) the revolutionary sector, legally unregulated and under the regime's direct authority (Mattes, "Formal and Informal Authority in Libya," in *Libya since 1969: Qadhafi's Revolution Revisited*, edited by Dirk Vandewalle (New York: Palgrave Macmillan, 2008), 58.

16. "Colonel Qadhafi called for the creation of revolutionary committees within the structure of the Basic People's Congresses as a means of stimulating revolutionary spirit and creativity among the masses" (El-Fathaly and Palmer, *Political Development and Social Change in Libya*, 173).

17. Ibid., 198.

18. See Edward Evan Evans-Pritchard, *The Sanusi of Cyrenaica* (Oxford: Clarendon Press, 1949); Farah Nejm, *Tribe, Islam and State in Libya*, unpublished PhD thesis (London: Westminster University, 2004).

19. John Davis, *Libyan Politics: Tribe and Revolution* (London: IB Tauris, 1987), 142–49.

20. Mansour Omar El-Kikhia, *Libya's Qadhafi: The Politics of Contradiction* (Gainsville: University of Florida Press, 1997), 103.

21. Omar El-Fathaly et al., *Political Development and Bureaucracy in Libya* (Lexington, MA: Lexington Books, 1977), 92.

22. The *bay'a* was a formal, usually written recognition of a ruler's legitimate authority, granted traditionally in return for the ruler's recognition of communal or tribal rights.

23. Obeidi, *Political Culture*, 119–20.

24. The *saff* was a tribal alliance pattern, found across North Africa, whereby tribes split into opposing moeties (kinship factions), which then linked across tribes into two mutually antagonistic alliances, known in Libya as the *saff al-bahr* and the *saff al-fawqi*, the coastal and the inland alliances. This acted as a further innate mechanism for diffusion of power in addition to segmentary opposition by balancing tribal factions off against each other. In its modern variant, of course, it reflected pro- and anti-regime tribes, where the alliance patterns emerged immediately after the regime collapsed in 2011.

25. Lisa Anderson, "Qadhafi's Legacy: An Evaluation of a Political Experiment," in *Qadhafi's Libya*, edited by Vandewalle, 233–35.

26. Ali Abdullatif Ahmida, *Forgotten Voices: Power and Agency in Colonial and Postcolonial Libya* (London: Routledge, 2005), 82–83.

27. Mogherbi, "Social Change," 39–41.
28. Many Libyans had fled abroad after the 1973–79 restructuring of politics and the economy. Although some became absorbed into the multifarious opposition movements to the regime active abroad, many more—professionals and businessmen—sought to rebuild their fortunes in the countries that gave them asylum. Needless to say, those associated with formal opposition movements were not encouraged to return!
29. Nick Clark, "Education in Libya," *World Education News & Reviews* (July-August 2004) http://www.wes.org/ewenr/04July/Practical.htm.
30. Ibid.
31. Helen Chapin Metz (ed.), *Libya: A Country Study* (Washington, DC: Library of Congress, 1987) http://countrystudies.us/libya/56.htm.
32. Geoff Maslen, "Libya: Students May Become Refugees," *University World News,* March 9, 2011, www.universityworldnews.com/article. php?story=2011030911432924.
33. Lord Woolf, *An Inquiry into the LSE's Links with Libya and Lessons to be Learned,* (London: London School of Economics and Political Science, October 2011) www.woolflse.com/dl/woolf-lse-report.pdf.
34. The reasons for this are still a mystery, particularly as Saif al-Islam seems initially to have seen the insurgency in Benghazi as an opportunity for positive change. It has been suggested that it was the insurgents' refusal to accord a formal role for his father in the new Libya that radically and so rapidly changed his position. However, this is quite inadequate to explain the ferocity of the commitment he voiced toward his father's regime and against the insurgency in his television address on the evening of 20 February 2011, which marked the abandonment of his urbane image as reformer and liberal. Indeed, shortly before he actually made the speech, he had talked to a contact in Britain, expressing his belief that his moment for reform had arrived. On the other hand, he was always intimidated by his father, and the latter's adamant refusal to tolerate compromise may have psychologically forced Saif al-Islam to adopt an equally intransigent position. See Philippe Sands, "The Accomplice," *Vanity Fair,* August 22, 2011, www.vanityfair.com /politics/features/2011/08/qaddafi/201108#.
35. Mogherbi, "Social Change," 42.
36. Mohamed Eljahmi, "Don't Let My Brother's Death Be In Vain," *Forbes Magazine,* June 16, 2009.
37. Organisation Mondiale contre la Torture, "Libya: the Arbitrary Execution of Mr Hussain Saif Salim Al-Jadak, Torture of His Brother, Abdalwahab and Mr Mohamed Massuad Izbeda," (2002) [Case LBY 021002] http://www.omct.org/pdf.php?lang=eng&articleId=2468&t ype=print.
38. Evans-Pritchard, *The Sanusi,* 51–53.
39. Alia Brahimi, "Libya's Revolution," *Journal of North African Studies* 16, no. 4 (2011) (Special Issue, *North Africa's Arab Spring*): 611–12.

40. Bruce Maddy-Weitzman, *The Berber Identity Movement and the Challenge to North African States* (Austin: University of Texas Press, 2011), 140–43.

41. E. G. H. Joffé, "Chad: Power Vacuum or Geo-Political Focus?" in *The Geography of the Landlocked States of Africa and Asia*, edited by I. Griffiths, B. W. Hodder, K. S. McLachlan, and R. N. Schofield (London: UCL Press, 1996).

42. Jeremy Keenan, personal communication, 2011: this estimate comes from specialists on Saharan affairs in 2011.

43. *Al-Quds al-Arabi*, January 20, 2012.

44. Hervé Bleuchot, "The Green Book: Its Context and Meaning," in *Libya since Independence*, edited by J. A. Allan (London: Croom-Helm, 1982), 148.

45. George Joffé, "Qadhafi's Islam in Local Historical Perspective," in *Qadhafi's Libya*, edited by Vandewalle, 139–56; 144–52.

46. John L. Esposito, *Islam and Politics*, 4th edition. (Syracuse, NY: Syracuse University Press, 1998), 170.

47. Moncef Ouannes, "Chronique Politique en Lybie," *L'Annuaire de l'Afrique du Nord 2000* (Paris: La Documentation Française, 2001).

48. Five other extremist movements based in Europe also claim to have been involved in these activities, although there is virtually no independent evidence of their alleged activities.

49. Mohamed Abedin, "From Mujahid to Activist: An Interview with a Libyan Veteran of the Afghan Jihad," *Spotlight on Terror* 3, no. 2 (The Jamestown Foundation: March 22, 2005).

50. Elizabeth Rosenthal, "HIV Injustice in Libya—Scapegoating Foreign Medical Professionals," *New England Journal of Medicine* 355, no. 24 (December 14, 2006).

51. "Libya Suspends Interior Minister after Cartoon Riots," *The Guardian*, February 16, 2006, www.guardian.co.uk/world/2006/feb/18/muhammad cartoons.libya1 Accessed January 26, 2012.

52. David Brumberg, "The Trap of Liberalized Autocracy," *Journal of Democracy* 13, no. 4 (October 2002): 56–68; 56–57.

53. David Brumberg, "Democratization versus Liberalization in the Arab World: Dilemmas and Challenges for US Foreign Policy," *SSI Monographs* (Carlisle, PA: Strategic Studies Institute, July 2005).

54. E. G. H. Joffé, "The Arab Spring in North Africa: Origins and Prospects," *Journal of North African Studies* 16, no. 4 (December 2011), 514–17.

55. Johnnie Ryan, "Thinking Centrifugal; Fecundity and Hazard on the Net," in *Islamist Radicalisation in Europe and the Middle East: Reassessing the Causes of Terrorism*, edited by George Joffé (London: I. B. Tauris, 2012), 58–92. See also Mohammed Nanabhay and Roxane Farmanfarmaian, "From Spectacle to Spectacular: How Physical Space, Social Media and Mainstream Broadcast Amplified the Public Sphere in Egypt's 'Revolution,'" *Journal of North African Studies* 16, no. 4 (December 2011) (Special Issue: *North Africa's Arab Spring*), 573–604.

56. Jean-Pierre Filiu, *The Arab Revolution: Ten Lessons from the Democracy Uprising* (London: Hurst and Co, 2011), 84–85.

57. Nicholas Pelham, "Libya, the Colonel's Yoke Lifted," *Middle East Research and Information Project*, September 7, 2011, www.merip.org /mero/mero090711.

2

DYNAMICS OF CONTINUITY AND CHANGE*

Youssef Mohammed Sawani

INTRODUCTION AND STRUCTURE

Libya's contemporary history has been dominated by the "perpetual dynamics" of religion, tribalism, regionalism, and oil. After 42 years in power, Muammar Qadhafi was killed at the hands of his own people. Despite receiving powerful support from NATO and certain Arab governments, the 2011 uprisings were authentically Libyan and were yet another reflection of the supremacy of these four "perpetual dynamics." The purpose of this chapter is to analyze these dynamics and how they are echoed in post-Qadhafi Libya.

To set the stage, the chapter begins by elucidating the fundamental continuities that undergirded the 2011 uprisings. The next section entitled "Libya's Perpetual Dynamics and Their Constraints on the Future" provides an explanation of the history and role of religion, tribalism, regionalism, and oil in shaping contemporary Libya. Then, "The Interaction of the 'Perpetual Dynamics' and Their Political Manifestations" identifies how these dynamics have played out during the uprisings and in their aftermath. Next, "The Topography of the Institutionalized Forces" seeks to show how the perpetual dynamics explain the emergence of the different political, social, and military organizations that came into being during the uprisings. This treatment builds on George Joffé's illustration in Chapter 1 that the structure of the *Jamihiriyya* channeled opposition activism into preexisting social cleavages.

---

*This chapter draws on my "Post-Qadhafi Libya: Interactive Dynamics and the Political Future," *Contemporary Arab Affairs* 5, no. 1 (2012): 1–26.

Looking back, it is now quite clear that the spontaneous organizations produced by the uprisings drew upon the wellsprings of solidarity that religion, tribalism, regionalism, and oil exert in Libyan society. A final section, "The New Libya: Challenges and Opportunities," briefly treats the history of foreign involvement in the uprisings and their aftermath, exploring how this legacy entails both challenges and opportunities for post-Qadhafi Libya. (This issue is developed at greater length in Chapter 4.)

The 2011 Libyan Uprisings in Larger Perspective

Any assessment of the future of post-Qadhafi Libya must address the questions and challenges arising from the war that led to Muammar Qadhafi's fall. In that conflict, a variety of local and foreign forces of many nations played a decisive role. To discern the future outlines of Libyan politics, it is necessary to examine the orientations of the prevailing forces and their political and social topography.

The unpredictable course of events that has unfolded in Libya since 17 February 2011 was truly impossible to foresee. Military operations ended on 20 October 2011 and the National Transitional Council (NTC) became the formal sovereign and governing authority of a Qadhafi-free Libya—as the NTC had secured recognition from most of the world's states even if it did not happen to be in control of most of Libya's territory. In Qadhafi's wake, the situation on the ground has been far from peaceful. During the later stages of 2011 and the first half of 2012, armed clashes were frequent while the edifice of an effective government was essentially absent.

There was no common cause that brought together the different uprisings' armed forces or political leaders except the goal of completely eradicating the Qadhafi's regime. This unifying factor vanished after the killing of Qadhafi on 20 October and the concomitant fall of the last loyalist strongholds of Sirte and Bani Walid. The ensuing vacuum opened up new horizons with literally limitless possibilities for the future of Libya at the levels of identity, national integration, democratic transformation, and the determinants of a new political order.

An attempt will be made here to sketch the features of Libyan society and politics from a range of political, economic, and social perspectives. This approach will bring into focus the "perpetual dynamics" that constitute the fundamentals that have shaped the Libyan past as well as the foreseeable future of the country. After this, the analysis will proceed to present an overview of the various political forces and currents. This will serve, to the degree that it is possible, to predict their future trajectories on the basis of the elements and determining factors from which they have emerged.

This study derives, in the main, from the author's observations of the ongoing developments since the spark of revolution was ignited and what has been written in Arabic in both the popular press and scholarly literature. It balances published information about the activities of the various political currents present in post-Qadhafi Libya alongside discussions with some of their representatives.

LIBYA'S PERPETUAL DYNAMICS AND THEIR CONSTRAINTS ON THE FUTURE

The relations between society and the state in Libya have remained subject to the primary constraints of religion, ideology, tribalism, and oil. These were certainly the primary factors that defined the relations between the political authority and the Libyan social structure over the past four decades. Therefore, it is highly likely that these dynamics will play a similar role in the future of the country after the fall of Qadhafi.[1]

In order to grasp these dynamics, it is necessary to sketch a panoramic view of contemporary Libya. The discussion begins with the factor of religion, which has always had paramount relevance throughout Libya's history. Today, religion is also a primary vector in which information about the uprisings and the ensuing debates and political competition have come to be expressed.

Religion and Politics

Libya has been a Muslim community since the late seventh century AD.[2] Since the Middle Ages, Libya has been a completely Islamic polity—akin to those of the Arabian Peninsula. The vast majority of Libyans are Sunnis adhering to the Maliki *madhhab* (school of religious law). The only exception is the existence of a small percentage of Libyan Berbers in the Western Mountain (Jabal Nafusa) who follow the Ibadhi sect.[3] Throughout these centuries, Sufi orders have found Libyan soil especially hospitable—as was the case throughout North Africa. Attempts at spreading Shi'ism during the period of the Fatimid state failed completely,[4] as did attempts to spread other *madhhabs* subsequently. Almost all authorities that have ruled Libya over the last 14 centuries, including the Ottomans (and, strangely enough, the Italians and British as well), have claimed that they are ruling in accordance with Islam while surreptitiously fashioning their own novel interpretation of Islam which serves to legitimate their rule.

Though the Ottoman Empire always presented itself as a Muslim one, Libyans were not particularly keen on maintaining loyalty to it once a genuinely Libyan and Arab movement presented an alternative. In 1911, Libya became an Italian colony, and many Libyans blamed the Turks for abandoning them to their own fate. They fought the Italians under the banners of both Islam and Arabism, only incidentally aligning themselves with the Ottomans.[5]

Prior to the rise of Fascism, the Italians tried to establish their Islamic legitimacy by enshrining Idriss Al-Sanussi as Amir for noncoastal Cyrenaica during what E. E. Evans-Pritchard referred to as "The Period of Accords" from 1916 to 1921. However, the Fascist government that took power in Rome in 1922 went back on those agreements, choosing to employ repression to crush the resistance, further antagonizing the very elements it had previously desired to accommodate. Omar Mukhtar, a Sanussi Sheikh and teacher at a Quran school, became a prominent leader of the jihad, unifying the military wing of the Sanussi Order under his leadership. (He has remained a unifying, yet contested, symbol throughout Libyan history. Evoking his memory references the noble struggle against injustice, as well as the legitimacy to govern in its wake. Unsurprisingly, his image was appropriated in a wide range of contexts during the uprisings. A rendering of Mukhtar appears on the cover of this book evoking the various uses of symbols in the struggle for legitimacy in post-Qadhafi Libya.)

Although the 1930s saw a switch from repression to co-optation, the failure of Italy to "put an Islamic face" on its rule was further evident after the attempt of Mussolini to portray himself as a protector of Libyan Muslims. He visited Tripoli in 1937 and in a theatrical display was presented with "the Sword of Islam." This charade was organized so that Italy could claim that it was not an infidel power, but rather one that cared for the Muslims under its rule. Even the Italians' most "culturally sensitive" actions, like introducing Arabic into their system of schools, failed to attract Libyans in any significant number.[6]

In late 1942, the Italians were evicted by the British, who chose to administer Cyrenaica through methods of "indirect rule." They also attempted to cast their administration as defending Islam as a means to secure Libyan cooperation. The British policy of aligning with the Sanussi Order, rather than opposing it, was far more successful than the half-hearted efforts at cooptation practiced by the Italians. In 1949, with the failure of the British to control the international politics surrounding Libya's future, the British administration declared Cyrenaica a semiautonomous Amirate to be ruled by Idriss Al-Sanussi in order to strengthen his hand in internal Libyan struggles. This policy proved effective: over the next two years, Idriss was able—with much British, American, and UN help—to impose his will on other Libyan leaders and ascend to the throne of a federal Libyan monarchy created when independence was gained in 1951.[7] Subsequently, the British and the Americans lent full support to the monarchy and were rewarded with a permanent military presence in the country, in addition to advantages in securing certain oil concessions from 1955 onward. However, such gains were the target of the Qadhafi regime that overthrew Idriss's monarchy in 1969.

The Qadhafi regime also met with failure in its attempt to reformulate the Islam of Libya in accordance with Qadhafi's own personal political and religious theses, especially those pertaining to the *hadith* and the *sunna* (i.e., the normative practice of the Prophet Muhammad as reported in the *hadith* literature). Despite Qadhafi's overt suppression of all Islamists, their most extreme variants—the socially oriented Salafists and military-oriented jihadists—gained a presence in Libya's eastern Green Mountain region. (The processes of Islamist confrontation with, and later co-optation, by the Qadhafi regime is discussed at length in Chapter 7.)

Religion remains the central component of Libyan identity. Each new set of rulers in Libya has tried to spread its own new form of Islam. Qadhafi sought to instill his own religious ideology, which stressed heterodox ideas such as personal *ijtihad* (legal reasoning), questioning the authority of the *hadith*, and individual interpretation of the Quran.[8] Moreover, he claimed that the ideology of his *Green Book* was in keeping with—and even derived from—Islam. But Libyan society did not embrace his idiosyncratic and heterodox ideology. The orthodox interpretation of Sunni Malaki Islam has always constituted the core of the Libyan value structure and the framework of its social system. This "perpetual dynamic" acquired special significance after the fall of Qadhafi's regime unleashed a wave of new ideological currents all claiming to derive from (or at least pay lip service to) Islam. Unsurprisingly, despite claiming to be rooted in Libyan Islam, many of the new political parties espoused mutually contradictory social and economic doctrines.

Thus, the ability of Libyans to hold on to their traditionally moderate form of Islam will be subject to serious tests as extremist trends attempt to use the vacuum of authority to make inroads. The debates that characterize post-Qadhafi Libya attest to the fact that Qadhafi's attempts to change Islamic practice inside Libya lacked any long-term influence. Though echoes of his stance against the Muslim Brotherhood could be seen in the discourse against them, Libyans seemed well determined to distance themselves from every remnant of

Qadhafi's discourse on Islam. In short, a new and familiar struggle is afoot to lay claim to the mantle of Libyan Islamic legitimacy.

Tribalism, Regionalism, and Political Authority

Libya is rich in tribes whose members are scattered throughout the country, such as the Warfalla and Zuwaya, while also possessing numerous geographically concentrated tribal enclaves like those of the Rajban in the Nafusa (Western) Mountains, Warshafana in the Jafara Valley, and the Barasa in Cyrenaica. Libyan society is basically a tribal one and—despite the advances and modernization of the last century—tribal loyalties are still powerful. Individuals may very well act rationally in their personal choices when doing so does not require making delicate or problematic choices between potentially divergent sources of their identity. Once the average Libyan has to make a difficult choice, the outcome is likely to align with the preferences of his tribe.[9]

Both the regimes of King Idriss and Colonel Qadhafi drew their top administrators from specific tribal groupings. Both also pitted opposing tribal confederations against each other. While the monarchy relied on Cyrenaican and Sanussi tribal alliances to give it legitimacy and to staff its ministries, Qadhafi's regime worked at reinvigorating the effectiveness of tribal alliances based around Sabha, Sirte, and Bani Walid, while at the same time endeavoring to activate the role of ideology in reshaping not only political structures, but also tribal structures. Qadhafi's regime went to great lengths to reinforce the traditional tribal alliances among the Qadhadhifa, Maqarha, and Warfalla through its preferential staffing policies in the military establishment. This is the mirror image of what the British, and later Idriss, did with the *Sa'adi* tribes of eastern Libya in staffing Idriss's Praetorian guard—the Cyrenaican Defense Force. (It also illustrates the notion of tribal inversion discussed in Chapter 1.)

It is important to take note of the amorphous nature and fluidity of tribal alliances in Libya, along with the tendency of most tribes to ally themselves with whatever political authority is in power, in order to gain economic handouts. Qadhafi exploited this tendency to manipulate tribal power structures. Similarly, Qadhafi's ideology of "statelessness" led to the undermining of the various administrative institutions and in many instances paved the way for regime domination of tribal alliances, thereby exacerbating factionalism. This process atomized the state and the relations of the tribes to it, consolidating a sense of regionalism. Consequently, part of Qadhafi's legacy is that, after his demise, conditions were conducive to debates on the reinstitution of the federal system in Libya, along lines similar to those that existed between 1951 and 1963.[10] The tribal nature of Libyan society and the role of tribal cleavages in the 2011 uprisings are discussed in greater depth by Wolfram Lacher in Chapter 5. Lacher argues that a resurgence of tribal institutions has contributed to the central authority's inability to consolidate its grip on the countryside.

While a post-Qadhafi Libya is in dire need of a strong and efficient central government, one that can undertake the herculean tasks of reconstruction and reconciliation while transitioning to democratic governance, the fact that regionally focused uprisings gave more strength to local and tribal forces was reflected by the unilateral declaration of a federal *Barqa* (Cyrenaica) following the convening in Benghazi on 6 March 2012 of the "The Barqa Conference of the People of Cyrenaica." Such separatist tendencies may spread to other regions unless a strong and efficient central authority is able to respond to the concerns and needs that were behind the regional uprisings. (The possibilities for secessionist tendencies surfacing in the south are discussed in Henry Smith's Chapter 6.)

Tribes have not been transformed into institutions that can work in harmony with the institutions of a modern state and its central bureaucracy. Moreover, given Libya's history, it is likely that tribal culture and the tribe as an institution will continue to exert a great and centrifugal influence on sociopolitical interactions as well as on individual and group identities in Libyan society. This will be the case so long as Libyans do not perceive the existence or relevance of alternative institutions and civil society organizations. It goes without saying that the existence of a vibrant Libyan civil society that enjoys independence from the state, religious structures, and the tribes is a prerequisite for a decline in tribalism.[11]

Qadhafi's tribal politics relied on manipulating tribal alliances within the state apparatus, particularly in the security and armed forces. Economic rewards and state projects were distributed mainly according to such alliances. Therefore, for decades tribes such as the Warfalla were the cornerstone of the security and state bureaucracies. But once elements of this tribe were involved in an attempted coup in 1993, the entire tribe was ejected from sensitive posts, and Qadhafi used tactics to inflict harm to their internal tribal cohesion. The regime, faced with the loss of the strong support the Warfalla had previously offered, promptly created the Popular Social Leadership (PSL) to institutionalize the security role of all tribal leaders in protecting the regime. (For more on this, see Chapter 1, pages 30–36)

Though the PSL institution and its subsidiaries were meant to represent tribes and their leaders to the government, they were simultaneously designed to help Qadhafi maintain strict control over the tribes. Most members were Qadhafi loyalists, comrades, revolutionary elements, security forces, or army generals. Most possessed close enough connections to him to be entrusted with decision-making authority. The PSL was not a part of the governance structures Qadhafi described in *The Green Book*, so he sought to bestow it with a different source of legitimacy as deriving especially from Libyan history and functioning as the embodiment and guardian of social values and ethics. It was supposedly the highest moral body in Libyan society to which official institutions had to listen and to whose guidelines they were forced to adhere. Qadhafi himself was declared the "supreme social leader," and in theory, this reinforced the fact that no one would question the legitimacy of his decisions, even though he "officially" had no governmental role.

In reality, however, the PSL was an informal institution that functioned in parallel to the formal bureaucracy, which it sought to control.[12] Since most of its leaders were given artificial "social" authority by Qadhafi and they were not truly rooted in the Libyan social system, they simply disappeared from their posts during the uprisings, as they no longer enjoyed sufficient support for their roles. Although a majority of the social leaders sided with their revolting tribes, some of the PSL leaders were active in rallying the support of their tribes on behalf of Qadhafi through propaganda-like tribal conferences.

Although 80 percent of the inhabitants of Libya now live in "urban areas," the Libyan sociologist Mustafa al-Tir asserts, "the vast majority of Libyans still speak of tribal belonging." This dichotomy derives from the fact that 90 percent of the grandparents of urban dwellers were themselves rural or semiurbanized. Al-Tir attributes these orientations to what he has termed the "ruralization" of cities whereby:

> The major urban areas developed as a result of emigration from the countryside and not as a result of natural increase [in population]. Thus, the tribe is still present today in the memory of a large number of urban dwellers. Instead of those coming from the countryside integrating into the life of the city and adopting the ways and modes of urban life, they entered the cities...and imposed [the] various particulars of rural life.[13]

This persistence of tribal loyalty impinged on the entire process of modernization. Al-Tir argues that "when [tribal] loyalty encroaches upon necessary qualifications, then discussing modern institutions becomes meaningless!"[14]

Both the Qadhafi regime and the partisans of the uprisings employed calculated appeals to tribal identities when it suited them. Qadhafi portrayed the uprisings and their leaderships as driven by tribal interests and separatist orientations. Conversely, the NTC consolidated its legitimacy through tribal declarations of allegiances and by discrediting Qadhafi's claim to enjoy overwhelming tribal support. The NTC sought to demonstrate that most of the tribal leaders brought in by Qadhafi to attend the Tripoli tribal gathering on 5 May 2011 had done so because they feared reprisals by Qadhafi if they had acted otherwise.[15]

Qadhafi endeavored to represent the uprisings as though they were limited to particular regions or tribes in an attempt to foment divisiveness and deepen intertribal fissures. The NTC that led the uprisings also utilized tribes in order to win advocates—as vividly demonstrated in the Council's co-optation of members of Qadhafi's own Qadhadhifa tribe in order to deprive him of legitimacy and counter his tribal propaganda. Such tactics serve as a reminder of the role tribalism played during the Italian occupation of Libya when both resistance and collaboration were primarily conducted using the tribes as organizational vehicles. Thus, throughout Libya's history, tribal loyalty or identity has proven a useful instrument to generate tribal consensus for the purpose of affirming or denying the legitimacy to rule the country as well as in organizing resistance or collaboration. There is no doubt that it will retain a weighty influence in the future as well.

This continuity has already dramatically manifested itself. The results of the 7 July 2012 elections provided ample evidence that Libyans favored independent or local candidates with whom they were likely to share regional or tribal connections over those linked to political parties with whom they might only share ideological connections. The fact that the National Forces Alliance, composed along regional, tribal, and personality lines gained most of the seats assigned to political parties further indicates the significance of factors other than ideology. Furthermore, the results of local council elections attested to the primacy of tribal association over political orientation.

In summation, despite the importance of tribes as a focal point for collective action, there were no vast social divisions of the sort that could have decisively undermined the uprisings' goal of toppling the dictator. Many held views that the regime was favoring certain areas and tribes at the expense of the rest, and of course, these cleavages were instrumental in channeling certain groups to rise up in greater numbers.

Yet, even in what were largely passive or ostensibly pro-Qadhafi areas, the majority of ordinary Libyans were either clandestinely supportive of the uprisings or voluntarily confined themselves to the privacy of their homes. Therefore, the vast majority of Libyans, whatever their tribal background, were ready at the end of the uprisings to attempt to integrate into the new Libya. This is not to say that tribal elites who enjoyed privileged positions in the Qadhafi era, such as those of the Maqarha, Qadhadhifa, and Warfalla have not sought to contest the spread of post-Qadhafi national authority to their areas in an attempt to maintain their local fiefdoms. This crucial theme is treated extensively in Chapter 5.

OIL AND THE CHALLENGES OF MODERNIZATION

Oil was and will remain an essential ingredient in the process of political, economic, and social transformation in Libya. Libyan sociologist Mustafa Al-Tir has noted that, unfortunately, modernization and rationalization of the Libyan economy did not result from the oil boom. In fact, prevailing economic, social, and political structures were co-opted and entrenched. Qadhafi's regime attempted to restrict oil-related transformations and contain their impact in order to minimize their effect on society at large. These processes happened differently than in the Gulf—where oil wealth led to a massive welfare state and urbanization, with foreign cultural influences seen as destabilizing but where economic modernization has been widely accepted. In contradistinction, in Libya the Qadhafi regime was keen on combating forces of political, social, and economic modernization. It also sought to keep "disruptive" foreign technological and societal influences from impinging on the traditional framework of Libyan society. The outcome of these policies was to place obstacles in the path of the modernization of Libyan society and its institutions.[16] (Qadhafi's various unsuccessful attempts to restructure Libya's economy and spur competitiveness, diversification, and job creation are discussed by Ronald Bruce St John in Chapter 3.)

Material abundance constituted the primary driving force that fueled Qadhafi's internal and external adventures. Yet, the most dangerous repercussion of oil wealth was that it accorded the regime the financial power necessary to achieve two contradictory ends simultaneously. The first pertained to providing the state with favorable conditions to penetrate society and create a system of local compradors.

The abundance of petrodollars enabled the state to practice subjugation in all its forms without the need to impose taxes. Similarly, oil wealth liberated the government from any need to reconcile itself to the demands of the people politically. Current academic literature on the Gulf States refers to a quid pro quo between the bestowing of state largesse and the populace's accepting the state's legitimacy. Although not the form envisioned by Rousseau, this is certainly a form of social contract.[17] Since the Libyan government had infinite material means from the hydrocarbon wealth at its disposal, democratic concessions were not a part of this social contract.

Oil also played a crucial role in determining the strategies of international and global powers toward Libya. The powerful influence of Libya's energy resources was clearly evident in the debate to impose United Nations sanctions on Libya from 1992 to 1999 in retaliation for Lockerbie. It took lengthy discussions among international actors—especially Germany, Italy, and the United States—to come to agreements on imposing sanctions. The fact that many European countries relied heavily on Libyan oil supplies, whereas the United States did not, made a consensus difficult to reach. Notwithstanding, America was also a prominent actor in the hectic international effort to rehabilitate Qadhafi and to "bring him in from the cold," so Libya might become a partner with which the global community could do business.

Recalling their stances in the 1980s and 90s against the American, British, and French marginalization of Qadhafi from the world scene, at the start of the 2011 uprisings, Germany, Turkey, and Italy were again quite reluctant to join in the alliance against Qadhafi. These countries had a clear national interest in maintaining oil and/or gas supplies from Libya and the prospect of early military action appeared to put these interests in jeopardy. (This dynamic is discussed in Chapter 4.)

Once the eastern part of the country was Qadhafi-free, Benghazi witnessed an influx of Western companies and government officials keen on displaying support for the revolt, but also eager to secure existing or new oil deals.[18] Viewed in this light, it is not possible for any analyst to ignore Libya's energy resources as a determinant of the country's future.[19] The contemporary history of Libya and the developments since February 2011, in conjunction with the position that major powers adopted against Qadhafi, has only intensified the strategic role of oil.

As far as tribe and oil are concerned, their dual influence on the past, present, and future of Libya must not be overlooked. The most important example pertains to the form the Libyan state will take, whether unitary, federal, decentralized, or other. In 2007, a Libyan intellectual described the negative impact of decentralization on the Libyan reality as it was practiced during the monarchy and the Qadhafi era:

> The disintegration of the center has limited the possibility of creating civil centrism as a driving force within a unified strategic vision...to become instead a sphere for competition between dispersed regions over resources...Experiments of decentralization always ended in the distortion of democracy. Decentralization strengthens local reactionary forces and weakens general political consciousness...from another angle, the tribal structure for the formation of Libyan society, which was revitalized through decentralization, imposed its traditional culture on the instruments for executing development and modernization projects in a society in need of employing the greatest measure of scientific and technical qualifications and capabilities.[20]

THE INTERACTION OF THE "PERPETUAL DYNAMICS" AND THEIR POLITICAL MANIFESTATIONS

This chapter has made it abundantly clear that preexisting dynamics figured prominently both politically and socially since the start of the revolt against Qadhafi. The most prominent manifestations are that groups associated with Islam expect their political role in the new Libya to be large, while even nonreligious groups must pay lip service to conservative Islamic practice to survive politically. Domestic Islamist movements today share a commitment to the goal of realizing an Islamic state. They see this as in fitting with Libyan history. None of the prominent political forces overtly rejected democracy, though the Salafist current underlined the contradiction between democracy and the Islamic precedent of the *salaf as-salih* (pious ancestors.) Salafists stress the historical precedents of *shura* (consultation) and the role of the *ahl al-hall wa al-'aqd* (those charged with the authority to conclude and dissolve agreements).

The *Ikhwan al-Muslimiyyin* (Muslim Brotherhood) were better organized than other Islamist groups, and they also shared reservations about democracy, notably those expressed by Ali Sallabi in his book on *shura*, where he considers shura to be legally binding and an authentically Islamic alternative to representative democracy, which is seen as a Western transplant.[21] They view democracy as an instrument or technique to be utilized in creating a governance mechanism whose underlying structures and legitimacy must come from within

Islam. They attempt to project a modern character by voicing no objection to a *dawla ma'adaniyya* (civil state) so long as that does not clash with the primacy of Islamic shari'a in legislation—in fitting with Sayyid Qutb's formulation. However, they vociferously denigrate and disavow any call for secularism.

As for liberal, nationalist, and leftist currents, these did not constitute clearly organized entities—despite certain claims of their supporters to the contrary. Their representatives also advocated a civil state, yet they warned that the danger to democracy is not only in its being divested of any social or economic content, but also in its potential to be hijacked under an Islamic rubric. They criticized the use of religion to control the public and accused Islamists of camouflaging their real intentions by employing democratic facades, where the appearance of democracy is only maintained until their arrival in power, at which time the democratic system will be subtly overturned. These "liberal" currents suffered from lacking effective organization at the grassroots level. Their leaderships did not pay enough attention to conceptual and organizational questions and seemed content to wager on the traditional, religious moderation of Libyans.

The State of Play after the GNC Elections

As of the end of 2012, it remains too early to tell if these "liberal" positions and their victory in the General National Council elections of July 2012 are likely to decisively quell the fervor of the Islamists. The heated debates that went on in the lead up to the elections highlighted the intrinsic antagonism between the liberal and Islamist currents. This was abundantly evident in reported incidents of personal defamation and verbal political assaults on the leadership of other political currents. However, despite this trend and Muhammad Sawan's (the leader of the Muslim Brotherhood's Justice and Construction Party) statement on 13 July 2012 that "Mahmoud Jibril shared Qadhafi's views on the shari'a," by the end of 2012 it appeared that a modicum of pragmatism was likely to prevail allowing limited cooperation between previously antagonistic groups.[22] Moderate Islamists and liberals do not disagree about issues of national unity, development of nation-wide infrastructure, and integration with the global economy. Hence the two currents face a strong logic to cooperate in the face of the tribalists, regionalists, local militias, and extremists who oppose such policies.

Such antagonism as prevailed during the transitional phase appears most clearly in the case of Islamist forces, at the forefront of which are the Muslim Brotherhood and the Islamic Movement for Change (IMC) led by Abdul-Hakim Bilhajj, one of the former leaders of the Libyan Islamic Fighting Group (LIFG). Bilhajj resigned his post as the chairman of Tripoli's Military Council and publicly affirmed his belief in democracy and a civil state.[23] He formed a political party, *Hizb al-Watan* (Homeland Party) and ran in the elections. Many still questioned his real intentions, close links to Qatar, and indications of his preparations to resort to violence in order to advance his ambitions. The abject failure of his Homeland Party in the elections could be interpreted as not only the Libyans' rejection of all forms of confronta-tionalist Islamist leaderships but also a strong indication of their disap-proval of foreign involvement in the transitional process. (Chapter 7 delves deeper into the attempts by Islamists—namely the Muslim Brotherhood, LIFG, and the Salafists—to transform themselves into viable political parties with genuine roots in the Libyan social system. It is shown that only the Brotherhood succeeded in this process.)

Localism

What also commands attention in the wake of the 7 July 2012 GNC election results is the strong emergence of localist and regionalist senti-ment within the Congress. The revolt against Qadhafi generated many groupings with a fanatical adherence to local interests—especially in the regions or cities such as Misrata, Benghazi, and Zintan—that had some prominence in advancing the revolution. This is evident in the call for Benghazi to be the new capital or to accord Misrata with a dis-proportionately large share of government positions. It is also exem-plified by the fact that immediately after the elections, both Misrata and Zintan did not reveal any desire or willingness to hand over to the central government the huge arms caches they had stockpiled. The issue of the powerful peripheries ceding their power to the weak center is one that will likely take years to play out in Libya.

In eastern Libya, where tribalism/localism plays a conspicuous and influential role, the call for federalism or a privileged position for Benghazi did not necessarily coincide with the interests of the Islamist political forces. In fact, the tribal factor had in many ways more at stake here and overlapped with calls for regional separatism. The federalist/ separatist "National Gathering for the Inhabitants of Cyrenaica," held in Bayda in October 2011, was fundamentally a tribal gathering.

By referring to the progressive emergence of the power of the periphery and the resurgence of tribal politics in eastern Libya, one may understand the position of the powerful al-Obeidat tribe, centered on

Darna. The tribe issued an emotionally charged statement advocating for decentralization after the killing of their member, Brigadier General Abdul-Fattah Yunis al-Obeidi, on 28 July 2011. Yunis defected from Qadhafi's forces in the early days of the uprisings to lead the NTC's army.[24]

The situation differed in the region of Misrata where there appeared to be a connection between the Islamist current and local sentiments. Misrata enjoys a position of great strength in the new Libya and does not need to advocate for federalism for its interests to be secured. It shares this perspective with the Islamists who also tend to oppose federalism and seek to control the Libyan center. This tacit "alliance" was clear both Islamists and Misratans called for the censure of some leading figures of the progressive and liberal current in the interim government.[25] Along with this development, Misrata was the most independent locality in Libya as it largely conducted its own administration and external relations without reference to the NTC.[26] Similarly, the leaders of Misrata have called for the displacement of the dark-complexioned inhabitants of the neighboring town of Tawergha, and NTC officials were powerless to prevent the realization of this agenda. This ongoing ethnic cleansing clearly sets a precedent fraught with risk. Even though there is a near-national consensus over what many Tawerghans have done to Misratans—ranging from killing, rape, assault, vandalism, and theft—the call to displace their whole village exceeded all expectations and proportionality.

As for the Nafusa Mountain region, the situation seems to be polarized into an Arab-*Amazigh* (Berber) dichotomy that prompted intense rivalry among the anti-Qadhafi ranks. Qadhafi's attempts to play on the issue in order to stop the revolt against him failed as most areas of the mountain quickly joined the uprisings. The fact that the Arab tribes of Zintan had acquired a huge cache of all types of weapons had led neighboring *Amazigh* tribes to follow suit and attempt to control their own territory. Local rivalries, predictably, fell along tribal lines, while others harbored some connection to the Arab-*Amazigh* dichotomy. Evidence points to Zintani alliance building as an attempt to offset the ethnic dichotomy. Yet, the precondition for such alliance building is that the Arab Zintanis establish themselves as the undisputed leaders of the whole region. Throughout the transition period, they appear to be using their capture of Saif al-Islam to do exactly this.

The Zintan situation is not unique. In a visit to the Mashasha area during the third week of October 2011, the author identified four towns and villages that were completely deserted. Their residents cannot go back to their homes for fear of persecution. They are labeled as Qadhafi loyalists and are accused of supporting his killing machine during the revolt. The author's discussions with leaders from the local council of Zintan reveal that the return of thousands of displaced people to their homes remains very problematic. It also highlights the prime importance and necessity of initiating a national reconciliation and implementing just judicial processes.

In connection with the rise in the importance of local identities, the *Amazigh* held a general conference in Tripoli on 26 September 2011—a move unprecedented in the history of contemporary Libya. The conference was the platform for advocating and securing the rights of the *Amazigh*—specifically, the constitutionality of their language as a national language written in the neo-Tifinagh script. Even though the general orientation of the *Amazigh* did not suggest any threats to national unity, some of the leading figures of the *Amazigh* movement in Libya put forth destabilizing demands. They voiced a desire for a type of regional autonomy and affiliation to the rest of the *Amazigh* of North Africa. A prominent *Amazigh* leader even expressed hostility toward Arabism and sympathy with Israel.[27] It is unclear whether the *Amazigh* will develop along the lines of other tribal or regional cleavages prevalent throughout Libya, or if they will become uniquely mobilized as a distinct ethnic/political party with positions and politics that differ markedly from their Arab neighbors.

No doubt these various levels of polarization render economic or political matters, particularly those related to democratic transition, highly subject to the maneuvers of different local forces. Of grave concern, for example, is that any attempt to discuss publicly the oversized roles of the "perpetual dynamics" in Libya's post-Qadhafi political life or to write about it in newspapers invites danger to the extent that the militias threaten those who bring up such issues with physical liquidation. Along these lines the editor-in-chief of the *Arus al-Bahr* newspaper was threatened with death if he continued criticizing Islamists. The editor published the content of the threat he received in a phone call from a supporter of Islamists. He obviously had no protection other than to resort to addressing a plea to some NTC authorities who probably did not have the capacity to protect him.[28]

ON THE CENTRALITY OF THE TRANSITIONAL PHASE: DEFINING THE RULES OF THE GAME

The National Transitional Council that initially convened in Benghazi on 27 February 2011 and was officially established on 5 March, allocated to itself the task of political leadership of the anti-Qadhafi uprisings and subsequent leadership of Libya during the post-Qadhafi transitional phase.[29] It obtained international support and the recognition of various Libyan cities sufficient to enable it to impose a degree of control and authority. It set out to carry its self-defined mandate until after military operations ended in order to supervise the election of a founding assembly—the General National Congress—which would both govern the country and draft a constitution to be put up for popular referendum. Despite this bold and noble mission, the council—constituting the "center" of the Libyan polity—possessed only moral, legal, or ethical authority while its many opponents and Libya's competing militias—constituting the "periphery"—had access to vast supplies of arms and local networks giving them de facto political authority.[30]

Even though the NTC approved an unprecedented 68.5 billion Libyan dinar budget for 2011 (approximately US$50 billion at January 2012 rates) and announced that its interim government would have a transitional program in place, implementation was still lacking on the ground. Most old state institutions and ministries, as well as the new ones that the NTC established, were largely unable to implement coherent reconstruction, development, or economic policies. National institutions of defense and security have been almost dysfunctional, with matters related to law and order largely in the hands of the militias. Bold action by the NTC (and later GNC) was still lacking even in instances when the Council's and Congress' building suffered attacks by armed militias or when armed confrontations and clashes took place throughout the country. The inability of the NTC to perform was related to a lack of capacity and to the fact that its actions were taken only after the cumbersome task of trying to build consensus which was subject to negotiations involving recalcitrant local and tribal elements. At the early stage of its authority, and especially immediately after the fall of Tripoli, the NTC could have taken bold actions since its approval ratings were fairly high and there was a desire to rally together around the common cause. However, since the Liberation was achieved and the NTC failed to successfully consolidate its authority, its inaction resulted in the loss of almost all of the popular leverage it once possessed. Resultantly, it was exposed to harsh criticism and even outright rejection as the new Libya's sovereign body. Certain groups called for the setting up of an alternative elected body, which would have led to an even more protracted transitional phase.

It may be fair to say that the core success of the NTC was the proclamation of the Temporary Constitutional Decleration and a road map for a transition to an elected authority, both of which

aimed to establish legitimate governance in Libya.[31] This Temporary
Constitutional Decleration promulgated on 3 August 2011 addressed
the hopes of the Libyan people by clarifying its orientation toward "a
society of citizenship, justice, equality, progress, and comfort in which
injustice, autocracy, tyrannical excess, exploitation and rule by a single
individual are impossible."[32] It set out a road map for the transition to
a permanent democratic government, reflecting the interaction of the
many political and armed elements that made up the NTC itself. In
this document, however, it was clear that the emphasis was on gener-
alities and commonalities, and there was a marked absence of details.
Although this reflected aspirations that were agreed upon during the
struggle against Qadhafi, it merely pushed potential divisive issues
further down the road. The fact that the desire to oust Qadhafi was
the core shared objective uniting the center and the periphery was
reflected in the temporary constitution: its provisions were meant to
cement the gains and unity of the uprisings by catering to all factions
in a generalized way. However, once the common goal was achieved,
myriad problems reared their heads and led to strong disagreements.

As discussed earlier, this is because the center and various components of the periphery were divided by the cleavages of religion, oil,
tribe, and region that have always characterized Libyan history. As
soon as the transition process began, disagreements on many issues
and demands for amendments to the constitution were strongly voiced.
Some of these disagreements and struggles between various local actors
and the new organizations created by the uprisings are addressed in
greater detail in the other chapters of this volume as they constitute "the
struggle for post-Qadhafi Libya." This chapter provides both an analytical framework to analyze these struggles (i.e., the perpetual dynamics detailed above) and a description of the multiple organizations and
institutions which were created by the uprisings—treated below.

One of the unique features of the 2011 Libyan uprisings was the
sheer number of spontaneous organizational bodies it spawned. The
Arab Spring events in Tunisia and Egypt gave rise to temporary neighborhood councils and a fleeting national leadership. In Libya, an abu-
dance of competing local militias, local councils, religious parties, and
citizens' organizations were created by the very multiplicity of the
uprisings and then flourished into the post-Qadhafi period. Moreover,
as discussed in the Introduction to this volume, the sovereign national
political institution forged by the 2011 Libyan uprisings, the National
Transitional Council, represented a far more dramatic instance of institutional change, than what happened in Egypt or Tunisia. This section
seeks to present the origins of the various institutional bodies created

by the uprisings and then briefly sketch how competition among them has been the defining constant of post-Qadhafi Libya.

THE TOPOGRAPHY OF THE INSTITUTIONALIZED FORCES

The National Transitional Council (NTC)

At the very start of the uprisings in mid-February 2011, the brutal onslaught of repression and killings at the hands of Qadhafi brigades appalled many regime officials. In fact, many senior bureaucrats and diplomats promptly adopted stances in line with the dictates of conscience and patriotism defecting before the end of the first week of the uprisings. As a result, the uprisings benefited from the services of many experts qualified to deal with the international aspects of the crisis. They understood the ways and means for obtaining global support while simultaneously addressing the domestic challenges associated with bringing together distinct revolutionary groups. This influx of Western-educated personnel to the side of the rebels inherently led to brainstorming about the creation of institutions to represent the political face of the uprisings and the mass of the Libyan people who otherwise had no viable means to express their opinion. Mahmoud Jibril, the first chairman of the NTC's executive arm, explained the Council's origins as his own brainchild. He understood the need for such a mechanism to represent the multiplicity of the uprisings under one roof in order to have a single organizational interlocutor to solicit international support. He then proposed the idea to Ali Issawi, Libya's ambassador to India. The two decided to send their proposal to Mustafa Abdul-Jalil in Bayda through Issawi's brother living in Benghazi, who received it by fax and drove to Bayda to deliver it.[33] Both Issawi and Jibril were technocrats who had advocated Washington Consensus–style reforms from within the Qadhafi regime. Their pro-business orientation was imprinted early on to the NTC. In the words of Jason Pack, on 9 March 2011 in the *Wall Street Journal*, "By putting Jibril and Issawi on the list [of the rebel's top political leadership], they're sending a message to foreign companies that the future Libyan government is interested in foreign investment and privatization."[34] According to Jibril's account, the Council was formed not by design but by an incidental process of gatherings of personalities from various regions and their struggles to cope with local and international pressures. Some members were rather independent, while others represented a range of political forces.

The NTC was a mix of reformist intellectuals, academics, journalists, lawyers, and human rights activists alongside defectors from Qaddafi's regime and many former Qadhafi opponents who had either lived outside Libya or had spent years in Qadhafi's prisons. It also included representatives of regions and tribes who reflected the diversity of Libya's tribal structure and pragmatists who were willing to negotiate with Qadhafi in order to avert further bloodshed.[35] Consensus around a unified position was thus difficult to attain. Only at later stages, after the liberation of many regions, did representatives of local or regional councils join the NTC, which further reinforced the primacy of such regional and tribal dynamics within the Council.

The NTC was therefore both an ad hoc creation and a highly heterogeneous one. It is not an exaggeration to say there were no common denominators except the will to stand up against Qadhafi. The NTC's great successes in gaining approval and recognition from many corners may be partially attributed to Qadhafi's shortsightedness. He believed that the West was always hypocritical and driven only by its interests. He wagered that since he himself posed no threat to the West, this should serve his purpose of convincing the West that it was the uprisings that actually constituted the threat instead. For this reason, Qadhafi failed to grasp that he had no real friends, and that his policies and personality were actually disdained by world leaders.

Subsequently, NTC members opted to institutionalize their activities, and the Council assumed the power of a parliament that also exercised some executive authority. The NTC's scope of authority had widened in theory; such expansion did not, however, lead to a consolidation of its power. After its formation, the NTC asserted its sole right to speak on behalf of the rebels and play the role of a political leadership for the multiple uprisings unfolding across Libya. Once liberation was attained, this body assumed the highest formal authority and was recognized internationally as sovereign. Not all Libyans however acknowledged this.

Therefore, the council became the target of many criticisms. Calls were voiced to expand the NTC's representative base so as to encompass all of Libya's regions. Others felt that the council's "revolutionary legitimacy" was insufficient. The NTC displayed a willingness to yield to pressures coming from regional, tribal, and ideological quarters to transform itself. Its expressed desire was to accommodate and build consensus. Sadly, due to a failure to achieve consensus on which reforms should be implemented, the end result was only further fragmentation, with the NTC's power and legitimacy suffering in the process.

The attacks on the NTC and its leadership came from all directions, but the most obvious danger stemmed from the armed militias that maintained an independence from the NTC and its policies.

The Local Councils

Majalis mahaliyah (local councils) were established during the uprisings through secret initiatives for the purpose of assuming the responsibility of administering each city or region after its liberation from the control of the ancien regime. Some were elected, others were not. It is indeed ironic that the Qadhafian ideal of local people's councils could provide a model for waging a sophisticated and institutionally well-developed anti-Qadhafi revolution. The irony was especially pronounced given that Qadhafi had failed to establish an effective system of committees and congresses to perform local government duties because of his maintenance of absolute power and his anti-institutional tendencies. The occurrence of fighting and armed clashes notwithstanding, once liberated from his control, Libyans were able to make a similar system to his Basic People's Congress system operate efficiently and succeed, to varying degrees, in the setting up of effective local authorities in the entire country, perhaps taking advantage of their previous experience and expertise in the management of service organizations and government.[36]

Some initially unelected local councils held elections after there was enough security to do so. In many areas—including Zawara, Misrata, and Benghazi—the newly elected councils were entrusted with the role of local administration of the various government and service sectors. Some of these councils have military wings nominally subject to their authority. Others function at the behest of dominate militias over which they have no control. After the liberation, there were many calls to dissolve the remaining unelected councils. To that end, in the weeks before the NTC's dissolution, it passed Law 59 of 2012 calling for the election of local councils.

The 17 February Coalitions

The 17 February Coalitions were associations formed spontaneously to "guard the revolution," but not to administer the cities like the local councils. They comprised political activists, human rights campaigners, and revolutionary partisans who participated in the first wave of protests. It became apparent that the urban 17 February Coalitions were closed organizations that did not allow outside membership.

They based their discourse on, and justified their actions according to, "revolutionary legitimacy." They attempted to exercise authority on almost all matters within their reach. This gave rise to problems and contradictions that appeared early on in Benghazi, and subsequently in Tripoli.

The vast majority of the members of the Benghazi Coalition elected to dissolve it or to withdraw from it. They explained this by their desire to submit to a single legitimate authority represented by the NTC. Zahi Mogherbi, one of its founders, explained in a phone conversation with the author that they took this decision so that the Coalition would not assume a position similar to that of Qadhafi's Revolutionary Command Council (RCC), which had announced after seizing power in 1969 that it would hand over power to the people only to consolidate one-man rule instead.[37] This is a clear indication of fear that the Coalition members felt regarding the risks of resorting to "revolutionary legitimacy," which threatens stability and democratic transition. Later the 17 February Coalition in Benghazi transformed into a civil society organization.

In Tripoli, the Coalition continued throughout the transition period to engage in a wide range of activities using the cover of its revolutionary legitimacy. A number of its members with whom the author met expressed their anger and resentment over practices that they attribute to the Muslim Brotherhood, which attempted to dominate the Tripoli Coalition. This has led many Coalition members to cease participation in its activities.[38] Though the importance of 17 February Coalitions waned at the regional level with the end of the transition period, many secret Coalitions were set up in ministries, government agencies, state-owned companies, and private corporations. These entities function as clandestine politburos and attempt to exercise influence in all matters they can get their hands on.

Islamic Political Groups

Despite their small size in terms of membership, the Islamists are highly organized and their members have both strong self-discipline and respect for their leadership figures. The most prominent of these is the Muslim Brotherhood, which has an organizational history in Libya dating back to the 1950s. As soon as specific Libyan regions were free of Qadhafi's control, the Muslim Brotherhood (MB) leadership rapidly emerged to occupy a prominent place, especially in the spheres of influential media such as *Al-Jazeera*, the Internet, and the Friday pulpits of mosques.

In March 2012, the Brotherhood formed their own political party, the "Justice and Construction Party," and the group has been engaged in setting up new civil and religious organizations and infiltrating similar entities. It exerts great efforts to expand its media presence through new satellite channels, mosques, *awqaf* (charitable foundations), *fatawi* (legal rulings), committees of *ulama*, public lectures, etc. They have professed their intention to abide by a civil state following Sayyid Qutb's formulation as well as their acquiescence to democracy within the confines of Islamic jurisprudence.

The NFSL, which was transformed in March 2012 into the "National Front Party," has historically been the largest of the Libyan Islamist-dominated movements. Its leadership adheres to many different theological and political orientations. Its current leadership seemingly has Sanussi tendencies. This may be traced to the political program of the NFSL and the statements it issued, expressing a clear attachment to the constitution as it was under the Sanussi monarchy.

Since its foundation in the early 1980s, the NFSL was subjected to dispersion by the Qadhafi regime and the voluntary desertion of many exiles from its ranks. The reasons for this fragmentation are related to differences in the Libyan exiled opposition since the failure of what was known as the National Conference of the Libyan Opposition (NCLO) in 2005. The NCLO was set up to unify and coordinate the efforts of opposition forces opposed to Qadhafi, but actually led to further divisions. However, despite the shrinking of its ranks, the NFSL constituted a preeminent media and political presence during the uprisings and before the liberation of Tripoli, after which its influence waned.

The most important, "non-moderate" Islamists are the Wahhabis and Salafis. Salafis come in many varieties, but all of them are associated with the theological/political concept *uli al-amr*—the Quranic term meaning "those who have been delegated responsibility for affairs." Despite the ambiguous position of this current, many of its leaders took a position that might at least be described as ambivalent towards the revolt against Qadhafi. Despite this they have spread among the ranks of the lesser educated groups of the population and youth.

After the no-fly zone was announced, the Salafi movement began supporting the uprisings and opening organizations and branches in many cities. As of the end of the transition period, they had not expressed a political position vis-à-vis the struggle of the other competing social forces. They did, however, exploit the absence of an effective governmental authority to control certain mosques and engage in proselytization (*da'wa*) in the street. Some of its members are directly engaged in *al-amr bi-l-ma'ruf wa al-nahi 'an al-munkar* (commanding what is right and forbidding what is unjust) in some neighborhoods of Tripoli. This included, for example, informing ladies' hair salons that they are no longer tolerated. They have also offended mainstream public opinion by their frequent destruction of graves with prominent Sufi tomb markers.

Among clandestine jihadist organizations, the Libyan Islamic Fighting Group (LIFG) was historically the most prominent, but the events of the uprisings transformed it into an aboveground military force that was initially important in the conquest and administration of Tripoli but rapidly lost power afterward. Abdul-Hakim Bilhajj's attempt to turn his military prominence and strong connection with the Qataris into political power was an abject failure. (The ways in which the main Islamist currents—LIFG, Brotherhood, and the Salafists—responded to the outbreak of the uprisings and engaged in a scramble for power in the wake of Qadhafi's ouster is dealt with in great depth in Chapter 7.)

Some extremist Islamists and militant jihadists are not part of any organized political or social movement and operate as "freelancers." During the NTC period (November 2011-August 2012), they failed to announce their political intentions clearly. They then reemerged into public prominence with the attack on the American mission in Benghazi on 11 September 2012, which killed Ambassador J. Christopher Stevens as well as three other Americans. The Ansar al-Sharia militant group was believed to be responsible, leading to widespread popular denunciations against it, and a fear that—in Cyrenaica in particular—freelance cells of jihadists were planning to undermine Libya's progress to security and stability.

LIBERAL, NATIONALIST, AND NON-ISLAMIST POLITICAL CURRENTS

The post-Qadhafi political scene contains a range of non-Islamist factions spanning from leftist and liberal to popular and Arab Nationalist. They all proclaim loyalty to liberal democracy. Some of the leaders were active in the field of human rights advocacy during Qadhafi's reign. Others were members of the exiled opposition. Yet others were organized around prominent urban merchant or elite families and comprise a very narrow membership.

During the transition period, some of these elements began to set up political parties or civil society organizations that echoed their views.

This came at a time when many of those involved found themselves drawn into political side-battles imposed upon them by the Islamists with the aim of dissipating their forces. It is difficult to produce a comprehensive outline of the political parties that were publicly announced or that undertook preparations to emerge and compete in the 7 July 2012 elections. Benghazi witnessed the birth of the first political parties, and by August 2012 there were at least 200.

Long before the NTC adopted legislation governing political parties and entities in March 2012, these groups proliferated in almost all Libyan cities and regions. They can loosely be classified into three major trends: regional, ideological, or personality-centered. Observers of their activities can attest to the lack of clarity in their attempts to formulate clearly defined political programs. They also lack clear-cut political identity and positions toward current issues. The rapid increase in the number of political parties was not matched by their ability to play any effective role in political life as shown in the results of the elections in July 2012, where only a few parties managed to win seats in the GNC. In fact, the GNC elections saw the main currents of Islamism, regional affiliation, former anti-Qadhafi opposition leaders, and technocrats loosely associated with the reformist current in the old regime remain the primary standard-bearers in Libya's political life today.

Mahmoud Jibril, former chairman of the NTC's Executive Council, seen as a prominent leader of the liberal trend, set up a political organization, the National Forces Alliance, in February 2012, and he was officially elected its chairman on 14 March 2012. The Alliance is an umbrella organization comprising 44 political parties including the National Centrist Party, also founded in February 2012 and headed by Ali Tarhouni, the minister of finance in Jibril's government, which served from March to October 2011. The alliance also has in its membership a whole host of organizations, 236 NGOs, and hundreds of prominent regional leaders who share a liberal nationalist orientation. Jibril explained that his Alliance is guided by adherence to preserving Libya's sovereignty, establishing a democracy, and instituting moderate Islam, national unity, and territorial integrity in a unified state that—while acknowledging the need for decentralization, sustainable regional development, and local administration—is in fact staunchly against federalism.[39] Given its composition and representation of all of Libya's major regions, the Alliance gained 39 seats out of the 80 seats designated for party lists in the 7 July 2012 elections. It is likely to play a key role in Libyan politics in the GNC and beyond.

CIVIL SOCIETY

Civil society organizations crop up almost daily in the major cities of Libya. Many focus on human rights, women's rights, or humanitarian issues. While it is apparent that there is an active presence of Islamists in a large number of these organizations, it is also clear that non-Islamists also find them to be a suitable forum for representation. The Internet is brimming with Libyan websites, and social networks host growing numbers of web groups and communities. The fact that there is an absence of effective political authority in the country renders this phenomenon more related to the chaotic political reality on the ground and less an expression of a culture that intrinsically values civil society. Despite the announcement of the formation of a number of umbrella unions, associations and coalitions of civil society organizations, it is doubtful if these genuinely reflect what their names imply.

The danger of ideological currents, tribalism, and political parties exploiting the institutions of civil society for their own ends has come into prominence. The challenge facing civil society organizations lies in the extent of their ability to facilitate the process of democratic transition through their commitment to liberating the sentiments and attitudes of individuals from the dominance of the state. This trend, if it occurs, would lead to the creation of a wider sphere for democracy without hindering the realization of democracy itself.[40]

THE NEW LIBYA: CHALLENGES AND OPPORTUNITIES

Given the nature of the struggle and its consequences, Libyans are in need of an extended period to deal with the consequences of Qadhafi's rule and the negative impact of his policies. Qadhafi destroyed the concept of a state comprised of neutral institutions—which stand above society and encourage its natural development—choosing instead to use the state to make war on Libyan society. The worst of his deeds were not those connected to brutality or squandering national resources but rather his undermining the value system of society and upsetting the components of its natural political culture.

The 2011 Libyan uprisings in their initial stages had no natural leadership and did not express any specific political or ideological orientations. This conferred on the revolution a capability to liberate itself from the impediments and sources of weakness associated with ideology and partisanship and the shackles they necessarily impose. Lacking true political ideology, the postliberation ideological divisions map onto the preexisting cleavages of tribes, religion, region, and oil. The transitional period illustrated that the initial strengths represented by the lack of ideology had transformed into an element of weakness, impeding the development of political organizations and an effective genuine civil society conducive to democratization. Only genuine civil society, responsible media, and political parties based on implementable programs can deliver Libya from the potential danger of exploitation of the rhetoric of the revolution and the blood of its martyrs for political agendas. Similarly, only civil society can safeguard against forces desiring to preserve the status quo in order to exercise influence as well as against any foreign actor desiring to play a dishonest role by intervening to mold the form of the new Libyan political entity.

* * *

The Libyan revolution was genuinely popular in its origins and orientations. Libyans ventured into the midst of the revolution without any political experience, political culture, or tradition of mass movements that would strengthen their ability to guide their revolution in the direction they desired. Libyans were compelled to accept the intervention of the North Atlantic Treaty Organization (NATO) as the only alternative to the savagery of Qadhafi and his brigades. The moral and political instigation by politicians, opposition figures, and satellite TV channels like *Al-Jazeera* played a decisive role in charging their emotions. While Qadhafi's killing machine was committing barbaric acts, Libyans sensed that their country could be plunged into a war of extermination without mercy, and hence there was no choice but to appeal to world conscience. This immediately immersed their revolution in the game of nations. This geostrategic element made Libya a pawn in a larger game and subjected it to pressures that only reinforced the existing political fragmentation and the role of the "perpetual dynamics." Should the new authorities not articulate a fresh role in the world, such inaction opens up possibilities of a resort to tribal, regional, or factional protectionism and, hence, the potential corruption of the climate of political competition.

A LOOK AHEAD

The most serious of Qadhafi's crimes were those he perpetrated upon the foundations of the Libyan value system by disrupting the preexisting culture of the political community, thereby undermining its natural potential for the evolution of the cultural components required for development and modernization. Furthermore, Qadhafi's foreign policy adventures greatly distorted Libyans' and outsiders' perceptions of Libya's place in the world. Altogether, these raise enormous challenges that may hinder social reconciliation, democratization, and reconstruction, while placing obstacles on the path of state building.[41] Arguing that the uprisings were dominated by the periphery, Jason Pack and Barak Barfi wrote that "[Libya] is not prepared for the shocks that the periphery can deliver to the center." The fact that the country lacks civil society institutions and local governance implies the need for "a paradigm shift [among policy makers leading to the] recogni[tion] that connecting the periphery to the center has become the top priority."[42]

Despite the importance of balancing national expectations and taking into account foreign interests—particularly those of countries that supported the revolution—the real objective remains that of reinventing the Libyan polity and undoing its dependency on tribes, oil, and religion. This process has been hindered by the institutional and leadership weaknesses at various levels. The fact that many of Libya's current political leaders in both the GNC and the militias are more concerned with partisan, regional, and tribal politics suggests the greater need for consensus-building measures.

Given the link between developments in Libya and the outside world, lack of strong leadership opens the door to yet more foreign influence. Although all foreign powers publicly expressed respect for the will of the Libyan people, it remains a legitimate concern as to the actual extent of outside support for genuine democracy in Libya.[43] Many Libyan commentators, analysts, members of social networks, politicians, and indeed people on the street raised eyebrows as to the real aims behind the Qatari activities and involvement in Libyan affairs. Skepticism about Qatar's role was so widespread that it appears that Qatar's support of Abdul-Hakim Bilhajj's Homeland Party was one of the reasons for its failure in the elections for the GNC. Yet, many of the individuals concerned about Qatari influence fail to recognize that different foreign powers such as Italy, Turkey, France, the United Kingdom, and the United States have different interests in today's Libya and support different actors in the local scene. Richard Northern and Jason Pack present a different take on the roles of foreign actors in post-Qadhafi Libya in Chapter 4. They assert that the relative paucity of effective foreign assistance in reconstruction and capacity building derived from the hands-off position taken by the major Western powers and was one of the factors that inhibited Libya from building the strong institutions needed for a democratic transition.

Post-Qadhafi Libya has become a theater for the interplay of the perpetual dynamics that have long dominated its modern polity. The country's first elections after Qadhafi gave ample evidence that such dynamics remain at work. The results of the elections demonstrated that a majority of candidates calculated their appeal and managed their campaigns along lines related to these dynamics. Therefore, the results mirrored not ideological divides but rather tribal and regional factors. Though a strong rivalry existed between the Islamists, particularly the Brotherhood, and the "Liberals," represented by the National Forces Alliance, the significance of this rivalry is less important than the regional and tribal factors. The contested 120 individual candidate seats in the GNC were along regional, tribal, and personality lines, further attesting to the main premises underlying this chapter and further dissected elsewhere in this volume. The inherent divisiveness of the "perpetual dynamics" appeared poised to dominate the GNC's attempts to select a prime minister, approve his cabinet, select a constitutional committee and preside over the constitutional process.

NOTES

1. A. Mislmani, *Huquq al-Insan fi Libya: Hudud al-Taghyir* (Cairo: Markaz al-Qahirah li-Huquq al-Insan, 1999), 66–75.

2. For an excellent treatment of Islam in Libya see, Alia Brahimi, "Islam in Libya," in *Islamist Radicalization in North Africa: Politics and Process*, edited by George Joffé (London: Routledge, 2011).

3. Ibadhism is not technically a *madhab,* but is sometimes considered one in the Libyan political context to downplay the differences between Ibadhis and Sunni Malikis.

4. Helen Chapin Metz, ed., *Libya: A Country Study* (Washington, DC: GPO for the Library of Congress, 1987), http://countrystudies.us/libya /10.htm.

5. See Rachel Simon, *Libya between Ottomanism and Nationalism: The Ottoman Involvement in Libya during the War with Italy, 1911–1919* (Berlin: Klaus Schwartz Verlag, 1987).

6. See Matteo Pretelli, "Education in the Italian Colonies during the Interwar Period," *Modern Italy* 16, no. 3 (August 2011), and Ali Abdullatif Ahmida, "When the Subaltern Speak: Memory of Genocide in Colonial Libya 1929–1933," *Italian Studies* 61, no. 2 (Autumn 2006).

7. Jason Pack, *British State-Building in Cyrenaica during the War Years (1941–1945)*, MSt. Thesis (University of Oxford, 2011).

8. Mahmoud Ayoub, *Islam and the Third Universal Theory: The Religious Thought of Mu'ammar al-Qadhdhafi* (London: Routledge, 1991).

9. For a treatment of this issue, see, Amal Obeidi, *Political Culture in Libya* (Richmond: Curzon, 2001).

10. Mislmani, *Huquq al-Insan fi Libya*, 77–82; Jason Pack and Ronald Bruce St John, "Libya's Missteps Threaten Descent into Federalism," *Al Jazeera* Opinion June 14, 2012, http://www.aljazeera.com/indepth /opinion/2012/06/2012614115342445476.html.

11. Obeidi, *Political Culture*,16.

12. For more on the PSL, see Mohamed Zahi Mogherbi, "Social Change, Regime Performance and the Radicalisation of Politics: The Case of Libya," in *Islamist Radicalisation in North Africa: Politics and Process*, edited by George Joffé (London, Routledge, 2011). For a detailed treatment of the competition between formal and informal authority, consult Hanspeter Mattes, "Formal and Informal Authority in Libya since 1969," in *Libya Since 1969: Qadhafi's Revolution Revisited*, edited by Dirk Vandewalle (New York: Palgrave Macmillan, 2008).

13. Mustafa Al-Tir, "Tahaddiyat al-Tahawwul ila al-Dimuqrat iyah fi Libya," *Sahifat al-Watan al-Libiya al-ʾ al-ā al-ʾIlʾ*, September 23 (2011) *All quotes from Arabic are the author's translations.*

14. Ibid.

15. Miranda Leitsinger, "Gadhafi, Rebels Vie for Loyalty of Libyan Tribes," *MSNBC*, May 18, 2011, http://www.msnbc.msn.com/id/43049164 /ns/world_news-mideast_n_africa/t/gadhafi-rebels-vie-loyalty-libyan -tribes/#.T2M894FqO1s.

16. Al-Tir, "Tahaddiyat al-Tahawwul."

17. See, Yousef K. al-Yousef, *Majlis al-taʾawin al-khaliji fi muthalith al wiratha wa la naft wa al qouwa al ajnabiayah* (The Gulf Cooperation Council in the Triangle of Hereditary, Oil and Foreign Powers), (Beirut: Center for Arab Unity Studies, 2012).

18. Al-Ahram al-Iqtisadi online, *Man sa yfouz bi al kaʾkat al Libiyah baʾd sukut al qadhdhafi* (Who Will Win the Libyan Cake after Gaddafi's Fall), http://digital.ahram.org.eg/Economy.aspx?Serial=632702.

19. Youssef M. Sawani, *Libya al-Muʿasirah: Qadaya wa Tahadiyat* (Tripoli: al-Markaz al-ʿAlami, 2006).

20. S. al-ʿAwkali, "al-Mirʾath wal Yutubya: Niqash Hawl al-Dimuqratiyah fi Libya," *Arajeen*, no. 6 (January 2007): 95.

21. Ali al-Sallabi, *al-Shura* (Beirut: Dar al-Maʿrifah, 2010), 6–21.

22. "Justice & Construction Leader Confirms NFA Not Part of Coalition Plans; Likens Jibril to Qaddafi," *Shabab Libya*, July 13, 2012 http:// www.shabablibya.org/news/justice-likens-jibril-to-qaddafi.

23. "Libya's Belhaj Quits Military Post for Politics," *BBC News*, May 15, 2012, http://www.bbc.co.uk/news/world-africa-18078436.

24. Ashraq al Awsat editorial staff, "wathaʾiq jadidah aʾn maqtal Abdul-Fattah Yunis" (New Documents on the Killing of Abdul-Fattah Younis), *Ashraq al Awsat*, October 11, 2011, http://www.aawsat.com/details .asp?section=4&article=644479&issueno=12005.

25. Emma Farge, "Libya Islamist Calls for PM Jibril's Exit," *Reuters*, September 20, 2011, http://www.reuters.com/article/2011/09/20/us-libya-ntc-opponent-idUSTRE78J4SH20110920.

26. It is worth noting that the chairman of the Cyrenaican Council considered Misratah independent of the NTC.

27. "Amazighiyi Libya: Amazigh Libya La Yajidun Ay Haraj fi al-Ta'amul ma' Isra'il mn Ajl Maslahat al-Amazigh fi al-Libya," http://www.al-shouraffa.com/?p=4030/.

28. F. Bin, 'Isa Is Tahdidat bil-Tasfiyah al-Jasadiyah li-'Iskatiha Isk 'Arus al-Bahr Tuhammil al-Wata ni al-Mas'uliyah," *Sahifat 'Arus al-Bahr* 6, no. 22 (2011): 3.

29. NTC Website, *'an al-majlis* (About the Council), http://www.ntc.gov.ly/index.php?option=com_content&view=article&id=4&Itemid=2.

30. Jason Pack and Barak Barfi "In War's Wake," *Washington Institute for Near East Policy*, February 2012, http://www.washingtoninstitute.org/policy-analysis/view/in-wars-wake-the-struggle-for-post-qadhafi-libya.

31. For more on the circumstances of the drafting of the temporary consitutional declaration and how it defined the rules of the game of the transition period while also channeling opposition to the NTC and unleashing a contest for legitimacy in post-Qadhafi Libya, consult Youssef Mohammad Sawani and Jason Pack, "Libyan Constitutionality and Sovereignty Post-Qadhafi: The Islamist, Regionalist, and Amazigh Challenges" (Forthcoming, Publisher TBD).

32. NTC Website. About the Temporary Constitution (Page no longer accessible).

33. Mahmoud Gibril, "Libya: Where to?" *al-Mostaqbal Al-Arabi* (May 2012): 103.

34. Charles Levinson, "Rebel Leadership Casts Wide Net," *Wall Street Journal*, March 10, 2011, http://online.wsj.com/article/SB10001424052748704629104576190720901643258.html.

35. Nicolas Pelham, "Libya in Balance," *Middle East Research and Information Project*, March 15, 2011, http://www.merip.org/mero/mero031511.

36. Jason Pack, "Qaddafi's Legacy," *Foreign Policy*, October 20, 2011; Jason Pack, "Post-Gaddafi Libya Should Think Local," *The Guardian*, October 20, 2011.

37. Zahi Mogherbi, telephone conversation with the author, October 13, 2011.

38. Al-Mashriqi, "Kawalis I'tilaf 17 Fibrayir: Khada'una fa Iltahamuna wa Qalu I'tilaf," *Sahifat Arus al-Bahr*, June 22, 2011.

39. Jibril, "Libya: Where to?" 110–12.

40. Obeidi, *Political Culture*, 16.

41. UN General Secretary "Report on UN Mission in Libya, 1.12.2011," http://unsmil.unmissions.org/LinkClick.aspx?fileticket=v_-F2Xr3c9I%3d&tabid=3543&mid=6187&language=en-US.

42. Pack and Barfi, "War's Wake," 15, 40.
43. David Roberts, "Behind Qatar's Intervention in Libya: Why Was Doha Such Supporter of the Rebels?" *Foreign Affairs,* September 28, 2011, http://www.foreignaffairs.com/articles/68302/david-roberts/behind -qatars-intervention-in-libya.

3

THE POST-QADHAFI ECONOMY

Ronald Bruce St John

Following the discovery in 1959 of oil deposits in commercially exploitable quantities, Libya abruptly transformed from an impoverished desert economy into a rentier state flush with cash.[1] After September 1969, the revolutionary government of Muammar Qadhafi repeatedly attempted to lessen the nation's reliance on income from the sale of hydrocarbons. Nevertheless, in the spring of 2011, Libya remained a classical rentier state with 95 percent of export earnings and 80 percent of government revenue deriving from the sale of hydrocarbons. This chapter examines the surprising extent to which the Libyan economy and the 17 February revolution impacted upon one another. It also examines the challenges and opportunities of the post-Qadhafi Libyan economy.

IN THE BEGINNING

When Libya achieved independence in late December 1951, around 80 percent of the population was engaged in agricultural activities that generally yielded pitiful returns due to limited rainfall, tired soil, destructive desert winds, primitive farming methods, and occasional locust swarms. The industrial sector offered even less potential than agriculture. Libya lacked the economic factors necessary for a successful industrial base: raw materials, capital, skilled manpower, and a known energy source. Consequently, the formal economy in the early years of independence relied on the export of castor seeds, esparto grass, and scrap metal scavenged from World War II military vehicles, together with bilateral and multilateral aid.[2]

The lingering aftereffects of World War II compounded the economic problems of Libya. The Italian banks had closed all of their branches by 1943, and they did not begin to reopen them until 1951.

In the intervening period of the British Military Administration, Barclays was the only bank operational in Libya, and it served largely as a central bank for the military administration. With the banking system shut down and credit virtually nonexistent, commerce was paralyzed. The indiscriminate use of land mines during the war—estimates reach as high as 12 million mines across North Africa—hampered air, land, and sea transport, as well as agricultural development.[3]

The human resources of Libya also suffered from quantitative and qualitative limitations. The small, scattered population of a little more than 1 million people enjoyed a relatively high birth rate, estimated at 4 percent a year; but primitive conditions and poor health care resulted in a similar death rate, with the result that annual population growth did not exceed 1 percent. Qualitative shortcomings were largely the product of limited educational and vocational training opportunities during the Italian colonial era (1911–1943), which left 90 percent of the population illiterate at independence. Throughout the Italian occupation, educational facilities mostly targeted Italian children. During much of World War II, schools were closed. In 1950, the United Nations estimated that only 20 percent of those eligible were actually in school.[4]

OIL POLICY

As early as 1914, traces of petroleum were found in Tripolitania. However, it was not until 1959 that American prospectors discovered oil deposits in commercially viable quantities. The Sirte basin, the location of most of the early oil fields, contained large oil deposits of high-grade "sweet" crude. "Sweet" crude oil is low in sulfur, a desirable quality in an increasingly environmentally conscious world, and one which furthermore reduces the cost of refining. Located nearer to Europe than its competitors, Libya also enjoyed an advantage in terms of transportation costs, and was less vulnerable to supply disruptions since it did not depend on pipelines, the Suez Canal, or transit around the Horn of Africa to reach its markets.[5]

In August 1961, Standard Oil of New Jersey, operating through its Libyan affiliate, established a posted price of $2.21 per barrel for Libyan base crude of 39° API gravity with a ceiling of $2.23 for 40° API gravity and above. As a result of the concessions granted to foreign companies under the 1955 Oil Law, Libyan royalties in the form of taxation derived from the posted price and not the profits actualized by the companies. The ensuing decade saw dramatic increases in both production and revenues, but not in the posted price of oil. From the start, the monarchy argued that the posted price was too low and that it was being shortchanged on its rightful revenue. However, given the dominant position of the oil companies, the monarchy was powerless to do more than launch a formal protest each time it received a payment. Concerned that a price dispute with the oil companies would slow industry development, the monarchy pursued a volume-oriented as opposed to a price-oriented policy.[6]

The volume-oriented policy followed by the monarchy resulted in sustained revenue growth at the expense of the rapid depletion of an exhaustible resource. In 1961–1969, revenues from petroleum exports increased from $3 million to $1.175 billion, and Libya became the world's fourth-largest exporter of crude oil, a rate of production and revenue growth previously unknown in the industry. In the process, Libya moved from being a capital-deficit to a capital-surplus state, and from being an aid recipient to a donor nation. By 1969, Libya's daily oil production was comparable to that of Saudi Arabia, although its known reserves were far less. Libyan oil production peaked in April 1970 at 3.7 million barrels per day (b/d), almost three times its level four decades later.[7]

In December 1969, the Revolutionary Command Council (RCC), which had seized power from the monarchy on 1 September 1969, moved to assert full Libyan sovereignty over its hydrocarbon resources and in the process to increase the posted price of its crude. The RCC focused on the smaller, independent oil companies, notably Occidental Petroleum, because they were the most dependent on Libyan crude for their worldwide production, and thus were the most vulnerable to reduced production quotas on a company-by-company basis. Under pressure from the revolutionary government, Occidental scrambled to find alternate sources of supply, but none of the larger oil companies extended a helping hand. In a matter of months, the hard-line policy pursued by the RCC had ended the myth that the oil producers alone could set the posted price of crude oil, changing forever the geopolitics of oil.[8]

On the fourth anniversary of the revolution, the RCC nationalized 51 percent of all foreign oil-producer assets. One month later, at the beginning of the October 1973 Arab-Israeli War, it imposed a partial oil boycott, which was supported by other Arab states, leading to a doubling in the posted price of oil. When OPEC ended the oil boycott in April 1974, the higher prices stuck. By the beginning of the following decade, the global price of oil had increased from a little over $2 a barrel in 1969 to as much as $41 a barrel in 1981.[9]

As the RCC moved to increase the price of oil, it also changed the terms of its contracts with the oil companies. In 1974, Libya converted all concessionary agreements to exploration and production sharing agreements (EPSAs), the form of contractual agreement still in place today. The EPSA phase I agreements provided for 35-year contracts with five years allotted for exploration and 30 years for production. When a second phase was initiated in 1980, the terms of the EPSA agreements resembled the first with the significant exception that the production-sharing pattern varied in accordance with the assumed prospects of the acreage. Together, the agreements concluded in EPSA phases I and II resulted in 694 exploratory wells, 270 of which were successful, and the discovery of some 8 billion barrels of crude oil and 45 trillion cubic feet of natural gas.[10]

Despite the relative success of EPSA phases I and II, oil exploration and development declined appreciably in the 1970s and again after 1980. In response to higher oil prices, consumers developed energy-saving technologies and diversified energy sources, while oil suppliers outside OPEC reduced the organization's ability to influence a shrinking market. As both global oil prices and Libyan exports declined, Libya experienced a serious recession. Oil production, which averaged 1.8 million b/d in 1980, dropped to 1.2 million b/d in 1981, stabilizing at around 1.0 million b/d for the next few years, and annual oil revenues in 1982–1986 dropped from $21 billion to $5.4 billion. At the same time, Libya had to adjust to the economic sanctions imposed by the United States in response to Qadhafi's support for global terrorism. In 1982, the United States banned imports of Libyan oil and prohibited the export of oil and gas machinery to Libya. Three years later, it ordered American oil companies out of Libya.[11]

LIBYAN SOCIALISM

In 1969, the agricultural sector employed approximately 20 percent of the workforce but contributed less than 3 percent of GNP, and its export value was negligible. The manufacturing sector represented less than 2 percent of GNP, employed less than 5 percent of the workforce, and produced an equally unimpressive output. The development plans of the RCC called for the rapid creation of viable and productive agricultural and industrial sectors. The first five-year plan (1976–1980) called for an annual increase of 10 percent in GNP, 25 percent in industrial output, and near self-sufficiency in food output, targets unrealistic to the point of being ludicrous. When the agricultural sector failed to respond to the unrealistic demands placed upon it, industry received a higher allocation than agriculture in the second five-year plan (1981–1985), and self-sufficiency in industrial production became a stated regime goal although it was never achieved.[12]

In both the agricultural and industrial sectors, human resources remained a problem. The monarchy and the revolutionary government invested heavily in educational facilities; nevertheless, overall levels of education remained low. In a system biased toward general education, the number of scientifically and technically qualified Libyans was exceptionally small, and the shortage of capable administrators and technicians limited the regime's ability to spend the funds allocated in their development budgets. A related objective of the industrialization policy—job creation for auxiliary and service workers—also went mostly unrealized. In response, the regime imported large numbers of expatriate workers who brought with them indirect costs, such as the import of a wide variety of consumer goods from their home countries, paving the way for the rise of complex social problems in a hitherto largely insular society.[13]

In spite of the many problems encountered, by the end of the 1970s, a social revolution had taken place in Libya, modifying long-standing economic and social structures. The management of the economy became increasingly socialist with housing, capital, and land redistributed and subject to arbitrary seizure by the government. Private enterprise was almost totally eliminated, replaced by a centrally controlled economy. Arbitrary assaults on the individual accumulation of capital became commonplace with increasingly tight control of individual banking transactions providing both the means and the pretext. By 1980, agriculture was the only economic sector in which a significant share of production remained in private hands, and even there, the public share of production had increased threefold since 1969 due to government projects in coastal areas and in the south.[14]

In the course of the 1980s, Libya was forced to curtail or abandon several important development projects which would have led to a greater diversification of the economy because the regime refused to curtail military expenditures even as revenues dropped due to declining oil prices. The third five-year plan (1981–1985) was drafted on the basis of oil production at 1.4 million b/d and revenues of around $20 billion per annum. Instead, revenues over the period were barely $10 billion per annum. The Qadhafi regime responded with painful austerity measures that prolonged the deep recession plaguing the economy.[15]

REFORM EFFORTS

In March 1987, Qadhafi announced the first in a series of economic and political measures (*infitah*) intended to return Libya to a more open, free-enterprise system. Describing the new policies as a "revolution within the revolution," he envisioned a new role for the private sector, together with limited political liberalization. Later, he called for reforms in the agricultural and the industrial sectors, including a reversal of import substitution policies and the adoption of modern management practices. In September 1988, Qadhafi called for an end to the state monopoly on trade and lifted some injunctions on retail trade with the result that *suqs* and small urban shops began to reopen.[16]

In December 1988, Pan Am flight 103 exploded over Lockerbie, Scotland, killing 270 people, and nine months later, UTA flight 772 exploded over Niger, killing 179 people. When Libya failed to cooperate fully with American, British, and French officials investigating those attacks, the United Nations on 15 April 1992 imposed mandatory sanctions. From 1992 through 1997, issues related to the UN sanctions regime blocked any progress on the economic reforms introduced after 1987. In August 1998, Libya accepted an Anglo-American proposal to try the two Libyan suspects in the Lockerbie case at The Hague under Scottish law. Once Libya had remanded them into UN custody, the UN suspended its sanctions regime, and with the conclusion of the trial and Libyan compliance with all applicable Security Council resolutions, the multilateral sanctions were lifted permanently in September 2003.[17]

As the Qadhafi regime moved to end its commercial and diplomatic isolation, officials at home and abroad aggressively marketed investment opportunities in Libya, especially in the agricultural, tourism, and trade sectors. Unfortunately, real performance seldom approached official rhetoric. With most of the economic reforms implemented in an ad hoc, opaque manner, potential investors faced a range of obstacles, including inadequate legal protection, ambivalent attitudes toward foreign workers, and a dearth of Libyan private sector business partners. In addition, risk-averse officials in Libya were hesitant to repeat earlier failed attempts at diversification, especially when oil and gas prices were at relatively high levels and production was expected to increase.[18]

With hydrocarbons continuing to make up some 95 percent of exports and 70–80 percent of government revenues, Qadhafi in June 2003 announced a major shift in economic policy, telling the General

People's Congress (GPC) that the public sector had failed and should be abolished. He called for the privatization of the hydrocarbon industry, together with other sectors of the economy, and pledged to bring Libya into the World Trade Organization (WTO). Four months later, Libya published a list of 360 state-owned enterprises targeted for privatization or liquidation. In conjunction with Qadhafi's call for economic reform, Shukri Ghanem was appointed prime minister. Ghanem, previously the minister of economy and foreign trade and a former head of research at OPEC, was a strong proponent of privatization. In December 2004, Ghanem outlined a new development strategy centered on economic diversification.[19]

With proven oil reserves at the time estimated to be 39.1 billion barrels—the largest in Africa—a core objective of the Ghanem administration was to reach a level of oil production of 3.0 million b/d no later than 2015. This was to be accomplished in two stages: first, an increase to 2.0 million b/d by 2010; and second, by achieving the final target of 3.0 million b/d by the end of 2015. In support of this objective, Libya in August 2004 announced a new round of exploration and production-sharing agreements, EPSA, phase IV, which offered enhanced incentives for oil and gas exploration in an open, competitive bidding environment. When the final results of EPSA, phase IV, were announced in early 2008, 36 companies from 19 countries had been awarded new contracts. As EPSA, phase IV, unfolded, oil production in 2006 approached 1.8 million b/d, so the target of 2.0 million b/d by 2010 appeared possible. However, the target of 3.0 million b/d no later than 2015 had been questionable from the start. In June 2009, Libya lowered its 2013 production forecast by almost 25 percent to 2.3 million b/d. In December 2009, it extended the much ballyhooed target of 3.0 million b/d out to 2017.[20]

Despite the best efforts of the Ghanem administration to steer Libya on a firm course of economic liberalization, concrete progress outside the hydrocarbon sector was limited and tentative. At every step of the way, hard-line elements within the Qadhafi regime opposed any change that might move Libya away from its centralized economic system. The hard-liners sought to protect their own sinecures, which true liberalization would destroy. Public criticism of liberalization policies intensified in mid-2005 when the government imposed a 30 percent hike in fuel prices and doubled the price of electricity for consumers of more than 500 kilowatts a month. A related decision to lift customs duties on more than 3,500 imported commodities raised concerns for job security in inefficient factories unable to meet foreign competition. At the same time, core elements of the reform process were increasingly compromised by changes in personnel. In March 2006, Qadhafi appointed Ghanem the chairman of the National Oil Corporation (NOC), replacing him as prime minister with his more malleable and more conservative deputy, Baghdadi al-Mahmudi.[21]

In September 2008, Qadhafi repeated an earlier charge that government ministries were centers of mismanagement, graft, and corruption, suggesting their budgeted funds should be distributed directly to the people. In March 2009, the GPC endorsed the concept of wealth distribution but only after "appropriate measures" had been put in place. The GPC's decision to delay implementation of wealth-distribution policies amounted to a rejection of Qadhafi's attempt to shift blame for the country's economic problems. In effect, Qadhafi had sought to deflect blame from himself and the ideology of *The Green Book* onto a state administration that he had long dominated but had now belatedly recognized as inefficient and corrupt. In the interim, charges of inconsistency, lack of transparency, and favoritism continued to plague the reform process. Libyan officials also continued to promote "people's capitalism," a halfway house between socialism and capitalism, described by them as looking like capitalism but acting like socialism. People's capitalism was nothing more than window dressing designed to mask the obvious differences between the anachronistic socialist ideology of *The Green Book* and the current economic reality. Official attempts to rationalize privatization, clearly outlawed in *The Green Book*, as the "extension of popular ownership" fell into the same category.[22]

QADHAFI'S SOCIOECONOMIC LEGACY

The early days of the 17 February revolution highlighted the impact of Qadhafi's socioeconomic legacy. The uprising began in eastern Libya, a region that suffered deliberate economic marginalization after 1969. Early support also came from deprived and persecuted minorities, notably the Tubu in the southeast and the *Amazigh* (Berber) minority in the west (see Chapter 6). Inspired by events in neighboring Egypt and Tunisia, Libyan demonstrators in mid-January 2011 clashed with police in Bayda, east of Benghazi, demanding job opportunities and a more dignified way of life, including better housing (see Chapter 4 note 3). In the first week of February, Jamal al-Hajji, a well-known lawyer and prominent Libyan political activist, was detained by Libyan authorities in connection with his human rights activities. On 15 February, Fathi Terbil, the convener of a group that had campaigned on behalf of the victims of the 1996 Abu Salim prison massacre, was arrested, prompting riots in Benghazi.

As the main thrust of the protests shifted away from complaints about socioeconomic issues, such as the shortage of housing, limited social services, and no job opportunities, toward a call for regime change, the demonstrators proclaimed 17 February—the fifth anniversary of antiregime riots in Benghazi sparked by cartoons of the Prophet Muhammad—a day of rage. The Qadhafi regime responded with force, killing as many as 50 demonstrators in Benghazi alone. As discussed in the previous two chapters by Joffé and Sawani, as well as in the Introduction by Pack, after an initial wave of repression, which only served to fan the flames of the disparate uprisings, the Qadhafi regime quickly melted away in the eastern part of Libya (see map 1). Its bureaucratic and military institutions ceased to exist as they fled or defected wholesale over to the rebels. Over the next few weeks in Libya's west— where the regime faced uprisings and protests, but not as widespread as those in the east—it continued to attack unarmed civilians, restoring order in most places other than Misrata and the Jabal Nafusa (see map 2). After that consolidation, the regime intended to recapture the recalcitrant east. In response, the UN Security Council imposed a no-fly zone over Libya and authorized "all necessary measures" to protect civilians from regime forces.

When Qadhafi and the Free Unionist Officers seized power from the monarchy on 1 September 1969, Libya was the classic example of a rentier state, and when the 17 February revolution began in mid-January 2011, it remained one. Well over five decades after the discovery of oil deposits in commercially viable quantities, Libya remained economically one of the least-diversified economies in the world. Largely due to the socialist ideology that dominated Libya for almost four decades, private investment at the end of the Qadhafi era was dormant at around 2 percent of GNP, and some 75 percent of employment remained in the public sector. Ironically, diversification of other economic sectors remained contingent on an increase in the productivity and competitiveness of the hydrocarbon sector, the country's only engine of economic growth.[23]

The Libyan people are intelligent, hardworking, entrepreneurial, and capable of the highest ethical standards. Unfortunately, the socialist regime created by Qadhafi did not encourage or reward these virtues. Advancement in his command economy more often than not depended on family, clan, and tribal ties or other forms of nepotism and cronyism. Graft and corruption were pervasive, especially over the last decade when the lifting of UN and US sanctions opened multiple new commercial opportunities. Qadhafi's family dominated the most lucrative sectors, and although most Libyans suspected the extent of their activities, the release of the Wikileaks cables at the end of 2010 revealed the horrific extent of nepotism for all to see. Qadhafi's eldest son from his first wife, Muhammad, was chairman of the General Post and Telecommunications Company; Qadhafi's third son, Sa'adi, was head of a construction company involved in most of the major construction projects across the country; his fifth son, Hannibal, was the first marine consultant to the management committee of the General National Maritime Transport Company with a near monopoly on the transport of Libyan oil and natural gas; and his second son, Saif al-Islam, was chairman of a diverse portfolio of companies known as the One Nine Group. Therefore, it became increasingly difficult to pursue any commercial opportunity in the country without first getting one or more of Qadhafi's children involved. Although Qadhafi and his family are now gone, the legacy of abuse and corruption they engendered remains, threatening Libya's political stability and economic growth. For example, the interim finance minister, Hassan Zighlam, admitted in early April 2012 that millions of dollars of Qadhafi family assets returned to Libya by European countries soon left the country, stolen by corrupt officials.[24]

The culture of entitlement that permeates contemporary Libyan society is an equally devastating legacy of the Qadhafi era. Over the last 42 years, Libyans have grown accustomed to a wide variety of free or state-subsidized social services, from food to education to housing to medical care, with the state also serving as the major employer in the country. In post-Qadhafi Libya, independent militias acting in the name of the revolution have become one of the largest sources of corruption, in large part because their members continue to be motivated by this sense of entitlement. An estimated 25,000 fighters took part in the uprisings; nevertheless, the NTC announced in May 2012 that the Warriors' Affairs Committee had already made $1.4 billion in payments to some 250,000 men, most of whom falsely claimed to be fighters. In another example, the interim government estimated that no more than 10–15 percent of Libyans treated overseas as part of an $800 million program for war wounded were actually eligible for treatment. Local authorities in charge of administering the program simply exploited it on behalf of family and friends. Finally, the revolutionaries in Zintan holding Saif al-Islam al-Qadhafi refused in May 2012 to release him to the NTC until the latter paid their salaries for the previous six months, an estimated $1.36 million.[25] (Additionally, the populace's insistence that the NTC continue Qadhafi-era subsidies guarantees that Libya's porous borders remain a contested site for competing smuggling networks. For more on this, see Chapter 6.)

Turning to the commercial environment, outstanding issues inherited from the Qadhafi regime include a lack of transparency, limited institutional coordination, and the absence of a comprehensive development plan. Policy areas long recognized as in need of major reform include incentive and regulatory regimes, exchange rates, trade practices, fiscal and monetary policies, and the quantity and reliability of economic data. To encourage private sector development in the post-Qadhafi era, NTC priorities included simplifying the approval process, reforming the labor code, and replacing the progressive corporate tax rate with a low flat rate that is competitive with other states. To promote foreign investment, the legal framework requires modification and modernization, to include the regulation of foreign direct investment, capital markets, intellectual property rights, insurance, and property rights. At the same time, economic reforms in themselves offer only a partial, incomplete solution to the manifold problems facing the Libyan economy. The radical changes required to ensure effective economic growth in post-Qadhafi Libya are incompatible with the retreat of the state called for by Qadhafi in his final years. Paradoxically, even though a bloated state is responsible for most of Libya's problems, the state will need to be intensively involved in the economic life of Libya for a substantial period of time if meaningful and sustained economic reforms leading to the diversification of the economy are to be implemented.[26]

At the outset of the 17 February revolution, Libya's physical infrastructure was in poor shape, and months of intense fighting in cities like Misrata made a bad situation worse. With the exception of electricity and water, Libya before the uprisings ranked low regionally in all metrics related to the quality of infrastructure, especially communication and transportation. The low level of infrastructure development reflected limited public investment and almost no private investment for many years. In the final days of the Qadhafi regime, the underdeveloped state of the telecommunications network, which suffered from a lack of expertise and competition, was especially significant. A well-developed and efficient telecommunications system is central to state-of-the-art information and communication technology, which in turn is a necessary condition for economic growth and entrepreneurship.[27]

Another significant legacy of the Qadhafi regime is a legal system in shambles. Post-Qadhafi Libya faces a formidable task in the creation of a modern legal system. All aspects of the current structure, including law schools, the bar, and the judiciary require a massive overhaul.

For example, the criminal justice system suffers from pervasive issues concerning due process, in part because the criminal law has not been amended since 1953. A contributing factor to the wider problem is that the Libyan public as a whole has little understanding of basic due process rights, a situation not surprising after 42 years of Qadhafi's rule. The lack of a credible justice system draws attention to high-profile cases like those of Saif al-Islam Qadhafi, held by revolutionaries in Zintan, Abdullah Senussi in Mauritania/Tripoli, and Baghdadi al-Mahmudi, in Tunisia/Tripoli, as well as the NTC's failure to substantively investigate the circumstances of Qadhafi's death. Additionally, as of August 2012, upwards of 7,000 POWS were still being held around the country, often in rudimentary facilities controlled by the militias.[28]

Throughout the region, demographics have become an increasingly powerful motor for change. Libya possesses the highest rate of population growth in the Maghreb, and the failure of the Qadhafi regime to create new jobs through a well-thought-out, long-term strategy proved a recipe for disaster. At the outset of the 17 February revolution, at least 30 percent of the Libyan population was unemployed or underemployed, a labor pool which represented both huge, untapped potential for the country as well as a steadily growing liability. In the course of the fighting, levels of unemployment and underemployment escalated, and when combined with the culture of entitlement inherited from the old regime, they proved a volatile mix. With productivity outside the hydrocarbon sector extremely low, the scarcity of technically skilled managers and workers is a core human resource issue in an economy that needs to promote diversification and entrepreneurship. In its closing days, the Qadhafi regime pursued a policy of Libyanization in an effort to increase private-sector job opportunities. However, in practice, the policy simply reinforced the culture of entitlement with foreign firms replacing the state as the provider of largesse, and meritocracy scarcely found in either the public or the private sectors.[29] To respond to the current needs of the job market and develop the skills and attitudes necessary to create new products and services, Libya will need a thoroughly revamped education system. Post-Qadhafi Libya would also benefit from a program that encourages diaspora Libyans to return home in order to leverage their experience and expertise.

CHALLENGES AND OPPORTUNITIES

When the Libyan revolution is compared to the popular uprisings which took place in other Arab states, notably Egypt, Syria, Tunisia, and Yemen, there are obvious similarities in the daily challenges the citizens of these countries face. For decades, they have all suffered from high unemployment and even higher underemployment, poor and limited housing, increasing food prices, and systemic graft and corruption. Over time, the citizens of these states have also gained increased access through the Internet to new forms of internal and external communication, attaining proficiency in social networking sites such as Facebook and Twitter.

There are also important differences between Libya and the other countries of the Arab Spring. Libya has enormous hydrocarbon reserves—the largest known oil reserves and the second largest gas reserves in Africa—and thus is a relatively wealthy state compared to Egypt, Syria, Tunisia, or Yemen. As discussed in the Introduction, in contrast to states like Egypt or Tunisia where political parties, trade unions, and other civil bodies existed throughout most of the Mubarak or Ben Ali eras, Libya at the outset of the revolution was a state with no operative civil society because the Qadhafi regime had systematically destroyed civil society organizations. In response, Libyans in the wake of the 17 February revolution moved quickly to create a plethora of civil bodies, together with the democratic processes and procedures necessary to conduct multiparty elections for a General National Congress (GNC) on 7 July 2012.

Religious Cohesion

Libya has a homogenous Muslim society with 99 percent of the population Muslim and 97 percent Sunni Muslim. This is in contrast to the religious divisions found in Egypt (Coptic Christians, Sunni Muslims, and Muslim minorities) and Syria (Alawites, Druzes, Christians, and Sunni Muslims). In part due to this homogeneity, fundamentalist Islamist movements and radical organizations like Al-Qaeda have found only limited indigenous support in Libya, unlike Egypt (the Muslim Brotherhood, Salafists), Tunisia (Al-Nahda, Al-Qaeda in the Islamic Maghreb), and Yemen (Al-Qaeda in the Arabian Peninsula). Tribal identities also remain strong in Libya, similar to Yemen, but unlike in Egypt, Syria, and Tunisia.[30]

Hydrocarbons

Libya today holds an estimated 46.4 billion barrels of crude oil reserves and some 55 trillion cubic feet of natural gas reserves. In the wake of the 17 February revolution, the NOC has issued highly optimistic projections about oil and gas production, estimates which often included condensate and liquefied petroleum gas (LPG) in their totals and that generally referred to maximum achieved output as opposed to sustained capacity. By the end of 2012, Libya achieved sustained production at near to prerevolution levels. However, the challenges which frustrated the Qadhafi regime's attempts to increase oil production beyond 1.7 to 1.8 million b/d will remain critical issues into 2013 and beyond. For example, British Petroleum (BP) has been slow to resume operations in Libya, in part due to security concerns, and in May 2012, Royal Dutch Shell abandoned two exploration blocks due to harsh contract terms, prevailing insecurity, and disappointing results.[31] Whatever production levels are achieved, Europe will remain the principal market for Libyan oil and gas. American companies will remain significant upstream players in the hydrocarbon industry; however, the main concern of the US government downstream will be to avoid delivery disruptions to Europe that could compromise US supply sources elsewhere in the world.

Investment Opportunities

As for future investments, historical patterns of regime change in countries like Iraq suggest that looming demands for large-scale infrastructure and welfare spending will slow Libyan investment in hydrocarbon exploration and enhanced recovery techniques. This gap will open up new opportunities for international investment. State-owned companies are also scheduled for privatization once new laws are established. In addition, Libya will need outside investment to rebuild other sectors of its economy, resulting in multiple new investment opportunities for international companies. For example, Monoprix Tunisia, an affiliate of the French supermarket giant, announced in late May 2012 plans to open ten new stores in Libya by the end of 2013. At about the same time, Qatar's Al-Meera Consumer Goods Company also announced plans to expand to Libya. As to whether or not members of the NATO coalition will receive special treatment in the awarding of contracts in Libya, this may happen on a symbolic level; however, Libyans have earned a well-deserved reputation for being tough negotiators and hard-headed businessmen, and these traits will soon trump goodwill. In the short term, political strife—together with uncertain investment laws and the unclear fate of business deals with the former regime—will dampen business prospects until an elected government under a new constitution is installed, probably no sooner than mid-2014. In the longer term, post-Qadhafi economic policy probably will be a mix of a strong government role in reconstruction efforts and social welfare services, with an emphasis on market-oriented reforms elsewhere in the economy.[32]

Civil Society

Once it had consolidated its power, the Qadhafi regime systematically destroyed civil society in Libya. There were no political parties, independent trade unions, Lions Clubs, or parent-teacher organizations in Libya before the 17 February revolution. Qadhafi was fond of describing a multiparty political system as one in which people are "rode on like donkeys" and derided the very idea of civil organizations, arguing his system of direct democracy made them redundant. Concerned that civil organizations could become centers of opposition, Qadhafi allowed only those groups, like the Boy Scouts and the Red Crescent, which he approved and the regime controlled. The last to be approved was the al-Qadhafi Charitable Foundation, headed by Saif al-Islam al-Qadhafi and created well over a decade ago. With civil society organizations prohibited, Libyans turned to the family for individual support and the tribe for group support. As described in Chapter 2, post-Qadhafi Libyan civil society is flourishing and the sheer number of organizations and media outlets is astounding. However, it will take time for these organizations to learn to organize and campaign in support of individual rights, democratic institutions, and a free-market economy.[33]

Islam

Libya has been, is, and will be an Islamic society where the Islamic shari'a is considered important to the formulation of law. The 1951 constitution stated that Islam was the "religion of the state" although a subsequent article did call on the state to "respect all religions and faiths." A 1953 statute establishing the Supreme Court specified that at least two well-qualified experts in Islamic law must be appointed judges to the Supreme Court. Both civil and shari'a courts functioned in Libya throughout the monarchical era (1951–1969). In 1969, the Revolutionary Command Council replaced the 1951 constitution with a constitutional proclamation. It protected religious freedom "in accordance with established customs" but also declared Islam to be the "religion of the state." The Qadhafi regime later proclaimed shari'a to be the principal source of all legislation and established a High Commission to examine existing legislation to ensure it was

consistent with Islamic principles. In 1972, a new law aimed to rationalize women's rights in marriage and divorce with shari'a. A year
later, another law merged civil and shari'a courts. From the Qadhafi
regime's inception it employed religious rhetoric for political purposes, a phenomenon discussed in more depth in Chapter 7. When
Qadhafi's controversial interpretations of the basic tenets of Islam
were challenged by religious leaders, he took steps to undermine their
power base, purging the members of the orthodox religious establishment critical of him.[34]

Contemporary Libya is a homogenous Islamic society; almost 100
percent of the population is Muslim. The Libyan people are conservative in outlook and deeply religious in nature, but with a few exceptions,
they have never displayed any real appetite for the radical Islam advocated by the Taliban, Al-Qaeda, or its North African affiliate, Al-Qaeda
in the Islamic Maghreb (AQIM). Equally important, the general public
has shown little interest in an Islamist alternative to the nonideological
17 February revolution. The Qadhafi regime succeeded in suppressing
the Muslim Brotherhood and more militant Islamist groups, including
the Libyan Islamic Fighting Group (LIFG). However, it was unable
to prevent the growing religiosity among Libyans that has taken hold
elsewhere in the Arab world.

From the start, moderate Islamic movements were expected to do
well in the July 2012 election; however, it was always unlikely that the
general public in Libya would embrace the message of fundamental
Islamist groups or welcome the current of Salafism, which has gained
prominence elsewhere in the region. Persecuted by Qadhafi, the fall of
his regime emboldened the Salafists in Libya, and they increased their
public presence, clamping down on the illicit sale of alcohol, demol-
ishing the tombs of saints, and attacking the beliefs of Sufi Muslims
and others as heretical. However, these violent acts generated Western
media coverage out of all proportion to their numbers and influence.
The Salafists will to continue to play a role in Libyan society, but as
expected, they were bit players in the July 2012 election.[35]

Tribal and Ethnic Divides

Libya is a tribal society, and its tribal element sets it apart from Egypt,
Syria, and Tunisia. Recognizing the power of traditional tribal leaders
and fearful that they would oppose his radical reform agenda, Qadhafi
initially tried to eliminate their role and influence. When those efforts
failed, he reversed field in the late 1970s and turned to them for

political support. The 17 February revolution was not based on tribalism, and in the course of the uprisings, some tribes joined the rebels while others remained loyal to the Qadhafi regime. At the same time, many tribes tried to remain neutral throughout the fighting, either because they were too small or poorly placed to affect the outcome or because they were waiting to see which side would gain the upper hand. In the post-Qadhafi era, tribal identity and loyalty will hopefully become less important in socioeconomic and political interactions as a new civic culture based on alternative institutions and civil society organizations develops. In the run-up to the July 2012 election, an astonishingly large number of new political associations, women's movements, and youth groups appeared. Although many of them will not endure, those that do will begin to erode the traditional power of both the family and the tribe in Libya.[36]

Governance and the Electoral Process

The Temporary Constitutional Declaration for the Transitional Stage, released on 3 August 2011, outlined a 13-month process leading to general elections and the formation of a new government.[37] With the release of the draft election law on 8 February 2012, the process outlined in the Declaration was already four months behind schedule, and the timetable later slipped further still. Following the General National Congress (GNC) elections, the NTC dissolved itself and handed over power to the GNC on 8 August 2012. The GNC then appointed a prime minister to form a new interim government to rule until a constitution is approved and general elections are held sometime in 2013.

As the process leading to the election for the GNC unfolded, political uncertainties and security concerns combined to limit economic development and hamstring investment opportunities. The NTC and the interim government faced a number of related challenges, including a lack of transparency, dialogue, confidence, and legitimacy. Most of their meetings were held behind closed doors with no minutes issued. Both bodies lacked a framework for working with recognized experts and interfacing with civil society organizations. The lack of public confidence stemmed largely from the NTC's failure to effectively address key issues, such as establishing security and articulating a framework for national reconciliation. Paradoxically, the NTC argued that it could not implement more forceful policies to demobilize the militias until security was achieved, but its failure to exercise its authority against the militias perpetuated the insecurity and lawlessness that inhibited bold initiatives. The competing revolutionary narratives of the militias, many of whom professed exaggerated roles in the revolution and offered contrasting versions of legitimacy, were central to this dilemma. Their subjective views of the past often translated into unrealistic expectations leading either to apathy or radicalization.[38]

Outstanding issues for the new interim government include increased recognition of and accommodation to the demands of women, youth, and ethnic minorities. Critics argue that all three groups need to be made more aware of their rights, enjoy equal opportunities to influence governance, and have sufficient access to justice to redress violations of their rights. The youth movement, which played a central role in the revolution, is a key political constituency in a country in which approximately one-half of the population is under 25 years of age. In the case of women, the establishment of an agreed-upon legal framework within which the rule of law can be exercised and the promotion of women's rights are connected issues as women make up a majority of the lawyers in Libya and of the students in colleges of law.

Various calls for decentralization or special regional autonomy agreements, often dubbed federalism in Libya, also merit thought and discussion. Mostly calls for the delegation of vague, autonomous, and overlapping powers to local or regional councils, they bear little resemblance to federalism as found in India, Switzerland, or the United States. Proponents of decentralization appear to forget that the United Kingdom of Libya emerged as a federal state in 1951, and for the next 12 years, four governments sitting in two national and three provincial capitals ruled Libya. Liaison between the federal and provincial governments and between the three provincial governments was poor, often resulting in conflicting policies and a duplication of services. With the deficiencies of a federal system painfully obvious, it was abandoned in 1963 in favor of a unitary state. By that time, the number of people employed by the federal and provincial governments had mushroomed to 12 percent of the labor force, the highest level in the world at that time.[39] In the short term, a decentralized government, with the Economy and Oil Ministries in Benghazi, the Culture Ministry in Zintan, the Finance Ministry in Darna, and so forth, would be popular with powerful regional constituencies (and their militias). However, in the long run, it would result in bloated bureaucracies and dysfunctional governance. The related talk of creating 50 local councils and administrative offices, each with its own budget, would only add to the confusion and waste. Instead of returning to past practice, Libya must seize the opportunity to chart a new path toward the diversification and privatization of the economy within a centralized government.

Regional Concerns

Informed estimates suggest it will take up to five years to build a national army capable of policing the frontier; therefore, Libya will be unlikely to secure its borders anytime soon. Concerns over border security explain in part recent initiatives toward Algeria, Chad, Egypt, Niger, Sudan, and Tunisia. Unrest in the Sahara and Sahel—notably in Chad, Mali, Mauritania, and Niger—has been fueled by the proliferation of arms from Qadhafi's arsenals; the return of armed veterans of the Libyan army; racist attacks in Libya against black Africans, refugees and related displacement issues; the volatile situation along the unsecured border; and the Tuareg's loss of a key sponsor with the fall of Qadhafi.

In northern Mali, a secular Tuareg independence movement, *Mouvement National de Libération de l'Azawad* (National Movement for the Liberation of Azawad or MNLA) was formed with the intent to create a new state, *Azawad*, out of Mali's Gao, Kidal, and Timbuktu regions. It consisted of a mixture of veteran rebels, defectors from the Malian army, and recently returned Tuareg veterans of the Libyan army. In March 2012, the MNLA and *Harakat Ansar al-Din* (Movement of Religious Supporters), a Tuareg-based Islamist movement, seized control of the northern half of Mali, precipitating the overthrow of the Malian government, and in late May 2012, the two groups declared an independent Islamic state in the north, an area the size of France.[40] Gradually al-Qaeda affliated Islamists came to overpower the Tuareg veterans of the MNLA and seize sole control of the key towns of northern Mali. They then pushed southward, threatening Bamako itself. This prompted the French—in collaboration with ECOWAS and the Malian government in Bamako—to launch an invasion of *Azawad* in January 2013 which led to the dispersal of the MNLA, the *Harakat Ansar al-Din*, and various al-Qaeda offshoots.

In retaliation to the French invasion, jihadists seized the In Amenas gas facility in January 2013 holding hostage and killing some of its Western workers. The Algerian government responded brutally retaking the facility and killing attackers and hostages alike. Algeria has long been concerned with Mali's failure to secure its northern territories, which provide bases for the Saharan and Sahelian branches of AQIM. Algerian relations with the new Libya have been strained because Algeria did not back the 17 February revolution, was slow to recognize the NTC, and gave refuge on humanitarian grounds to Qadhafi's wife, daughter, and two sons. There was also concern that the availability of looted Libyan weapons could allow the formation of new armed groups in West Africa, like *Jama'at Tawhid wa'l-Jihad fi Gharbi Afriqqiya* (Movement for Oneness and Jihad in West Africa or MOJWA), an Al-Qaeda splinter group dedicated to the spread of jihad throughout the region.[41]

In the short term, the unrest on Libya's borders restricts trade and investment with neighboring states, including many countries where the Qadhafi regime once lavished business projects and other forms of largesse to purchase power and influence. For example, Libya and Tunisia before the revolution enjoyed the highest volume of trade between any two North African countries, and that volume increased an average of 9 percent annually in 2000–2009. In the first quarter of 2012, Tunisian exports to Libya dropped 34 percent and imports fell 95 percent due to the outbreak in fighting. Equally important, 100,000 Tunisian workers in Libya returned home, and the remittances they had been sending to families in Tunisia, an estimated $76 million, disappeared. In total, the Qadhafi regime hosted approximately 1.5 million guest workers, and their abrupt departure during the fighting drastically reduced remittances in virtually every neighboring state, adding to an already large pool of unemployed in the home countries. The Libyan Investment Authority (LIA), a sovereign wealth fund established in March 2007, was charged with investing the financial assets of six extra-budgetary funds; and while the bulk of its investments were in Europe and the United States, a relatively large amount of money was invested in Africa. In light of recent disclosures of poor management, cronyism, and a lack of checks and balances, better and more transparent management of Libya's sovereign wealth funds will be crucial to the country's economic recovery.[42]

The long-term role Libya will play in Africa is unclear; however, the disruption of regional alliances and the weakening of regimes bankrolled by Qadhafi have set the stage for policy change. Early signs suggest that Libya will turn toward North Africa and the Middle East as well as Europe to the detriment of sub-Saharan Africa. At the recent African Union (AU) summit in Addis Ababa, Ashur Bin Khayal, the interim Libyan foreign minister, emphasized that Libya would reorient its role toward its African neighbors, stressing the need to strengthen Libya's southern borders to stem the flow of contraband, drugs, and migrants. He also vowed to end the nefarious activities of the Qadhafi regime in a variety of African states, noting that the former regime had used its diplomatic missions in at least 11 countries to store and smuggle explosives and weapons. The interim government's intent to review all Qadhafi-era investments, in general, and its aggressive pursuit of investments made in Africa, in particular, are further indications of a more business-like approach toward sub-Saharan Africa. These statements and actions are encouraging as they suggest that Libya's post-Qadhafi economy will not be hijacked by political considerations. However, until the overall security situation improves, including border security, it will remain a drag on much-needed foreign investment.

Economic Prospects

The Libyan economy is at a critical juncture with authorities facing the twin challenges of economic stabilization and responding to the aspirations of the revolution. Following the election of the GNC and the appointment of the new interim government, short-term challenges include a normalization of the security situation, management of the political transition, and the exercise of budgetary discipline while maintaining macroeconomic stability. The NTC's interim finance minister, Hassan Zighlam, emphasized the importance of the security issue in a 25 July 2012 press conference. He stressed that the security situation in Libya had not improved enough for foreign companies to return and the absence of foreign companies, in turn, restricted Libyan expenditure of the redevelopment budget. In a country with limited democratic experience, the development of a working consensus in the GNC, the appointment of an effective interim government, and the drafting of a new constitution will be difficult and time-consuming tasks. Libya can afford for some time the elevated levels of current expenditures necessary to satisfy revolutionary expectations during the transition period. However, increased subsidies and higher wages will inevitably undermine fiscal sustainability. In the longer term, Libya needs to address a variety of related issues, like job creation, increasing capacity building, improving the quantity and quality of education, rebuilding infrastructure, reducing hydrocarbon dependence through diversification, and establishing an effective social safety net.[43]

Fortunately, the swift restoration of hydrocarbon production has enabled economic activity to recover rapidly. Total real GDP in 2011 was 60 percent lower than in 2010; however, according to the

International Monetary Fund (IMF), economic growth in the first half of 2012 rebounded to 116.6 percent. The IMF forecasts that growth will settle at 16 percent in 2013, declining to 13 percent thereafter. The high level of financial reserves has preserved confidence in the currency and mitigated much of the potentially destabilizing economic impact of the revolution. Most of the UN sanctions freezing Libyan assets, estimated at some 200 percent of 2010 GDP, were lifted on 16 December 2011, enabling the Central Bank of Libya (CBL) to provide liquidity to banks and normalize banking operations. Compared to a budget surplus of 16.2 percent of GDP in 2010, the budget deficit in 2011 was 27 percent of GDP due to the fall in hydrocarbon exports. However, contrary to expectations, the interim finance minister announced in July 2012 that there would be no budget deficit in 2012. As crude oil production approached preconflict levels over the summer of 2012, it was hoped that by the end of 2012 reconstruction expenditure and the release of pent-up private capital would improve growth in the nonhydrocarbon sectors of the economy. The risks to an otherwise positive economic outlook include a failure to normalize the security situation, ongoing political uncertainty, and a fall in hydrocarbon prices.[44]

CONCLUSIONS

The 2011 uprisings in Libya began on the periphery in economically marginalized areas but soon spread to other parts of the country dissatisfied with the socioeconomic and political policies of the Qadhafi regime. The socialist economy of the Qadhafi era and its debilitating pattern of political management based on patronage networks were at the heart of the widespread discontent that led to the overthrow of the regime. In turn, the physical damage caused by the uprisings, together with the social, economic, and political legacies of the war, will have a determining impact on future economic reforms and the eventual structure and operation of the Libyan economy.

The post-Qadhafi era offers Libya a fresh opportunity to reject the rentier state pattern, replacing it with a comprehensive, far-reaching strategy for sustained economic development. Nonetheless, the hydrocarbon sector will remain the centerpiece of the economy for years to come, and the new Libya will encounter the same problems the Qadhafi regime faced in achieving a major increase in oil and gas production. In lieu of a short-term focus on the more rapid depletion of a nonrenewable resource, the alternative is the creation of a long-term strategy of economic privatization, diversification, and development, designed to create job opportunities, grow the nonhydrocarbon sectors of the economy, and prepare Libya for the posthydrocarbon period. Despite the expressed interest in certain areas of the country in decentralization or "federalism," a strong central government, representative of and responsive to all segments of Libyan society, remains the optimum structure for the development and execution of a well-defined, coherent, and effective nationwide plan for economic development.

NOTES

1. A rentier state is one in which the economic rent derived from the sale of a single resource, often hydrocarbons, enables the state to act as the distributor of this rent in the form of socioeconomic benefits in return for political allegiance from its citizens.
2. Ronald Bruce St John, *Libya: From Colony to Revolution* (Oxford: Oneworld, 2012), 110.
3. Ibid., 110–11.
4. Shukri Ghanem, "The Libyan Economy before Independence," in *Social and Economic Development of Libya*, edited by E. G. H. Joffé and K. S. McLachlan (Wisbech, Cambridgeshire: Middle East & North African Studies, 1982), 148.
5. Keith S. McLachlan, "Libya's Oil Resource," *Libyan Studies* 20 (1989): 243–44; Judith Gurney, *Libya: The Political Economy of Energy* (Oxford: Oxford University Press, 1996), 4–5, 11.
6. Frank C. Waddams, *The Libyan Oil Industry* (London: Croom Helm, 1980), 117–24; Gurney, Libya, 56–58, 85–103.
7. Shukri Ghanem, "The Oil Industry and the Libyan Economy: The Past, the Present, and the Likely Future," in *The Economic Development of Libya*, edited by Bichara Khader and Bashir El-Wifati (London: Croom Helm, 1987), 58; Mustafa Bakar Mahmud and Alex Russell, "An Analysis of Libya's Revenue per Barrel from Crude Oil Upstream Activities, 1961–93," *OPEC Review* 23, no. 3 (September 1999): 215–16, 221–27; Gurney, *Libya*, 91–99.
8. Daniel Yergin, *The Prize: The Epic Quest for Oil, Money & Power* (New York: Free Press, 1991), 578–79; McLachlan, "Libya's Oil Resource," 245.
9. Yergin, *Prize*, 606–9, 613–32; Gurney, *Libya*, 58–61.
10. Waddams, *Libyan Oil Industry*, 260–63; Gurney, *Libya*, 67–70.
11. Ronald Bruce St John, *Libya and the United States: Two Centuries of Strife* (Philadelphia: University of Pennsylvania Press, 2002), 124–27, 131–35; McLachlan, "Libya's Oil Resource," 247–48; Mahmud and Russell, "Analysis of Libya's Revenue," 219.
12. Keith McLachlan, "Strategies for Agricultural Development in Libya," in *Libya since Independence: Economic and Political Development*, edited

by John Anthony Allan (London: Croom Helm, 1982), 17–20; John Anthony Allan, *Libya: The Experience of Oil* (London: Croom Helm, 1981), 187–91; Paul Barker, "The Development of Libyan Industry," in *Libya since Independence: Economic and Political Development*, edited by John Anthony Allan (London: Croom Helm, 1982), 56–69.

13. Allan, *Libya*, 190–91; Ghanem, "Oil Industry," 66.

14. Allan, *Libya*, 244.

15. John Anthony Allan, "Libya Accommodates to Lower Oil Revenues: Economic and Political Adjustments," *International Journal of Middle East Studies* 15, no. 2 (August 1983): 377–79, 381–82.

16. Dirk Vandewalle, "Qadhafi's 'Perestroika': Economic and Political Liberalization in Libya," *Middle East Journal* 45, no. 2 (Spring 1991): 216–31; Ronald Bruce St John, "The Changing Libyan Economy: Causes and Consequences," *Middle East Journal* 62, no. 1 (Winter 2008): 78–80.

17. Timothy Niblock, *"Pariah States" & Sanctions in the Middle East: Iraq, Libya, Sudan* (Boulder: Lynne Rienner, 2001), 35–94; Luis Martinez, *The Libyan Paradox* (New York: Columbia University Press, 2007), 13–14, 31–35, 39–41.

18. Ronald Bruce St John, "Libya: Coming In from the Cold, Ties Re-established in Europe and Africa," in *Africa Contemporary Record*, vol. 27 (1998–2000), edited by C. Legum (New York: Africana Publishing Company, 2004): B631-B633; Ronald Bruce St John, "Libya: Lockerbie Trial Ends, Sparking New Libyan Initiatives," in *Africa Contemporary Record*, vol. 28 (2001–2002), edited by C. Legum (New York: Africana Publishing Company, 2006): B643-B647.

19. Alison Pargeter, "Libya: Reforming the Impossible?" *Review of African Political Economy* 33, no. 108 (June 2006): 223; Ronald Bruce St John, "Redefining the Libyan Revolution: The Changing Ideology of Muammar al-Qadhafi," *Journal of North African Studies* 13, no. 1 (March 2008): 101–2.

20. World Bank, "Socialist People's Libyan Arab Jamahiriya: Country Economic Report," *Report No. 30295-LY* (July 2006), 1–2, 13; St John, *Libya: From Colony to Revolution*, 264.

21. Dirk Vandewalle, "Libya: Post-War Challenges," *African Development Bank Economic Brief* (September 2011): 8 http://www.afdb.org/filead min/uploads/afdb/Documents/Publications/Brocure%20Anglais%20 Lybie_North%20Africa%20Quaterly%20Analytical.pdf; Pargeter, "Libya," 224–26; St John, *Libya: From Colony to Revolution*, 249–50, 266–67.

22. Ronald Bruce St John, *Libya: Continuity and Change* (London and New York: Routledge, 2011), 107–9.

23. St John, *Libya: Continuity and Change*, 110.

24. Ali Shuaib and Christian Lowe, "Insight: In Muddle of Libya's Finances, Billions Go Missing," *Reuters*, April 9, 2012, http://www.reuters.com/article/2012/05/08/us-libya-finances-idUSBRE8470E2201

20508; Ronald Bruce St John, "The Libyan Economy in Transition: Opportunities and Challenges," in *Libya since 1969: Qadhafi's Revolution Revisited*, edited by Dirk Vandewalle (New York: Palgrave Macmillan, 2008), 26.

25. "Forces Holding Seif Delay His Transfer to NTC," *Tripoli Post*, May 30, 2012, http://www.tripolipost.com/articledetail.asp?c=1&i=8462; Ali Shuaib and Hadeel Al-Shalchi, "Libya Halts Cash for Ex-Fighters over Corruption," *Reuters*, April 9, 2012, http://www.reuters.com/article/2012/04/09/us-libya-corruption-idUSBRE8380QZ20120409; Susanne Tarkowski Tempelhof and Manal Omar, "Stakeholders of Libya's 17 February Revolution," *United States Institute of Peace, Special Report 300*, January 2012: 3 http://www.usip.org/files/resources/SR%20300.pdf.

26. St John, *Libya: Continuity and Change*, 111; Vandewalle, "Libya: Post-War Challenges," 10.

27. St John, *Libya: Continuity and Change*, 112.

28. Ronald Bruce St John, "A Transatlantic Perspective on the Future of Libya," Mediterranean Paper Series, The German Marshall Fund of the United States and the Istituto Affari Internazionale (May 2012): 4–5 http://www.gmfus.org/wp-content/blogs.dir/1/files_mf/1338296057StJohn_Libya_Apr12_web.pdf; United Kingdom Foreign & Commonwealth Office, *Human Rights and Democracy: The 2011 Foreign & Commonwealth Office Report* (2012): 281–82, http://www.fco.gov.uk.

29. St John, "Libyan Economy in Transition," 144–45.

30. Ronald Bruce St John, "Libyan Myths and Realities," Royal Danish Defence College, August 2011, http://forsvaret.dk/fak/eng/publications.

31. Marie-Louise Gumuchian, "Security Concerns Worsen for Oil Firms in Libya," *Reuters*, September 20, 2012, http://in.reuters.com/article/2012/09/20/libya-oil-attack-idINL5E8KJID220120920; Marie-Louise Gumuchian and Ali Shuaib, "Libya Sees Return to Pre-War Oil Output in October," *Reuters*, July 26, 2012, http://www.reuters.com/article/2012/07/26/ozabs-libya-oil-idAFJOE86P03H20120726; "Shell Abandons Oil Exploration on Two Libya Blocks," *Reuters*, May 29, 2012, http://www.reuters.com/article/2012/05/29/libya-oil-shell-exploration-idAFL5E8GTA7720120529; St John, *Libya: Continuity and Change*, 103–4.

32. Rory Jones, "Libya Readies for Dawn of New Economic Era," *The National*, July 1, 2012, http://www.thenational.ae/thenationalconversation/industry-insights/economics/libya-readies-for-dawn-of-new-economic-era; Reese Erlich, "Libya's Economy Facing Big Challenges," *Marketplace*, May 28, 2012, http://www.marketplace.org/topics/world/libyas-economy-facing-big-challenges; St John, "A Transatlantic Perspective," 14.

33. United Kingdom Foreign & Commonwealth Office, *Human Rights and Democracy*, 279–80; Ronald Bruce St John, "Libya: The Road Ahead,"

The Montréal Review, April 2011, http://www.themontrealreview.com/2009/Libya-The-Road-Ahead.php.

34. Omar Ashour, "Libyan Islamists Unpacked: Rise, Transformation, and Future," Brookings Doha Center, Policy Briefing (May 2012): 1–11; Ronald Bruce St John, "Libya Is an Islamic State," *Knox Reads,* February 13, 2012, http://knoxreads.knox.edu/?p=79.

35. Youssef Mohammad Sawani, "Post-Qadhafi Libya: Interactive Dynamics and the Political Future," *Contemporary Arab Affairs* 5, no. 1 (2012): 2–3, 5–7, 17–18; Tempelhof and Omar, "Stakeholders," 7–8; Alia Brahimi, "Islam in Libya," in *Islamist Radicalisation in North Africa: Politics and Process,* edited by George Joffé (London and New York: Routledge, 2012), 23–24; St John, "A Transatlantic Perspective," 7.

36. St John, *Libya: From Colony to Independence,* 18–19, 23–24; Amal Obeidi, *Political Culture in Libya* (Richmond, Surrey: Curzon, 2001), 108–35; Ronald Bruce St John, "Why Tribes Matter," *New York Times,* February 23, 2011; Sawani, "Post-Qadhafi Libya," 3–4.

37. For more on the circumstances of the drafting of the temporary consitutional declaration and its implications for post-Qadhafi Libya, consult Youssef Mohammad Sawani and Jason Pack, "Libyan Constitutionality and Sovereignty Post-Qadhafi: The Islamist, Regionalist, and Amazigh Challenges" (Forthcoming, Publisher TBD).

38. Ronald Bruce St John, "Libyan Election Breaks Arab Spring Pattern," *International Spectator.* 47, no. 3 (September 2012): 17–19; Pack and Barfi, "In War's Wake," 3–4; Tempelhof and Omar, "Stakeholders," 3.

39. St John, *Libya: From Colony to Revolution,* 111–15; Pack and Barfi, "In War's Wake," 9, 11–12; St John, "A Transatlantic Perspective," 5.

40. "Islamic State Declared in Northern Mali," *New York Times,* May 27, 2012.

41. Dario Cristiani and Riccardo Fabiani, "Al Qaeda in the Islamic Maghreb (AQIM): Implications for Algeria's Regional and International Relations," Istituto Affari Internazionali (IAI), Working Papers 11, no. 7 (April 2011) http://www.iai.it.

42. Yahia H. Zoubir, "Qadhafi's Spawn: What the Dictator's Demise Unleashed in the Middle East," *Foreign Affairs,* July 24, 2012, http://www.foreignaffairs.com; International Monetary Fund, *Libya beyond the Revolution: Challenges and Opportunities,* Middle East and Central Asia Department Paper 12/01 (April 2012): 6–7, http://www.imf.org; Libyan Investment Authority, "Management Information Report," September 2010 http://www.globalwitness.org; Martinez, *Libyan Paradox,* 127–28.

43. Sami Zaptia, "There Will Be No Budget Deficit in 2012, Libya Not Secure Enough for Foreigners—Finance Minister Zaglam," *Libya Herald,* July 26, 2012, http://www.libyaherald.com/2012/07/26/there-will-be-no-budget-deficit-in-2012-libya-not-secure-enough-for-foreigners-finance-minister-zaglam/; International Monetary Fund,

Libya—Staff Visit Concluding Statement, May 4, 2012, http://www.imf.
org; International Monetary Fund, *Libya beyond the Revolution*, 12–19.

44. Ronald Bruce St John, "A Transatlantic Perspective on the Libyan
Election," *Op-Med: Opinions on the Mediterranean* (August 2012):
2–3, http://www.gmfus.org/wp-content/blogs.dir/1/files_mf/1338
296057StJohn_Libya_Apr12_web.pdf; "Libya—Staff Visit Concluding
Statement by the IMF," *Libya Herald*, July 11, 2012, http://www
.libyaherald.com; International Monetary Fund, *Libya—Staff Visit
Concluding Statement*, May 4, 2012, http://www.imf.org.

4

THE ROLE OF OUTSIDE ACTORS

Ambassador Richard Northern and Jason Pack

INTRODUCTION

The Libyan uprisings began with demonstrations in Benghazi on 15 February 2011. Within ten days, the Qadhafi government had lost control of eastern Libya (Cyrenaica) and faced riots in disparate towns in the south and west—including Tripoli (see map 1). The precise sequence of events that led to the mass mobilization of the Libyan populace, the waves of defections from the regime's bureaucracy and military, and the formation of the rebels' political structures in Benghazi have been discussed in Chapter 2.

During the first three weeks of the uprisings, the rebels appeared to have the momentum. First, they consolidated their authority in the Cyrenaican heartland. Then, their ragtag armies gained territory by pushing westward from Ajdabiyya along the coastal road (see map 1). Each incremental rebel advance toward Sirte further fueled the isolated Tripolitanian uprisings, which had already erupted in Qadhafi-held territory in western Libya and the Nafusa Mountains. These disconnected uprisings were relatively successful at first: whole pockets of Tripolitania were temporarily liberated. Then on 6 March, the regime launched a counteroffensive. It reestablished control over towns such as Zawiyya and Zuwara to the west of Tripoli and pushed eastward from Sirte toward Benghazi, occupying key oil towns on the coastal road, such as Brega and Ras Lanuf. Almost immediately, the rebel-held cities inside Tripolitania succumbed, with the notable exceptions of Misrata and Zintan (see map 2).[1]

Over the next ten days, the regime gradually moved its military forces to the outskirts of Benghazi, in preparation for an assault on the city. Saif al-Islam Qadhafi claimed on 17 March that the rebellion would be crushed within 48 hours. Colonel Qadhafi himself warned in a defiant radio address: "Our troops will be coming to Benghazi tonight.... There will be no mercy."[2]

Despite the earlier upheavals in Tunisia and Egypt, the Libyan uprisings had nonetheless taken Western governments almost completely by surprise. There had been signs in Libya over the preceding months of discontent boiling up over issues of corruption, inequality of wealth, poor employment prospects for the growing numbers of youth entering the labor market, and the lack of housing for young families. Furthermore, the nation had been visibly unsettled by coverage on the Arab satellite channels of the events in neighboring Tunisia and Egypt. In fact, a week of spontaneous occupations of incomplete housing projects across Libya followed Ben Ali's resignation on 14 January.

On the surface, these housing riots appeared to be disconnected from the larger themes of the Arab Spring.[3] By the end of January, they had subsided in response to promises of increased welfare spending. In fact, the regime appears to have actually given a green light to the housing occupations as a safety valve to release growing tension about economic grievances. Therefore, right up until mid-February, almost all analysts, including those in the Libyan government, assumed that fear of brutal retribution and the regime's ability to buy off dissent would deter any wide-scale popular uprisings in Libya.

Yet, within five weeks of the first demonstrations, the United Nations Security Council adopted Resolution 1973 on 17 March authorizing the implementation of a no-fly zone (NFZ) and "all necessary measures" to protect the civilian population of Libya.[4] By the evening of 19 March, France, Britain, and the United States had launched military strikes to implement the resolution. As early as 26 February, in compliance with the earlier Resolution 1970, the International Criminal Court had launched an investigation, and the UN Human Rights Commission had appointed a Commission of Inquiry, into the Qadhafi regime's response to the uprisings. By the standards of international diplomacy, this was a remarkably swift, concerted, and coordinated reaction. This is all the more impressive given that no contingency plans existed for international intervention in a civil conflict in Libya.

Initially caught off-guard, the international community showed itself remarkably nimble, leading critics and supporters alike to speak of a "triumph of multilateralism" and of an "Obama doctrine."[5] In response to Qadhafi's repression of his own people, the international community had overridden its normal cautious instincts and bureaucratic constraints, and had created a new model for military intervention underpinned by a diplomatic and legal framework capable of addressing the unique strategic, humanitarian, and military aspects of the Libyan crisis.

*　*　*

This chapter begins with a review of the diplomacy that led to Resolution 1973. We then explore the motives and actions of the major international players (France, the United Kingdom, the United States, Qatar, the United Arab Emirates, Italy, Sudan, and South Africa). Next, we investigate the risk/reward calculations which confronted the allies as they weighed intervention. Later, we examine the relationships between the emerging National Transitional Council (NTC) and its foreign backers. Finally, we explain how the nature of the intervention, and the diplomacy behind it, defined and limited the role of external actors in the transitional period after the Liberation. The emphasis on swift humanitarian intervention, followed by a tacit consensus for effecting regime change, left little scope for postconflict nation building, which was seen as falling outside the coalition's original mandate, and for which it had surprisingly little enthusiasm given Libya's economic importance.

Over the course of the summer, the coalition eventually became the rebels' air force, simultaneously supporting different militias' aims militarily. Inadvertently, this strengthened the power of the key Western militias from Zintan and Misrata at the expense of the rebel's Cyrenaica-based political leadership. On the international scene, coalition members had recognized the NTC—becoming its financial and diplomatic sponsors—long before Qadhafi was defeated. This extensive, but hands-off, military and diplomatic support ensured that politics inside Libya would be driven by the struggle between the victorious militias and the NTC rather than by a dynamic between local actors and outside powers. The Libyan-led nature of the uprisings and of postrevolutionary politics is clearly illustrated in the other chapters of this volume. The international community attempted to help the NTC with capacity building, demobilization, security training, and election monitoring. But since 17 March 2011, its main focus had been on constraining, and then removing, the Qadhafi dictatorship which posed such a threat to Libyan civilians, ensuring that the uprisings were irreversible, and averting the risk of a humanitarian crisis when Tripoli fell. Once these goals had been achieved, the coalition was ready to stand back and let Libyans determine the country's future. As a result, the successes and failures of the National Transitional Council in governing post-Qadhafi Libya and in dealing with the local militias in their midst have been very much their own.

SECURITY COUNCIL RESOLUTION 1973

The French and British governments spearheaded the international response to the Libyan uprisings. They drafted and proposed the text of Resolution 1973, which Lebanon agreed to cosponsor. They adeptly built upon the provisions of the previous Resolution (UNSCR 1970 on 26 February) in favor of economic sanctions, an arms embargo, and a travel ban against the Libyan authorities. Their diplomats seized on the Arab League's landmark statement of 12 March, which called on the United Nations to impose a no-fly zone in Libya to avert the imminent threat to Benghazi, as a means to overcome the risk of a Russian or Chinese veto.[6] This was the first time that the Arab League had called for non-Arab military intervention in the internal affairs of an Arab state in its 65-year history. This step was highly indicative of the total death of Arab Nationalism and the ideology-free climate that prevailed in the Middle East during the Arab Spring. (For an exploration of this point, consult the Introduction.) Only in the wake of the Arab League statement did the US Administration, led by the proponents of liberal interventionism—Hillary Clinton, Susan Rice, and Samantha Powers—become fully ready to support the Anglo-French initiative.[7] (We consider the diplomatic aims and motives of each of the external powers below.)

By the time of Resolution 1973, many sub-Saharan African and non-Libyan Arab refugees had fled across Libya's borders to Egypt and Tunisia. Many of them had been guest workers. The loss to their home countries of their remittances, combined with the horrific conditions in which they had fled and in the refugee camps in which they were accommodated, constituted a humanitarian emergency.[8] On 17 March, as the Qadhafi regime prepared to overrun Benghazi, a city of nearly a million inhabitants, families began to leave the city in convoys heading toward Egypt (see map 2). A new humanitarian crisis loomed. This impending disaster, exacerbated by bellicose threats from Qadhafi spokesmen and by regime planes bombing residential areas of Ajdabiyya—south of Benghazi—made it relatively easy for the United Kingdom and France, along with their supporters, to secure a consensus in the Security Council in favor of imposing a no-fly zone and preventing a massacre of civilians in Benghazi (UNSCR 1973).

Five Security Council members (Russia, China, Germany, Brazil, and India) abstained from the vote which approved Resolution 1973, because of concerns about the wide-ranging authority it gave for external military intervention in an internal conflict. But none dared vote against or veto the resolution, partly because of the level of international concern about the threat to civilians in Libya and partly because of the Arab League statement. Without the Arab League's move, Russia and China would almost certainly have vetoed what they saw as an attempt to secure UN cover for Western military intervention in another Islamic country. Britain and the United States had lobbied the Arab League Secretariat (and other Islamic organizations) both directly and through Arab allies before the March 12 meeting to encourage a robust statement.[9] This helped produce the desired result, though subsequent statements from Arab League spokesmen during the uprisings were more nuanced, and sometimes criticized the coalition for going beyond its humanitarian mandate.

FRANCE

President Nicolas Sarkozy had been encouraged, by the freelance diplomacy of the philosopher and writer Bernard-Henri Lévy, into throwing his full weight behind the Libyan opposition from the outset.[10] Thus, France became the first country to recognize the National Transitional Council as the "legitimate government of Libya" on 10 March[11]—an unusual step and out of line with Western legal and diplomatic practice, which is to "recognize" states rather than governments, and to establish diplomatic relations only with governments which are able to demonstrate de facto control over their state's territory. This step led logically to the French calling for the international community to treat the NTC as Libya's sovereign authority in place of Qadhafi, at a time when other governments were more hesitant to state publicly that "regime change" was their objective.

Prior to the conflict, France had a highly unfavorable trade balance with Libya as French companies were behind Italian, British, and German competitors in both the oil and infrastructure sectors. For example, the French oil company Total produced only 55,000 barrels of oil per day in the country in 2010.[12] Yet, despite the low profile of its companies there, France was becoming increasingly dependent on Libyan oil, taking 15 percent of Libyan oil exports (which account for some 11 percent of French consumption).[13] Politically, France had not been central to Western diplomacy toward Libya during or after the Cold War. Although 54 French citizens were killed in the 1989 bombing of a UTA airliner over Niger, planned by Libyan spymaster Abdullah al-Senussi, France was not a driving force for sanctions against the Qadhafi regime in the 1990s, nor for their removal in the following decade. Both processes were led by Anglo-American cooperation on Libya, with the French playing a peripheral role.[14]

France's desire to use the uprisings as an opportunity to increase its limited diplomatic and economic involvement in Libya was consistent with Sarkozy's ambition to restore his country to center stage in international affairs. He had repeatedly advocated an "Atlanticist" foreign policy, under which France would not shy away from inserting itself into those overseas conflicts which were previously seen as the domain of the Anglo-Saxon powers. To this end, he increased French involvement in Afghanistan and rejoined NATO's military command, from which President de Gaulle had withdrawn in 1966.[15]

As the French were formulating their response to the initial uprisings, in mid-February and early March, Lévy met the NTC leadership in Benghazi and then directly contacted Sarkozy's office at the Élysée Palace. He insisted on keeping the French Foreign Ministry, who might have been more cautious, in the dark about his policy recommendations.[16] Furthermore, the French government's swift and deep engagement with the rebels in Benghazi must be seen in the context of its clumsy reaction to the earlier uprisings in Egypt and Tunisia. This had led to the resignation of the French foreign minister, Michèle Alliot-Marie, whose first instinct had been to offer support to President Ben Ali in the face of mounting popular protests. To compensate for that fiasco, President Sarkozy was keen to back the right side in Libya and to regain an influential role in Western diplomacy toward the Arab Spring. In short, French dynamism at the beginning of the Libyan uprisings sprang very much from the personal roles and instincts of President Sarkozy, his cabinet advisors in the Élysée, and Bernard-Henri Lévy rather than the Foreign Ministry's considered policy advice. Anecdotal evidence suggests that Sarkozy entertained Gaullist notions of projecting French power into North Africa, simultaneously seeking to win plaudits from a domestic audience for conducting a successful humanitarian intervention all the while diverting their attention from the failures of his promarket policies to alleviate the economic crisis in the run up to the Spring 2012 elections. A side benefit for Sarkosy's corporate allies would be a boost in France's hitherto disappointing trade with Libya. It therefore came as no surprise that, once the conflict ended, French ministers and businessmen wasted no time in visiting Tripoli to press for commercial rewards, or to deepen their ties with the authorities of post-Qadhafi Libya by offering security training and defense sales.[17]

UNITED KINGDOM

A year into his tenure in office, Prime Minister David Cameron was facing his first series of international crises. The Egyptian and Tunisian revolutions had required calm and authoritative handling. But Libya posed challenges of a different order—moral questions about humanitarian intervention and practical ones about committing the British government to the intensive international diplomacy needed to build and sustain a multilateral coalition, and making a prominent contribution to the military effort to back up intervention.

From the outset, the prime minister took control of the UK response using the government's new National Security Council as the forum for coordination and decision making. This ensured the active involvement of a range of senior ministers (including the foreign minister, deputy prime minister, defense minister, overseas development minister, and chancellor of the exchequer), who met regularly and remained personally engaged in coordinating and directing the UK diplomatic and military operations from start to finish. This hands-on, high-level political involvement at a level of operational detail normally left to departmental officials, gave great momentum to the humanitarian, diplomatic, and military campaign, ensured that human and financial resources were found to back it up, and guaranteed a consistent approach. But it also led to an overemphasis on short-term results and a focus on day-to-day domestic political headlines rather than the longer-term strategic objectives given higher priority by departmental experts.[18]

In opposition from 1997 to 2010, the Conservative Party had never supported the Blair and Brown governments' attempts to use incentives to encourage an evolution in the Qadhafi regime's external behavior, and had strongly criticized the Scottish Executive's decision in 2009 to release Abdul-Basset al-Megrahi, the Libyan intelligence officer convicted of involvement in the Lockerbie bombing.[19] Consistent with this stance, the Conservative/Liberal Democrat coalition government adopted a firm line with the Libyan regime, when it came to power in May 2010. It made warmer diplomatic relations with Libya conditional on progress in outstanding bilateral disputes dating back to the 1980s, notably the incomplete police investigations into the Lockerbie bombing, and the shooting of policewoman Yvonne Fletcher outside the Libyan embassy in London, and claims for compensation from victims of attacks carried out by the Irish Republican Army (IRA) using Libyan-supplied explosives. Therefore, the Cameron government had few a priori qualms about military intervention in Libya. They felt less constrained by Blair's earlier pursuit of détente with Qadhafi than a Labour government might have been.

Economic considerations did not drive the UK government's interest in intervention, despite the fact that the UK's economic stake in Libya had grown (from a low base) since 2003. BP and Shell had both invested heavily there. Neither was yet producing oil or gas, though BP's concessions, both onshore and offshore, were believed to have enormous potential. In the service sector (particularly education, training, health care, and energy services) British companies had established a strong foothold, though they lagged behind Italy and Germany in the supply of consumer and industrial goods. The United Kingdom was also host to the largest and most affluent Libyan expatriate community. From the outset its spokesmen were strong and effective advocates of the rebels' cause.

In its enthusiasm to be at the forefront of the international response to the crisis, the British government suffered two minor diplomatic mishaps. On 21 February, foreign secretary William Hague announced that Qadhafi had fled Libya en route to Venezuela. This was based on an unconfirmed eyewitness report. Later the very same day, Qadhafi appeared in Tripoli to demonstrate the inaccuracy of this claim. It subsequently transpired that the eyewitness had actually seen Qadhafi's son Mu'tasim Billah—who did fly to Venezuela and the Caribbean, but returned a week later. Second, a rushed attempt to put a UK "liaison" team into Benghazi ended in farce, when the team and its security escort—whose arrangements had not been properly coordinated with the NTC—were arrested on arrival and detained for several days in early March. Fortunately, neither mishap had longer-term implications for the British position in Libya.

UNITED STATES

In spite of having reached a diplomatic settlement with Libya in 2003 concerning compensation for American victims of Libyan terrorism and the normalization of Libya's relations with the West, the US government's relations with Libya remained cautious throughout the decade. By late 2010, these relations were again at a low ebb. American businesses had not achieved as strong a presence in Libya as their European counterparts. In their drive for reforms (2005–2008) to reduce the role of the state and open up and modernize the Libyan economy, Saif al-Islam and his circle had employed American management consultants. Despite some good intentions, many of these selectively enforced "reforms" functioned as smoke screens, and to varying degrees American consultants became complicit in this process. Crony privatizations followed, leading to state assets being "privately owned" by those associated with the Qadhafi family.[20] Furthermore, since 2008, hard-liners in the political system had moved to block or mitigate the impact of the reforms. One tactic they employed was to put pressure on American firms offering consultancy advice—some of whom were even involved in pro-Qadhafi political activities, in addition to their supposed role of encouraging liberalization—forcing them to leave the country. Although a few American companies did secure roles in major infrastructure projects, or oil concessions, up until the fall of the Qadhafi regime, new projects in the energy services, transport, health, and security sectors went predominantly to UK, European, Chinese, and Russian firms. Lingering suspicion of and hostility to the United States and American citizens persisted among hard-liners at all levels in the regime.

At the end of December 2010, the Libyans forced the American government to withdraw their ambassador, Gene Cretz, from Tripoli after his confidential cables to Washington were published by Wikileaks. Cretz had painted a frank, unflattering, and presumably accurate picture of Qadhafi as a ridiculous and a tyrannical despot. These cables infuriated the regime and undermined the aura of an all-powerful leader above criticism, which Qadhafi and his circle strived to maintain. They also revealed the extent to which Qadhafi's sons profited from official contracts and corrupt deals relating to the supposed "reforms." As Abdullah al-Senussi, Qadhafi's intelligence chief and brother-in-law, warned a state department visitor at the time, any Libyan who had dared to express such views in writing would have met a swift and certain fate.[21]

Having limited strategic and commercial interests at stake in Libya, and not wanting to be seen as following President Bush's controversial policy of American intervention in Islamic countries, the Obama administration was reluctant to lead the international response. It therefore encouraged European Union countries to do so, while making clear that it would lend its support. This support was essential, as the use of advanced US military technology was a sine qua non for the no-fly zone's success.

ITALY

Thanks to former colonial ties, as well as geography, Italy was by far Libya's biggest trading partner. Italy's largest company by market capitalization, ENI, was the biggest foreign oil producer in Libya—pumping approximately 17 percent of all Libyan crude. Italy was also the largest importer of Libyan oil, accounting for 28 percent of all purchases in 2010. ENI owns 50 percent of the Greenstream natural gas pipeline between Libya and Sicily that carries almost all Libya's gas exports (around 10.5 billion cubic meters in 2010), and provides Italy with 10 percent of its gas requirements. Indeed, Libya is ENI's biggest theater of operations, accounting for 15 percent of the company's total oil and gas production.[22] Furthermore, the Italian state owns nearly a third of ENI's stock and possesses a golden share granting the Italian government ample motives and levers to coordinate its policy with the oil giant.

Italy and Malta were also the first destinations for African migrants transiting Libya. These interests had led the Italian prime minister Silvio Berlusconi to build a close personal relationship with Qadhafi, signing the 2008 Treaty of Friendship with him, which required the payment of Italian reparations for colonial rule (in return for business contracts and cooperation in limiting flows of illegal migrants across the Mediterranean). Meanwhile, Qadhafi had invested part of his country's oil wealth in Italy. Even in 2012, Libya holds a 7.5 percent stake in the Italian bank UniCredit, a 2 percent share in Italian vehicle manufacturer Fiat, and a 2 percent interest in Italian defense contractor Finmeccanica.[23]

At the start of the uprisings, Italy's dependence on Libya for energy and capital might have tempted Silvio Berlusconi, as Qadhafi's best friend in Europe and the main beneficiary from the status quo, to sit on the fence. Indeed, this may have been the Italians' first impulse. Italian foreign minister Franco Frattini called on 14 March for Arab mediation and negotiations to end the violence in Libya and warned on 23 March that the no-fly zone should not become a "war on Libya."[24] But, once the decision was taken to implement a no-fly zone, Berlusconi saw that Italy's interests lay in joining the coalition and immediately made NATO and other bases in southern Italy and Sicily available to coalition aircraft. On 2 April, two days before Italy officially recognized the NTC as the "only interlocutor in Libya," ENI's CEO, Paolo Scaroni, met rebel officials in Benghazi, who were seeking to "restart cooperation in the energy sector and get going again the collaboration with Italy."[25] Unsurprisingly, Italy's already dominant economic position in Libya emerged further strengthened at the end of the conflict.

QATAR AND THE EMIRATES

If France and the United Kingdom pushed the Western powers to intervene in Libya, it was Qatar and the United Arab Emirates that worked behind the scenes to secure the Arab League statement, which enabled the UN Security Council to adopt Resolution 1973. Qatar also became the first Arab country to recognize the NTC on 28 March, calling it "the sole legitimate representative of the Libyan people."

The Qataris and Emiratis did not limit their efforts to diplomacy alone. Qatar sent six fighter jets; and the United Arab Emirates sent twelve.[26] They engaged in combat as well as surveillance missions. But Qatari military involvement went well beyond the few aircraft and crew provided. When it became clear that the NATO bombing campaign alone would not be sufficient to ensure that the rebels toppled Qadhafi, Doha played a crucial role in arming rebel militias. From April 2011 onward, it supplied French Milan antitank missiles and Belgian FN rifles. Over the course of the campaign, Qatar supplied more than 20,000 tons of weapons in 18 shipments. Qatar also brought hundreds of Libyan fighters to Doha for training. During the final assault to take Tripoli, Qatari Special Forces fought shoulder to shoulder with the militias and "supervised" their battle plans, according to the Qatari chief of staff.[27]

In Doha, Qatari authorities provided secure offices for the NTC's government in waiting, and made TV studios and broadcasting equipment available to *Libya al-Ahrar*, the NTC's station run mainly by young Libyan volunteers from the United States and United Kingdom, to broadcast anti-Qadhafi programs in Arabic into Libya.[28]

Both Qatar and the United Arab Emirates sent humanitarian supplies and financial aid. Qatar also offloaded a shipment of oil from the NTC-controlled terminal in Tobruk and sold it to raise funds for the NTC at a time when international companies were prohibited by UN sanctions from buying oil directly from Libya. Qatari readiness to provide generous political, military, and economic support to the NTC puzzled some. Their involvement was based on humanitarian, economic, and, more crucially, personal and strategic factors.

Over the past few years, analysts have concluded that "the only way [for Qatar] to protect their sovereignty against traditional Saudi meddling in their internal affairs is to act like a regional power. By pitching a stake in every major regional issue, they become more resilient to the frequent great power gales of the Middle East."[29] In contrast to the Saudis, who were slow to abandon their old allies in North Africa, Shaykh Hamad bin Khalifa al-Thani, Qatar's Amir, pursued a flexible foreign policy largely independent of Qatar's Gulf Cooperation Council partners. He had already acted as a mediator or host for peace negotiations in a range of international disputes. Within the Arab

Spring countries, Qatar sponsored a broad range of emerging political movements, especially moderate Islamists.

In the case of Libya there were also sentimental factors—Shaykha Moza, the influential second wife of the Amir, had lived for some years in Egypt and Libya, and had personal links with families associated with the former monarchy in Benghazi. There were also old scores to settle: Qadhafi had fallen out with several Gulf leaders, but his resentment over Sheikh Hamad's refusal to listen to his repeated demands to put pressure on *Al-Jazeera* TV, when he found its broadcasts unsympathetic to the Libyan *Jamahiriyya*, produced deep and long-running bad feeling on both sides. Qadhafi was also rumored to have refused to pay back money loaned by the Qataris to facilitate the release in 2009 of the Bulgarian nurses imprisoned after children at a hospital in Benghazi were infected with HIV.

Furthermore, the Amir of Qatar had said a number of times that Arab leaders should take responsibility for resolving disputes in the Arab world. Intervention in Libya posed no conflict of interest for him: backing the rebels was both a moral and a pragmatic choice. Qatari intervention was successful in boosting the capability of rebel armed forces, though the choice of individual Libyan leaders to act as channels for support did not always promote military or political unity in the longer term.

In addition to patronage for secular Libyans with long-standing ties to the Qatari royals, like the rebel's media expert Mahmoud Shammam, Qatar also funded Islamists, repeating the strategies it had used in Tunisia and Egypt. It built on preexisting Libyan diaspora networks based in Qatar and the United Arab Emirates. The most active of these was led by Ali Sallabi, an Islamic cleric and Libyan dissident jailed in the 1980s, who later lived in exile in Qatar putting down extensive roots. Despite his lifelong opposition to the Qadhafi regime, Sallabi was involved in Saif al-Islam's 2009 campaign to persuade the Libyan Islamic Fighting Group to renounce violence. During the uprisings, Sallabi served as an *Al-Jazeera* studio analyst. Qatar in turn used Sallabi's personal networks to fund the rebels. From the start of the conflict, Doha was channeling assistance to Fawzi Bu Katif's 17 February Brigade in Benghazi; from April onward, it became the primary patron of Abdul-Hakim Bilhajj's Tripoli Military Council.

In summation, during the uprisings, Qatar connected itself to secularists (Mahmoud Shammam), nonmilitia-aligned Islamists (Sallabi), Cyrenaican Islamist militiamen (Fawzi Bu Katif), and Tripolitanian Islamist militiamen with jihadist backgrounds (Abdul-Hakim Bilhajj) in addition to hosting Mahmoud Jibril and providing logistical and financial support to the NTC leadership. Its assistance was disbursed through different and uncoordinated elements of Libyan society and thus had a destabilizing influence after the end of hostilities. It did not aid the Libyan "center" in its struggle with the "periphery." Quite the contrary: the disparate networks of Qatari patronage have tended to aid peripheral elements in undermining the center's agenda.[30] The repercussions of Qatari support of Islamist currents are discussed in Chapter 7, while the backlash that recipients of Qatari aid faced from the Libyan electorate has been briefly covered in Chapter 2.

Like Qatar, the Emirates have a number of companies with investments in Libya and Emirati leaders had strategic and personal reasons for involvement in Libya. The Emirati al-Ghurair Group owns 50 percent of Libya's largest oil refinery (in Ras Lanuf), and it announced after the overthrow of Qadhafi that it would invest $1.5 billion to upgrade it. Other UAE ventures own stakes in the First Gulf Libyan Bank and power plants in Tripoli. But Emirati engagement was also a reaction to Qatari ambitions, in particular Qatari sponsorship of Islamic groups and the periphery. The Emiratis tried to counter this influence by channeling their own support through the National Transitional Council and their allies within it. They were well positioned for this role: former NTC prime minister Mahmoud Jibril, although based in Doha during the uprisings, had long-standing business interests in Dubai and quickly emerged as the key interlocutor for the Emiratis together with his ally, Arif Ali Nayed, who was later appointed Libyan ambassador to the United Arab Emirates. The victory of the National Forces Alliance in the July 2012 elections and the implosion of Bilhajj's Watan Party suggest that post-Qadhafi Libya may be more closely aligned with Emirati than with Qatari interests. If, however, the central government's authority fails to take root and peripheral power centers retain their independence, Qatar could be drawn into playing a more influential role in Libyan politics and economic development.

In the meantime, Qatar's links to Islamist and regional leaders in the periphery have aroused deep suspicion among the wider population about its long-term objectives. In October 2011, a group of rebels in eastern Libya visited Doha to seek support for their bid for independence for Cyrenaica. Attempting to build upon genuine local frustration at the lack of tangible improvements in daily life in the East after the revolution, their separatist campaign failed to attract wide support. Furthermore, the mere fact that they tried to ally themselves with Qatar—even though the Qataris may not have endorsed their cause or offered support—damaged their standing inside Libya.

THE RISKS OF EXTERNAL INTERVENTION

The military (and to a lesser extent political) risks of international intervention in Libya were lower than they might have been elsewhere. The country is sparsely populated; the open, desert terrain leaves ground forces vulnerable to air attack; and Qadhafi did not possess sophisticated, modern air defenses. NATO had access to military bases in Sicily, and in extremis in Malta, only 150 miles from the Libyan coast. Since the 1990s, the Qadhafi government has not been central to the Arab-Israeli dispute; Libya's relations with most other Arab countries have progressively deteriorated during the Qadhafi era. Lebanon—a firm antagonist of Libya since the disappearance of the Lebanese political and religious leader Musa Sadr during a visit to Tripoli in 1976—supported a firm international response in the Security Council. Other Arab leaders (e.g., the kings of Saudi Arabia and Morocco) had been the targets of unsuccessful assassination plots by Qadhafi. In fact, Qadhafi had few real friends outside Africa, other than Belarus and Venezuela.[31] Although occasionally supportive, even North Korea, Cuba, and Iran had their grievances with Qadhafi.[32]

Complex operations to evacuate foreign citizens by air and sea during February and early March had already brought NATO military aircraft and ships to Libya. This had enabled them to gather intelligence that would prove useful in the subsequent military campaign. The popular protests in Egypt and Tunisia had already shown that ordinary people in the region were no longer prepared to be excluded from political and economic freedoms by aging autocrats. Once they appreciated this, governments in the West saw the advantages of supporting the aspirations of these populations against their dictatorial rulers in the hope that this would lead to more representative forms of government, more open economies, and greater political stability on Europe's doorstep. Facilitating a successful evolution to democracy in Libya and working with the grain of popular opinion, might create a model for engagement in other Arab countries and restore the image of the West on the Arab street. Successful international involvement might also provide a strong precedent for future multilateral interventions to protect populations from repression and slaughter by autocratic governments. In addition, coalition governments expected to benefit directly from increased trade with, and reduced migration flows from, North Africa.

On the other hand, there were certainly some risks—most of them political and geostrategic rather than military. Air strikes and a no-fly zone might prevent Benghazi being overrun, but were unlikely in themselves to produce a quick and decisive result. Militarily, US defense secretary Robert Gates warned Congress at the beginning of March that implementing a no-fly zone would require the elimination of all Libya's air defenses and could become a "big operation in a big country."[33] Geostrategically, the stakes were high; and a failure to act could have had resounding regional consequences. Some Western governments feared that allowing Qadhafi to brutally suppress the uprisings might well stop the evolution of more representative government in Tunisia and Egypt in its tracks and extinguish the hopes raised by the Arab Spring elsewhere in the region.

Politically, it was hard to imagine what a Libya without Qadhafi would look like. His departure would doubtlessly leave an enormous vacuum. In Tunisia and Egypt, the armed forces had been able to maintain stability and order after the removal of unpopular presidents; and there were established opposition parties and institutions to lead and channel popular concerns. In Libya, there were no comparable independent social or political institutions. This raised crucial questions: What might replace Qadhafi and his *Jamahariyya*? Who would maintain order in liberated areas? How credible and effective would the rebel movement prove as a governing authority? How would the tendency for authority to fragment—so common in Libya's history and now reignited by the disconnected nature of the uprisings—be reversed in the aftermath of the conflict?

These imponderables weighed against military intervention as Western actors—especially, but not only, the United States and Britain—were determined not to become directly entangled in Libyan affairs or to be forced into yet another "nation-building" mission in a failed state. As a result, some US and UK politicians, bureaucrats, and think-tank specialists remained particularly wary about "going in" to Libya after the painful experience of Iraq and seeing that any military intervention, even without ground troops, might entail a costly nation-building program.[34]

Conversely, the uprisings were a genuine citizens' revolt, which had grown and spread thanks partly to public outrage at the regime's brutal reaction to early demonstrations in the East, and partly to the fact that communities throughout Libya had historically nurtured their own local grievances against the regime. The spontaneous civil unrest of mid-February had not been planned and had no leadership around which to coalesce. Organized Libyan opposition parties played no direct role in sparking it: they were small and their leaders in exile. Within the country, Islamist groups in the East had led the opposition to Qadhafi since the 1990s, but even in their heyday, they were too few in number to topple the regime. By 2010, most of these Islamist actors, such as the Libyan Islamic Fighting Group and the Muslim Brotherhood, had entered into tacit cooperation with the Qadhafi regime.[35] The emerging National Transitional Council, formed in Benghazi on 27 February, appeared to be led by former reformists from within the Qadhafi regime and to only tangentially interface with the established Islamist or exiled opposition. It was a wholly new kettle of fish. Crucially, it was unclear how deep the support for the NTC ran among local rebel military units leading the disparate uprisings in cities throughout Libya. Would they heed its commands and follow its political leadership?

These dynamics made it difficult for Western governments to know at the beginning whom exactly they might be supporting by intervening militarily and what these actors stood for.[36] Nor was there any prospect of promoting an early negotiated settlement, which would limit the need for external involvement. Qadhafi was not temperamentally inclined to compromise and prized loyalty above all else. Attempts by the African Union and South African president Zuma to mediate were manifestly stalling tactics designed to keep Qadhafi in power. We discuss them further below.

Thanks to Qadhafi's record of ruthlessly crushing dissent, the demonstrators knew that once they had fundamentally challenged his authority, there was no going back. Their struggle was a battle to the death. Unlike in Tunisia and Egypt, the "Brother Leader" was not going to be persuaded to step down in the face of popular protests. He identified himself with the very form of the Libyan state: the two were functionally inseparable in his mind. He saw it as his role and duty to defend his historic achievements as Leader and to defeat his enemies. For this reason, he was never likely to leave Libya or stand down under pressure. As multiple confidants of the Libyan Leader told the authors in early 2011, Qadhafi had been very shaken by Ben Ali's decision to flee rather than stand up to his critics in Tunisia; he resented the lack of gratitude and respect shown by Egyptian demonstrators toward Mubarak, whom he respected as an Arab hero for his role in the 1973 Arab-Israeli war.

The NATO-led coalition that sprang into action on 18 March had learned lessons from Iraq and Afghanistan. Experience in those conflicts had shown that any casualties, particularly tragic incidents involving civilian deaths, could quickly turn public opinion both in the region and at home against intervention. So NATO set restrictive rules of engagement to minimize the risk of such incidents. It was also determined not to assume responsibility (even temporarily) for administering or providing security for a post-Qadhafi Libya. This meant operating in a "supporting" role only, leaving Libyan opposition forces to conduct operations on the ground and define their political future. But it also limited coalition influence over the campaign's timescale as well as its precise outcome. These depended not on NATO, but on the ability of the revolutionary forces leading each of the disparate local uprisings to work together to overthrow the regime and administer the country—and to retain local Libyan and international support and respect while doing so. This made NATO military chiefs cautious initially. They could not be sure how or when their intervention would end.

DIPLOMACY

The two UN Security Resolutions, especially 1973, owed much to skillful and timely drafting and lobbying by the United Kingdom and allied missions at the United Nations in New York. Agreement on effective language was helped both by the Qadhafi regime's blatant disregard for civilian casualties and by the care taken to overcome suspicions that Western intervention in Libya might follow the pattern of Iraq. The drafters of the resolutions explicitly ruled out the use of ground forces in a foreign military invasion. Despite this, some Europeans remained unenthusiastic. A European Union summit in mid-March (prior to the Arab League's statement and to Resolution 1973) failed to agree on military action to enforce a no-fly zone. Some participants thought it might take weeks to put arrangements for a no-fly zone into effect.[37] Others, such as Germany and Poland, had serious reservations about military action, partly for domestic reasons and partly because they were reluctant to be drawn into another expensive military operation (after Afghanistan) in a country that did not pose even an indirect threat to themselves, and where the outcome seemed uncertain and the competence and worthiness of the rebels unproven. The German foreign minister, Guido Westerwelle, had described the consequences of military intervention in late February as "unpredictable" and fraught with "considerable risks and danger."[38] Some southern Europeans feared the impact of wider conflict in Libya on their own economies or increased flows of migrants across the Mediterranean. France and Britain were not deterred. They set about creating what President Sarkozy dubbed a "coalition of the willing," eerily echoing a phrase used previously by President Bush.

Within hours of a hastily arranged summit meeting in Paris on 19 March, President Sarkozy announced that French planes were already in action against Qadhafi's forces preventing their assault on Benghazi.[39] (See map 2 showing the farthest extent of loyalist advances.) The same day, American and British naval ships fired Tomahawk missiles, and the Royal Air Force launched air strikes on Libyan air defenses. Both before and after launching military action, the allies rightly attached great importance to securing and maintaining support from Islamic countries and organizations. They had worked hard to win diplomatic approval from the Arab League. Once Resolution 1973 was adopted, they encouraged Arab states to participate in its enforcement. As many Arab nations had been prominent in calling for intervention, as mentioned above, it was not difficult to get Qatar, Jordan, and the United Arab Emirates to send planes and cash.

The British government convened a ministerial conference in London on 29 March 2011 for relevant international organizations and for countries belonging to or supporting the coalition enforcing the UN Resolutions.[40] This "Contact Group" became the key forum for coordinating political and public relations aspects of the military campaign as well as maintaining its diplomatic momentum. Follow-up meetings were convened at monthly intervals by different coalition members. The list of participants grew each month.

National Transitional Council

A difficulty the British and others faced in the early weeks of the uprisings was how to identify, assess, and open dialogue with the emerging leaders of the Libyan opposition in Benghazi. Two ministers in Qadhafi's government—Mustafa Abdul-Jalil, the justice minister, and Abdul-Fattah Yunis al-Obeidi, the interior minister—were in Cyrenaica at the start of the uprisings and promptly defected to the rebels. They quickly emerged as go-betweens and focal points—known to Western governments and useful conduits to less known players within the rebel leadership. But even after the National Transitional Council (NTC) was formed, the rebel leadership had no clear structure or hierarchy. The NTC was not set up to function as a crisis government: it was established as a forum to represent the various views of different communities in Libya. Initially, the core membership comprised Benghazi lawyers and academics prominent in the disputes that had triggered the mid-February demonstrations. It held its first formal meeting in Benghazi on 5 March, gathering representatives of cities and tribes in the liberated areas. It seemed better at debate than decision making. Its leaders lived in fear of assassination and betrayal. They also lacked secure communications with each other and the outside world.

Mahmoud Jibril, a US-educated technocrat—who had recently run the Economic Development Board (EDB) in Tripoli, effectively a reform-minded Ministry of Planning, which lacked the power or tools to implement its ideas—was appointed Chair of the NTC's Executive Committee. He also took charge of international relations, working first from Cairo and later from Doha. Jibril was highly effective in this role. He visited Paris and London in March, meeting the US Secretary of State in both capitals. In London, with British government encouragement, he published a revised version of a Charter drafted by the National Transitional Council in Benghazi. It pledged respect for human rights, including freedom of speech and association. This document made it easier for the NTC to attract international support and to give substance to its claims to represent the uprisings and serve as their legitimate political face. It was superseded in August 2011 by a new and more detailed draft constitutional charter, setting out the NTC's plans for forming a government post-Qadhafi.[41]

THE LIBYAN DIASPORA

As soon as the uprisings started, Libyan expatriates in Europe, North America, and the Persian Gulf looked for an active role in helping to topple Qadhafi. Many had spent years outside Libya because of their opposition to the regime. They raised funds and shipped (sometimes at considerable risk to their own personal safety) humanitarian supplies to rebel communities. Libyan communities in the United Kingdom shipped supplies (humanitarian and other) to Malta and Tunisia and chartered vessels to smuggle them into Misrata and Zawiyya, even when the regime was blockading those ports. Prominent Libyans overseas also lobbied host governments to increase support for anti-Qadhafi forces. Some, like Anwar Fekini, a successful international lawyer, whose grandfather had led resistance to Italian colonial forces in Jabal Nafusa,[42] returned to Libya to fight for the opposition forces in their hometowns. Libyan expatriates with specialist expertise even managed to keep mobile telephone networks in eastern Libya operating after the regime had cut them off and monitored regime military communications.[43]

THE MILITARY CAMPAIGN

On 31 March, less than two weeks after the coalition's military intervention had begun, command of military operations passed from the United States to NATO. The United States continued to provide essential support and assets, but withdrew its planes from direct combat after 4 April. The burden of attacking Libyan ground forces fell predominantly to French, British, Italian, Danish, Belgian, Canadian, Emirati, Qatari, and Norwegian planes. Within the coalition, Jordan, Spain, Turkey, and the Netherlands limited their participation to routine air patrols and support roles.

Though the Libyan revolutionary forces lacked nothing in bravery and determination, most were untrained and poorly equipped. They also suffered from lack of organization and disagreements about tactics; the secondment of Western military advisers did little to alleviate this. Sporadic clashes soon settled into a war of attrition, lasting from April to July, waged between regime forces and the rebels along a front line on the Mediterranean coast from Brega toward Sirte, with neither side able to break through. The regime was constrained by NATO airpower, while the rebels suffered from lack of tactical knowledge, organization, and heavy weaponry.[44] (Map 3 reveals how even as Tripoli was encircled by rebel forces on 19 August, the stalemate still persisted on the coastal road from Brega to Sirte.)

Meanwhile, the NTC faced the challenge of administering liberated areas of Libya with limited resources and no administrative infrastructure other than the broken institutions it inherited from Qadhafi. With the help of NGOs, international agencies, and bilateral donors, they gradually overcame these challenges. On the political front, Jibril's Executive Committee secured diplomatic recognition—by July, all members of the Contact Group, including the United States and Britain, had recognized the NTC as the legitimate government of Libya. Jibril also mobilized Libyan exile communities and some senior Libyan ambassadors who had defected to the opposition to press host governments to deliver further financial and material support. The NTC needed this support to boost its authority in preparation for the decisive battle for Tripoli and the challenges of government.

Despite its success abroad, the NTC in Benghazi was slow to realize the importance of communicating with the population. They were notoriously bad at keeping the population informed about their decisions and achievements. Frequently, one spokesman contradicted another. The lack of clarity in NTC statements about the circumstances surrounding the killing of Abdul-Fattah Yunis al-Obeidi in July 2011, and their reluctance to identify those responsible, created suspicion and confusion. It also suggested weak leadership and damaged the NTC's image overseas, making it easier for the Qadhafi regime to convince those already skeptical about NATO's intentions that the rebels were a disorganized rabble propped up by NATO and lacking authentic popular support. The NTC leadership also found it hard to shed its habits of secrecy or to delegate effectively. For example, citing security concerns, it never revealed its full membership in spite of promises to do so.

With little movement on the military front between April and July, the United Kingdom, Italy, and France tried to weaken the regime's resolve to prolong the conflict by encouraging dissent and defections in its senior ranks. They had some successes from late March onward, most notably the defections of foreign minister Musa Kusa, the head of the National Oil Company (NOC), Shukri Ghanem, and the governor of the Central Bank, Farhat Ben Gdara. But the propaganda impact of these defections was short-lived. Other potential defectors hesitated to leave Tripoli because of the severe punishment that Qadhafi inflicted on the families and properties of those who showed disloyalty.

SUDAN

The Sudanese government intervened briefly in southeastern Libya. Khalil Ibrahim, leader of the Justice and Equality Movement (JEM), a Sudanese opposition movement sponsored by Qadhafi in Darfur, and his closest supporters had been living in Tripoli since May 2010.[45] As conditions in Tripoli deteriorated during 2011, they moved south intending eventually to return to Darfur. Alarmed by this development, Sudanese government forces crossed the porous border in June 2011 and occupied the Libyan town of Kufra, forcing the Qadhafi regime's border garrison stationed nearby to withdraw toward Sabha. The Sudanese army occupied the town for about two weeks.[46] Their aim was to prevent the JEM from using the town as a base for cross-border attacks. From Kufra, the Sudanese sent supplies to the NTC in Benghazi and protected their southern flank. (For more on developments in Kufra, Sabha, and of southern Libya during the uprisings, consult Chapter 6 by Henry Smith.)

AFRICAN DIPLOMACY

By early summer 2011, Africa had become the focus of international diplomacy surrounding the protracted conflict in Libya. Qadhafi sent envoys to fellow African Union leaders to lobby (often with financial inducements) for military supplies and diplomatic support in the form of African Union statements demanding a halt to NATO intervention and the launch of cease-fire initiatives. President Jacob Zuma and four other African leaders arrived in Tripoli on 10 April in an unsuccessful effort to promote cease-fire talks between the Qadhafi regime and the NTC as a basis for a political settlement and a suspension of NATO air strikes.[47] In Benghazi, they were met by hostile crowds who disrupted their meetings and made clear their opposition to any deal with Qadhafi based on promises of reform. Zuma was no more successful in persuading Qadhafi to compromise when he visited Tripoli again on 31 May.

At the same time, the United Kingdom, the United States, and France launched a diplomatic offensive to persuade African governments of the scale of human rights violations committed by regime forces (including those against African residents in Libya) and of the futility of promoting cease-fire talks on Qadhafi's terms. The coalition's diplomatic offensive had mixed success. The many eyewitness or personal accounts from residents fleeing Tripoli, Zawiyya, and Misrata gave harrowing details of arbitrary arrests and executions of rebel sympathizers as well as indiscriminate rape and intimidation of civilian populations. But some African leaders still instinctively felt uncomfortable about any military intervention by former colonial powers on African soil and about the principle of external encouragement of indigenous rebels. They understood how both precedents could be used in the future to undermine their own governments. Some may also have worried that a post-Qadhafi Libya might break up and destabilize the region. In addition, they did not know the NTC leaders personally or assumed (rightly) that they would not continue Qadhafi's policy of investing in the African Union and in their economies. In a few cases, such as Mali, Rwanda, Uganda, and Burkina Faso, African leaders themselves had become financially dependent on Qadhafi's largesse and stood to lose much if his regime fell.[48]

Despite diplomatic encouragement from coalition countries, the NTC leadership was slow to engage with African leaders and the African Union. They resented the resources Qadhafi had spent on Africa and the support African leaders continued to give him. They saw no reason to cultivate sub-Saharan Africa, and were more comfortable dealing with governments in Europe, North America, and the Middle East, who shared their outlook and aspirations.

SOUTH AFRICA

From the start of the uprisings, South Africa was the most important African interlocutor, both because of its powerful regional role and because it happened to hold a seat on the UN Security Council at that time. South Africa had voted for Resolutions 1970 and 1973, but had since become concerned—and regularly expressed this concern in international meetings—about a perceived change of emphasis in NATO's exercise of its mandate from protecting civilians to achieving regime change. This concern was shared by India at the United Nations and by certain Arab states (e.g., Egypt, Syria, and Algeria). President Jacob Zuma attempted to champion such sentiment. Qadhafi had been a longtime supporter of Nelson Mandela and the African National Congress in its struggle against apartheid and in its attempt to hold onto power in the new South Africa.[49] Zuma may therefore have felt he owed Qadhafi a personal debt of gratitude, and could repay it by mediating on his behalf. By doing this, Zuma hoped to establish South Africa as the spokesman for "African" interests on the international stage. But he seized on the wrong issue. His decision to act as an advocate for Qadhafi proved a serious miscalculation. It backfired, damaging Zuma's own international stature and reputation.

Zuma's unsuccessful initiatives to broker a cease-fire in Libya failed for many reasons. One was that the African Union membership was deeply split on the issue. Those members who backed the so-called peace initiatives (launched in response to appeals from Qadhafi) were already regarded by the NTC as closet Qadhafi supporters out to relieve mounting pressure on the regime. The African Union, therefore, stood no chance of being accepted as honest brokers. Meanwhile some AU leaders resented the failure of other organizations, including the United Nations, to defer to their authority over a dispute on "African soil." The UN secretary general had appointed a special envoy, Abdul-Ilah al-Khatib, a former Jordanian foreign minister, to try to achieve a peaceful, negotiated end to the hostilities. But, despite repeated efforts, Mr. al-Khatib had to report to the UN Security Council on several occasions that he had found no common ground between the two sides on which to build a peace process.

WIDENING THE CAMPAIGN

By June 2011, NATO coalition governments—though comfortable with the progress made—worried that an end to hostilities still looked a long way off. As long as Qadhafi remained in control in Tripoli, he felt he could stand defiant. On 7 June he proclaimed, "I will stay here until the end, victorious. Dead or alive, it doesn't matter."[50] For Qadhafi, survival and continued defiance represented victory. He believed that, as in Iraq, NATO's resolve to maintain its campaign would fade in the face of mounting international skepticism and in the wake of civilian casualties. The holy month of Ramadan would be starting on 1 August. NATO governments wondered whether this might have a negative impact both on the fighting and on international reactions to bombing raids. This added to mounting pressure to bring the intervention to an early conclusion.

After heavy loyalist losses as a result of precision coalition bombing in March and April, regime forces had shed their uniforms and dispersed their forces and armor into built-up areas, using schools, hospitals, or mosques as cover. They also began to deploy the same type of pickup trucks that the rebel forces were using. NATO therefore had fewer clear military targets and faced the constant risk of inadvertent friendly fire incidents. Arguing that it also needed to destroy command and control centers to relieve the threat to civilians, NATO widened the scope of its targeting in June, attacking military and intelligence agency buildings in Tripoli and repeatedly hitting complexes where the senior leadership had their homes and offices, including Qadhafi's Bab al-Aziziyya compound in central Tripoli. By now, coordination between NATO and rebel forces operating in Tripolitania and still surrounded by Qadhafi controlled areas—especially militias from Misrata and Jabal Nafusa—led to effective exchanges of information on targets and threats. According to press reports and the rumor mill, Qatari Special Forces on the ground played a key role as go-betweens connecting rebel forces with the coalition targeteers, who called down air strikes. By July, NATO was effectively acting as the air force of the anti-Qadhafi forces.

Lack of rebel military progress along the coastal road from Sirte to Brega led NATO to divert resources to relieve the siege of Misrata and to attack military targets in Jabal Nafusa. Initially, NATO was reluctant to make raids in the Jabal, because of its difficult terrain and the lack of accurate intelligence. The NTC in Benghazi had established communication with, and provided limited support to, communities in Misrata (by sea) and Jabal Nafusa (by land through Tunisia and by helicopter). But fighters in these centers had learned to improvise and organize themselves. They had become close-knit and self-reliant. Though they pressed the NTC for cash and weapons, they strongly resisted NTC attempts to impose leadership or command and control structures on them. By late June, rebel communities in Jabal Nafusa and Misrata, buoyed by increased NATO air support, were pushing back regime forces and enlarging rebel-held territory. On 29 June, the French government admitted to the press[51] that it had been dropping shipments of light weapons (including antitank missiles and rocket-propelled grenades) from the air to resupply besieged communities in the Jabal. NATO itself denied prior knowledge of these air drops and insisted that the coalition's policy remained to supply humanitarian materials only.[52] Meanwhile the Qatari government (which may have financed the French arms shipments) had sent military trainers, advisers, and special forces—together with new military equipment—to support the rebels in the Western mountains. This support was delivered primarily to specific groups, with whom Qatar was working closely. This included fighters from the town of Zintan. The Qataris also supplied and trained favored groups from Tripoli or elsewhere, such as the Tripoli Military Council, which had relocated to Jabal Nafusa, to prepare for an assault on the capital. (The impact of this assistance in propelling former jihadist fighters aligned with the Libyan Islamic Fighting Group to prominence in the assault on Tripoli and its immediate aftermath is dealt with in Chapter 7.)

The Qataris gave military and financial support to specific militia commanders, clerics, and political leaders rather than to the NTC as a whole. This created divisions within the opposition and raised questions about longer-term Qatari intentions. Qatari support actually proved a double-edged sword to its beneficiaries: in July 2012, the Libyan electorate shunned the primary recipient of Qatari aid, Abdul-Hakim Bilhajj and his Watan Party. (Youssef Sawani discusses this phenomenon in Chapter 2.)

The British government identified the Libyan regime's limited access to refined oil products, particularly fuel for military vehicles, as an exploitable weakness. It therefore devoted resources to monitoring international movements of oil products and helped NATO vessels in the Mediterranean thwart attempts by the regime to import fuel and export crude oil. This had an impact, though not a decisive one, on regime operations and morale. NATO decided, however, not to attack critical infrastructure, such as oil and water pipelines, on which the regime depended, because of the hardship this could cause to civilian populations, particularly in Tripoli. Interestingly, the Qadhafi regime, too, decided not to sabotage key pieces of infrastructure (except for a few raids on oil fields or pumping stations in the East), even when they had fallen into rebel hands. Qadhafi may have believed until the very end that he could win. The lack of damage to critical infrastructure was an important factor in the restoration of Libya's oil production and its future economic prospects. (This is discussed by St John in Chapter 3.)

Access to finance was a constant problem for the NTC throughout the spring and early summer. Most Libyan families were dependent on public sector salaries or government handouts. The NTC, therefore, had to find large sums of money each month to pay families living in areas they administered. In the early days, they were able to do so by drawing on aid or loans from international donors, particularly the Gulf States. They lobbied hard for Western nations to release frozen Libyan assets, but had to accept that the legal obstacles imposed by UN sanctions precluded this solution. In addition, donors worried about the NTC's ability to administer and disburse large sums of cash in a transparent and accountable way. The Contact Group therefore established a Temporary Finance Mechanism in Doha to ensure that money donated or released to the NTC would be held and managed properly.[53] By July, the UK government was able to provide some relief to the NTC by releasing a shipment of new Libyan banknotes, which it had impounded in February. This enabled the NTC to distribute some funds to isolated communities in western Libya.

By August the regime was weakened, but still in control of the capital and other cities in central and southern Libya. The main threat to Tripoli now came from rebel forces in Jabal Nafusa and Misrata as they expanded the territory they controlled (see map 3). Coordination between NATO, rebel units in these areas, and NTC representatives based in Tunisia and Tripoli was becoming more effective. In a carefully coordinated operation designed to follow up the fall of Gharyan, a garrison town at the edge of the Nafusa Mountains controlling the approach to Tripoli, NTC sympathizers in the capital rose up on the evening of August 19. They were supported by NATO precision strikes and by militia columns converging by road and sea on Tripoli from Misrata in the east, Gharyan in the south, and Zawiyya in the west. Within three days, and almost without a fight, the capital had fallen to pro-NTC militias. Key Qadhafi generals entrusted with Tripoli's security had secretly defected to the rebels. When the decisive battle began, they removed their troops from the capital. Two months later, on October 20, Qadhafi himself was captured and killed by militiamen from Misrata as they overran his hometown of Sirte.

RECONSTRUCTION

From April onward, several allied governments, particularly the United States and United Kingdom, did a great deal of contingency work on postconflict reconstruction scenarios for Libya, sending development experts and advisers to the NTC in Benghazi. In May, the United Nations agreed to take over the role of coordinating humanitarian assistance, planning for reconstruction, maintaining essential services, and organizing postconflict national elections.

By midsummer, the coalition concentrated on adopting whatever tactics and propaganda might deliver regime change most quickly. The air campaign had been welcomed on the ground, and had caused remarkably few civilian casualties. Military planners and policy makers were anxious to bring the campaign to a conclusion before any unforeseen accidents or humanitarian emergencies might turn public opinion against it. This meant arming, funding, and boosting the largest militias in western Libya capable of taking Tripoli. As the endgame approached, the allies had reason to believe that their contribution was nearing completion. Tripoli was captured with its critical infrastructure intact. Libyans from across the country had shown remarkable unity of purpose in overthrowing the regime.

The NTC had contingency plans to restore oil production quickly. They also had a plan and timetable for establishing representative government and agreeing on the processes for drafting and ratifying a new constitution.[54] The NTC would soon have access to vast resources although unfortunately it remained cash starved in the immediate aftermath of Qadhafi's fall as it took time to navigate the international legal obstacles necessary to unfreeze Libyan assets seized abroad by UNSCR 1970 and 1973. The various Libyan militias were made up of untrained volunteers, who might be expected to return to civilian life. The allies were content, therefore, for the transition to be Libyan-led, and confined their contributions to short-term, small-scale reconstruction initiatives, deploying professional advisers to ministries, and launching programs to prevent the proliferation of dangerous weapons.

The Western allies were reluctant to be drawn directly into nation-building during the transitional period for several reasons. Firstly, they knew that their electorates supported humanitarian intervention, but had no appetite for occupation or nation building after Iraq and Afghanistan. Secondly, they understood that Libyans themselves were wary of direct foreign involvement: Libyan politicians did not want to be seen as agents of foreign interests or have their integrity as nationalists impugned. Thirdly, they were optimistic that the transitional authorities had a feasible plan and timetable (which broadly suited coalition interests) for establishing an open political system. Moreover, there was no obvious threat from external neighboring or regional powers to subvert this political process. Finally, the allies knew that direct Western interference might prove counterproductive, provoking a hostile political reaction not only in Libya but also in the wider Arab world. By standing back, the allies have been able to criticize and avoid association with mistakes made by the transitional authorities (e.g., corruption and human rights abuses), while remaining confident that the transitional authorities and successor Libyan governments would look to the West for advice and assistance, when they do encounter problems or threats.

In spite of the favorable aspects of the postconflict situation mentioned above and the relative lack of external meddling, the transition period presented the NTC with serious challenges. The bureaucracy they inherited in Tripoli was dysfunctional. This restricted their ability to implement decisions or deliver services effectively. More importantly, the largest militias from the periphery, having been armed, funded, and supported in their campaign by coalition members, showed no inclination to lay down their weapons or withdraw from the capital, until they could be sure that the political and economic interests of their communities would be safeguarded. Their leaders, now powerful political figures in their own right, paid no more than lip service to central authority, and were in no hurry to merge their forces into a national army or police force to defend the central state. In general, militia members from the periphery were less educated and more devout than the general population (especially in the cities), as the results of the July 2012 national elections demonstrated. Their views were not representative of the population as a whole; but the NTC could not afford to ignore their demands. Libya was awash with heavy weapons, ordnance, and armed but poorly trained militiamen. The US government provided resources and expertise to help collect and destroy some of the most dangerous weapons (particularly MANPADS and remaining elements from Libya's weapons of mass destruction).[55] These teams made a significant contribution;[56] but many weapons had already been smuggled across Libya's borders into the hands of insurgents in the Sahel, and would later reach armed groups in Mali, Cote d'Ivoire, Syria, Gaza, and Sinai.

Attempts by external powers before the final collapse of the Qadhafi regime to help the NTC train and organize a national army and police force made little headway. Each local militia had begun by defending their homes, families, and territories. As they moved further from home, intermilitia suspicion and poor leadership prevented their assimilation into a coherent army. The uprisings had unleashed a torrent of forces that strengthened divisive peripheral loyalties over unifying central ones.

Revolutionary militias in Misrata and parts of Jabal Nafusa were battle-hardened by months of siege, during which they had had to rely on their own resources. When external assistance did arrive, particularly from Qatar, it was distributed through particular local commanders and leaders, strengthening their authority rather than that of the NTC leadership. As a result, when the NTC political leadership moved to Tripoli, they had to deal with powerful local militia commanders, who exercised de facto control over the city. The task of collecting weapons and returning militia members to civilian life, or enrolling them in the national security forces, proved daunting. They were unwilling to surrender their newfound authority and bargaining power. They also enjoyed the prestige of having overthrown Qadhafi and liberated the capital—something NTC spokesmen could not claim.

CONCLUSION

In its aftermath, NATO and its allies rightly judged their military intervention in Libya a success. They acted just in time to prevent Qadhafi's forces from overrunning the cities of eastern Libya—averting many civilian deaths. They also showed impressive determination and patience throughout the late spring and early summer, when revolutionary ground forces seemed unable to break through regime lines on the ground and (to certain observers) the outcome looked uncertain. This patience in the face of electoral and media pressures at home enabled them to confound Qadhafi's belief that they would not be able to sustain their resolve. They also proved Qadhafi wrong in his assumption that the reactions of Western powers are dictated by narrow self-interest or that the West would not consider intervention in Libya to be consistent with its long-term interests.

The circumstances in Libya that allowed for such a positive outcome were highly unusual. Qadhafi was almost isolated internationally, and faced ever-mounting discontent internally. Conversely, despite regional divisions, the rebel forces were remarkably socially, ethnically, and religiously homogenous. The fact that Qadhafi was so unpopular in the Arab world—and had alienated fellow Arab leaders to the extent that they were ready to call through the Arab League for swift foreign intervention to curb his aggression against the Libyan people—made it difficult for others, like Russia or China, to defend him or to argue persuasively against NATO intervention. The speed and skill of the diplomatic campaign to create the legal framework for intervention and to reassure potential skeptics in the Islamic world about Western intentions was remarkable. Never before had the UN Security Council acted so quickly and decisively on intervention in an internal conflict or agreed so early on a referral to the International Criminal Court.

The sanctions contained in the two UN Resolutions were remarkably far-reaching. They imposed indefinite international isolation on the Qadhafi family and regime. This was achieved by intensive diplomacy at precisely the moment when international outrage at the regime's behavior was at its peak.

There were diplomatic costs for being on the wrong side of history. Russia and China were caught off-guard by the coalition's wide interpretation of its mandate. Their public criticism of the NTC and of the coalition's bombing campaign proved ineffective. Russia in particular, had to accept the loss of extensive investments and strategic interests in Libya. But a perverse consequence of the success of international intervention in Libya was repeated Russian and Chinese obstruction of a coordinated international response to the situation in Syria in 2012 and early 2013. Never again would Putin succumb to humanitarian or popular pressure to grant UN sanction to a Western-led attempt to remove a Russian ally.

As a result of the spontaneous and haphazard way resistance to the Qadhafi regime developed—and was supported by the coalition in the interests of toppling Qadhafi as quickly as possible—independent power structures grew up, conferring authority on local militia leaders. The localized nature of the uprisings encouraged personal loyalty not to wider tribe, nation, or ideology, but to an individual's immediate community. Under Qadhafi's regime, citizens in the periphery had depended on Tripoli for salaries, handouts, favors, and services. They now felt ownership of their revolution, having liberated their home territories themselves, and felt empowered to insist on continued access to these entitlements—with their own local leaders as intermediaries. Meanwhile those who lived in communities that had not been directly involved in the anti-Qadhafi fighting, such as Bani Walid, felt overlooked and inadequately represented in the new interim central administration. Meanwhile long-standing rivalries or jealousies between neighboring communities resurfaced in the absence of a strong central authority. This made the task of reconciliation and reconstruction daunting for the first postconflict administration led by Prime Minister Abdul-Rahman al-Kib.

Generous support and detailed planning from the international community helped set the direction, but left the NTC to struggle with the implementation of reconstruction. Even with the benefit of hindsight, it would be wrong to judge the performance of Libya's transitional authorities harshly. Despite their myriad failings, they did restore oil production to pre-uprising levels, avert an overt civil war between peripheral actors, oversee a free and fair election, and hand over power to an elected government on 8 August 2012. Although they may not have taken full advantage of the capacity-building assistance offered by allied nations, they did govern post-Qadhafi Libya without falling prey to the charge that they had become puppets of Western interests. These are not insignificant achievements. Their mission was a challenging one. Reasserting the authority of the Libyan center over the newly emerged local leaders, and retaining the confidence of foreign investors and their own population, was bound to require exceptional patience, perseverance, and capacity for compromise. There was only so much outside actors could do to ease this process. The 2011 uprisings were Libyan-led—both their successes and their failures.

NOTES

1. International Crisis Group, "Holding Libya Together: Security Challenges After Qadhafi," *Middle East/North Africa Report no. 115*, Dec 14, 2011, 2, http://www.crisisgroup.org/en/regions/middle-east -north-africa/north-africa/libya/115-holding-libya-together-security -challenges-after-qadhafi.aspx. "As the uprisings in the west expanded [in late February], each town's militia retained its identity and sense of ownership based on its purported role and sacrifices. In March 2011, the most significant rebellions in the west took place in the cities of Zintan, Misrata and Zawiya, followed swiftly by Nalut, located in the Nafusa mountains south west of Tripoli. Qadhafi forces rapidly and ruthlessly crushed the revolt in Zawiya, helped by the city's proximity and accessibility to Tripoli. In contrast, Zintan and Misrata, both of which were on the frontline of the conflict between rebel and loyalist armies, put up strong resistance, becoming important bases for weapons distribution as well as for organising and consolidating the war effort."
2. Ian Black, "Gaddafi Threatens Retaliation in the Mediterranean as UN Passes Resolution," *The Guardian*, March 18, 2011, http://www.guardian .co.uk/world/2011/mar/17.
3. Initially, the housing riots were not connected to Ben Ali's resignation. Evidence suggested that they were caused by a misinterpretation of Qadhafi's 13 January speech at Sabha where he proclaimed in response to audience pressure, "We have built hundreds of thousands of homes...[Those Libyans who returned from Niger and don't have homes]...This is not a problem; you can live in them." However, the majority of Libyans who occupied unfinished housing in response to this pronouncement were neither those who had returned from Niger nor those Qaddafi supporters who heard the speech live in Sabha, but rather those from the disaffected east of the country, as well as some from the poorer suburbs of Tripoli. They were upset that long-promised and much-needed public housing projects had been stalled, often because the funding had been siphoned off by corrupt officials. The most prominent looting occurred in Darna at a construction site of a Korean company, Won. Some occupations evicted Western expatriates from their

accommodation, notably in Al-Marj. The above quote derives from a digital video of Qadhafi's speech in Sabha on 3 January. The footage was displayed on the *Jamahiriya News Agency* (JANA) website. The electronic record no longer exists as JANA's website was destroyed by the revolution. Parts 31–34 of Qadhafi's speech showed young Libyans returned from Niger complaining to the leader about housing. For online sources that are still accessible see: Ali Shuaib, "Libyans Occupy, Loot Homes Amid Shortage-Report," *Reuters,* January 17, 2011, http://af.reuters.com/article/tunisiaNews/idAFLDE70G1B220110117?pageNumber=1&virtualBrandChannel=0.

4. The relevant language of the resolution is as follows: "[Point] 4. Authorizes Member States that have notified the Secretary-General, acting nationally or through regional organizations or arrangements, and acting in cooperation with the Secretary-General, to take all necessary measures, notwithstanding paragraph 9 of resolution 1970 (2011), to protect civilians and civilian populated areas under threat of attack in the Libyan Arab Jamahiriya, including Benghazi, while excluding a foreign occupation force of any form on any part of Libyan territory...[Point] 6. Decides to establish a ban on all flights in the airspace of the Libyan Arab Jamahiriya in order to help protect civilians...[and Point] 8. Authorizes Member States...to take all necessary measures to enforce compliance with the ban on flights imposed by paragraph 6 above, as necessary, and requests the States concerned in cooperation with the League of Arab States to coordinate closely with the Secretary General on the measures they are taking to implement this ban." S/Res/1973(2011), http://www.un.org/Docs/sc/unsc_resolutions11.html.

5. Douglas Feith and Seth Cropsey, "The Obama Doctrine Defined," *Commentary Magazine,* July 2011, http://www.commentarymagazine.com/article/the-obama-doctrine-defined/; Lexington, "The Birth of an Obama Doctrine," *The Economist—Lexington's Notebook,* March 28, 2011, http://www.economist.com/blogs/lexington/2011/03/libya_4.

6. Richard Leiby, "Arab League's Backing of No-Fly Zone over Libya Ramps up Pressure on West," *Washington Post,* March 12, 2011, http://www.washingtonpost.com/wp-dyn/content/article/2011/03/12.

7. Tara McKelvey, "Samantha Power's Case for War on Libya," *Daily Beast,* March 22, 2011, http://www.thedailybeast.com/articles/2011/03/23/libya-war-samantha-power-and-the-case-for-liberal-interventionism.html.

8. "North Africa: New Threats to Migrants," *Africa Focus Bulletin,* March 5, 2011, http://www.africafocus.org/printit/mob.php? http://www.africafocus.org/docs11/na1103.php.

9. Authors' personal experience.

10. Karin Badt, "Bernard-Henri Levy and the West's Intervention in Libya: A Discussion with Experts," *The Huffington Post,* June 11, 2011, http://www.huffingtonpost.com/karin-badt/bernard-henri-levy-libya_b_1575573.html.

11. "Libya: France Recognises Rebels as Government," *BBC News*, http://www.bbc.co.uk/news/world-africa-12699183.

12. According to Total's self-published "Factbook 2010," 81.

13. French consumption of Libyan oil in 2010 was up more than 50 percent from 2009 according to the Institut National de la Statistique et des Etudes Economiques. We thank John Hamilton of Cross-border Information for insights into these figures.

14. Dirk Vandewalle, *A History of Modern Libya* (Cambridge: Cambridge University Press, 2006).

15. Modified short excerpt from Jason Pack and Barak Barfi, *In War's Wake: The Struggle for Post-Qadhafi Libya*, p.16 http://www.washington institute.org/pubPDFs/PolicyFocus118.pdf.

16. Kim Willsher, "Libya: Bernard-Henri Levy Dismisses Criticism for Leading France to Conflict," *The Observer*, March 27, 2011, http://www .guardian.co.uk/world/2011/mar/27/libya-bernard-henri-levy-france; Renaud Girard, "La campagne libyenne de Bernard-Henri Levy," *Le Figaro*, March 18, 2011, http://www.lefigaro.fr/international/2011 /03/18/01003–20110318ARTFIG00671-la-campagne-libyenne -de-bernard-henri-levy.php.

17. "L'Intervention Francaise en Libye, un 'Investissment sur l'avenir,' Assure Juppe," *Le Parisien*, August 27, 2011, http://www.leparisien .fr/flash-actualite-politique/l-intervention-francaise-en-libye-un-investi ssement-sur-l-avenir-assure-juppe-27–08–2011–1581271.php.

18. Authors' observation.

19. "Cameron Condemns Megrahi Release," *BBC News* report, August 2009, http://news.bbc.co.uk/1/hi/8212457.stm.

20. Ronald Bruce St John, "The Libyan Economy in Transition: Opportunities and Challenges," and Ethan Chorin, "The Future of the US-Libyan Commercial Relationship" in *Libya Since 1969: Qadhafi's Revolution Revisited* (New York: Palgrave Macmillan, 2008).

21. Reported to the primary author by US officials at the time.

22. Polya Lesova, "Italy's Ties to Libya in Spotlight Amid Unrest," *MarketWatch*, February 2011; for ENI's figures, see http://www.eni .com/en_IT/eni-world/libya/eni-business/eni-business.shtml#.

23. Giselda Vagnoni and Deepa Babington, "Factbox: Italy and Libya Share Close Investment Ties," *Reuters*, February 20, 2011.

24. "Focus-Libya: Frattini at the G8 Ministerial Meeting in Paris: Immediate Ceasefire the Only Solution," *Farnesina—Italian Ministry of Foreign Affairs*, March 14, 2011, http://www.esteri.it/MAE/EN/Sala _Stampa/ArchivioNotizie/Approfondimenti/2011/03/20110314 _Libia_Frattini_G8.htm; "Odyssey Dawn Should Not Mean War against Libya—Frattini," *Voice of Russia Radio* (March 21, 2011), http://www .english.ruvr.ru/2011/03/21/47734566.html.

25. "Focus-Libya: Frattini, the NTC Is Italy's Only Interlocutor," *Farnesina—Italian Ministry of Foreign Affairs*, April 4, 2011, http://

www.esteri.it/MAE/EN/Sala_Stampa/ArchivioNotizie/Approfondim
enti/2011/04/20110404_FocusLibia_frattinI_Cnt.htm; "Italy: Energy
Company ENI CEO in Libya for Talks," *Associated Press*, April 4, 2011,
http://seattletimes.com/html/businesstechnology/2014681612
_apeuitalylibyaoilcrisis.html.

26. Richard Norton-Taylor and Simon Rogers, "Arab States Play Limited
Role in Battle against Muammar Gaddafi's Regime," *The Guardian*,
May 23, 2011.

27. Sam Dagher, Charles Levinson, and Margaret Coker, "Tiny Kingdom's
Huge Role in Libya Draws Concern," *Wall Street Journal*, October 17,
2011; "Qatar Admits It Had Boots on Ground in Libya," *Agence
France-Presse*, October 26, 2011.

28. For more on the Qatari role in the establishment of the rebels' media
infrastructure, see Anja Wollenberg and Jason Pack, "Rebels with a Pen:
Observations on a Newly Emerging Media Landscape in Libya," *The
Journal of North African Studies*, Volume 18, Number 2, March 2013,
pp. 191–210, http://www.tandfonline.com/doi/abs/10.1080/13629
387.2013.767197.

29. Shashank Joshi and Jason Pack, "Qatar: Kingmakers in Syria?" *CNN
Global Public Square*, January 18, 2012, http://globalpublicsquare.
blogs.cnn.com/2012/01/18/qatar-kingmakers-in-syria/?hpt=hp_bn2.

30. Modified short excerpt from Jason Pack and Barak Barfi, *In War's Wake:
The Struggle for Post-Qadhafi Libya*, 17–18, http://www.washingtonin-
stitute.org/pubPDFs/PolicyFocus118.pdf.

31. George Joffé and Emaneulla Paoletti, "Libya's Foreign Policy: Drivers
and Objectives," Mediterranean paper series. Publisher: Washington,
DC. *German Marshall Fund of the United States (GMF)* 2010 http://
www.gmfus.org/wp-content/blogs.dir/1/files_mf//galleries/ct
_publication_attachments/JoffePaoletti_final_Oct10.pdf.

32. Relations with Iran were also affected by the disappearance of Musa
Sadr.

33. David E. Sanger and Thom Shanker, "Gates Warns of Risks of a
No-Flight Zone," *New York Times*, March 2, 2011, http://www.nytimes.
com/2011/03/03/world/africa/03military.html?pagewanted=all.

34. Richard Haass, President of The Council on Foreign Relations, spoke
to the Senate Foreign Affairs committee against the concept of a no-fly
zone and NATO intervention—even after the Arab League's March 12
statement.

35. For more on this process, consult Chapter 7.

36. See Jason Pack, "The Two Faces of Libya's Rebels," *Foreign Policy
Magazine*, April 5, 2011.

37. "Libya: US & EU Say Muammar Gaddafi Must Go," *BBC News*, March
11, 2011, http://www.bbc.co.uk/news/world-europe-12711162.

38. For more on Germany's position, please consult Reinhard Merkel, "Die
Militärintervention gegen Gaddafi ist illegitim," *Frankfurter Allgemeine*

Zeitung Feuilleton, March 23, 2011, http://www.faz.net/aktuell/feuil
leton/voelkerrecht-contra-buergerkrieg-die-militaerintervention-gegen
-gaddafi-ist-illegitim-1613317.html; Severin Weiland and Roland Nelles,
"Berlin lässt seine Verbündeten alleine kämpfen," *Der Spiegel Online,*
March 18, 2011, http://www.spiegel.de/politik/deutschland/libyen
-einsatz-berlin-laesst-seine-verbuendeten-alleine-kaempfen-a-751673.
html. We thank Florian Niederndorfer and Stefan Binder of *Der Standard*
of Austria for direction to and insights into these sources.

39. Embassy of France in Washington, text of statement to the press by
President Sarkozy after the Paris summit, March 19, 2011, http://
ambafrance-us.org/spip.php?article2241.

40. William Hague, British foreign secretary, statement on the conclusions
of the London conference and related documents, March 29, 2011,
http://www.fco.gov.uk/en/news/latest-news/?view=News&id=57507
6582.

41. For an explanation of the earlier (i.e., April) iteration of a constitutional
declaration, see Charles Levinson, "Libya Rebels Build Parallel State,"
Wall Street Journal, April 11, 2011, http://online.wsj.com/article
/SB10001424052748703648304576265021509675668.html. See also,
al-i'alan al-dusturi al-libiy http://www.hnec.ly/uploads/publisher/6
_ntc_2011.pdf, which is the text of the Temporary Constitutional
Declaration that was in force from 3 August 2011 until the approval of a
permanent constitution.

42. Angelo Del Boca, *Mohamed Fekini and the Fight to Free Libya* (New York:
Palgrave Macmillan, 2011). The Fekini family, traditional leaders of the
Arab Rajban tribe in Jebel Nafusa, played an important role in colonial
and postcolonial Libya. Rajban, like Arab Zintan and Berber Nalut in the
Jebel, was not a center of support for the Qadhafi regime and was quick
to join the uprisings.

43. Christopher Williams, "Libyan Rebels 'Hijack Mobile Network,'" *Daily
Telegraph,* April 13, 2011, http://www.telegraph.co.uk/news/world-
news/africaandindianocean/libya/8448482/Libyan-rebels-hijack-mobi
le-network.html.

44. Chris McGreal, "Undisciplined Libyan Rebels no Match for Gaddafi's
Forces," *The Guardian,* March 30, 2011, http://www.guardian
.co.uk/world/2011/mar/30/libyan-rebels-no-match-gaddafi; Peter
Graff, "Libyan Rebels Regroup but Battle Exposes Weakness," *Reuters,*
July 14, 2011, http://www.reuters.com/article/2011/07/14/uk-libya
-idUKTRE76C1H420110714.

45. Yehudit Ronen, "Between Arabism and Africanism: Libya's Involvement
in Sudan," at a conference Lecture on Libya's Pan-African Policies held
in Alexandria, VA, in October 2010.

46. Damien McElroy, "Sudanese Army Seizes Southern Libyan Town,"
The Daily Telegraph, July 1, 2011, http://www.telegraph.co.uk/news/
worldnews/africaandindianocean/Libya/8611199/Sudanese-army-seiz

es-southern-Libyan-town.html; "Libya's New Masters Are Thankful for Sudan's Military Support," *Sudan Tribune,* August 29, 2011, http://www.sudantribune.com/Libya-s-new-masters-are-thankful,39985; Authors' personal contacts.

47. Jason Pack and Dirk Vandewalle about the AU visit on the Riz Khan television program, "Can the African Union Bring Relief to Libya?" *Al Jazeera English TV,* April 13, 2011, http://www.aljazeera.com/programmes/rizkhan/2011/04/201141275720476652.html.

48. For a quick history of Qadhafi's largesse in sub-Saharan African and especially the roles of the Libyan Africa Investment Portfolio (LAP) and Libyan Arab African Investment Company (LAAICO) sovereign wealth funds, please consult Jon Rosen, "Wither the 'King of Kings?' How Qaddafi's Battle for Libya Will Impact Africa," *ISN Insights,* April 26, 2011, http://www.africanewsanalysis.com/2011/04/26/wither-the-king-of-kings-how-qaddafis-battle-for-libya-will-impact-africa-by-jon-rosen-for-isn-insights/.

49. Yehudit Ronen, *Qaddafi's Libya in World Politics* (Boulder, CO: Lynne Rienner, 2008).

50. "Libya Crisis: Gaddafi Vows to Fight to the Death," *BBC News,* June 7, 2011, http://www.bbc.co.uk/news/world-africa-13688003.

51. Alex Parry, "French Military Air-Dropped Arms to Libya Rebels," *France 24,* http://www.france24.com/en/20110629-french-military-confirm-airdropping-arms-libya-kadhafi-rebel.

52. Nick Hopkins, "NATO Reviews Libya Campaign after France Admits Arming Rebels," *The Guardian,* June 29, 2011, http://www.guardian.co.uk/world/2011/jun/29/nato-review-libya-france-arming-rebels.

53. Prior to a more comprehensive release of assets after the fall of Qadhafi, the NTC had access during the period of the uprisings to less than $1 billion of unfrozen funds through the Libya Contact Group's temporary financing mechanism. On 17 December 2011, the UN lifted its sanctions on Libya's Central Bank; See Patrick Worship, "UN Sanctions Lifted on Libya's Central Bank," *Reuters,* December 16, 2011. This triggered the US Treasury Department to issue General License 11, which unblocked most Libyan assets (except for Libyan Investment Authority funds believed to be under the control of certain members of the Qadhafi family or the former regime; the text of the Treasury order is available at http://www.treasury.gov/resource-center/sanctions/Programs/Documents/libya2_gl11.pdf). The European Union quickly followed the US lead and unfroze assets on 21 December; see http://www.consilium.europa.eu/uedocs/cms_Data/docs/pressdata/EN/foraff/127073.pdf.

54. The NTC's Temporary Constitutional Declaration was promulgated on 3 August 2011. It set out a road map for the transition to a permanent democratic government and a constitutional drafting process. Unsurprisingly, the NTC's vision of what constituted constitutional

legitimacy was not shared by all. For specific critiques of the NTC's Temporary Constitution Declaration and their implications on the struggle for legitimacy in post-Qadhafi Libya consult Youssef Sawani and Jason Pack, "Libyan Constitutionality and Sovereignty Post-Qadhafi: the Islamist, Regionalist, and Amazigh Challenges" (Forthcoming, Publisher TBD).

55. Factsheet: "Libya: Securing Stockpiles Promotes Security," *US State Department,* September 17, 2011, http://london.USembassy.gov/acda 047.html; Andrew J. Shapiro "Addressing the Challenge of MANPADS Proliferation," speech, Stimson Center, Washington, DC, February 2, 2012, http://www.state.gov/t/pm/rls/rm/183097.htm.

56. Andrew Chuter, "50,000 Libya MANPADS Secured", *Defense News,* April 12, 2012, http://www.defensenews.com/article/20120412/5–000 -Libya-MANPADS-Secured.

5

THE RISE OF TRIBAL POLITICS

Wolfram Lacher

The 17 February revolution saw the rise of the tribe, and tribal politics, as a central factor and key explanatory variable in the civil war.[1] For many, both inside and outside Libya, this was a surprising development. In the four decades preceding the revolution, the political role of tribal loyalties and tribal leaders in Libya did not attract sufficient scholarly attention. Leaving aside John Davis's seminal work on tribal politics in Ajdabiyya and Kufra during the late 1970s, it was only in the mid-2000s that researchers began to accord more importance to the tribal factor.[2] From the first weeks of the uprisings, however, tribal figures appeared on satellite television speaking for their constituencies, and the international media identified tribal loyalties as a key factor determining the course of events.

This chapter seeks to shed light on the role of tribal loyalties, divisions, and institutions during and after the civil war—that is to say from February 2011 until the end of the transition period in August 2012. It does not cover the historical background explaining how tribes came to play a significant role in Libya under Qadhafi and before, since this has already been addressed in Chapters 1 and 2. The focus of this chapter, therefore, lies on analyzing the degree to which political and military mobilization took place on a tribal basis during the civil war and in its aftermath.

It is argued below that in Jabal Nafusa, southern Libya, and certain parts of Cyrenaica, tribal solidarities and rifts were important determinants of mobilization into revolutionary brigades, as well as polarization into opposing camps during the civil war. Tribal institutions also played an important role in providing continuity and order as state control broke down. Conversely, the revolution should not be reduced to a tribal civil war, since urban and ideologically based networks—such as various Islamist currents—dominated the patterns of revolutionary mobilization in the big coastal cities. The rise of tribal politics was part of a larger phenomenon during and after the civil war, whereby the local level—tribes, towns, and cities—became the most important arena for political and military organization. In other words, the increasing role of tribal politics was part of the "ascendency of the periphery over the center" as has been referred to in the Introduction. Indeed, in many instances, it is difficult to draw a distinction between tribally based and other local structures.

Following an analysis of tribal politics during the civil war, the chapter explains the rise of conflicts between tribes and cities in the immediate postwar period, as well as the role of tribal leaders and councils as key actors in attempts to resolve such conflicts. Particular emphasis is placed on the case of the Warfalla tribe centered on the city of Bani Walid, as the most important example of tensions between the revolutionary camp and the constituencies of the former regime. Bani Walid's exclusion from and rejection of the revolutionary postwar order was coupled with attempts in the town to create its own autonomous governance structures, which were opposed by revolutionary forces as "threatening" the new order. This contributed to polarization throughout post-Qadhafi Libya and impeded attempts at reconciliation, prompting Warfalla leaders to build a coalition with other tribes considered as pillars of the former regime. The chapter concludes that politics in revolutionary Libya were partly defined by the interplay between tribal politics in the hinterland, and urban or ideological politics in the big coastal cities. Tensions between conservative tribal forces and the urban revolutionary camp represent a continuing source of structural instability in the new Libya.

WHAT IS A LIBYAN TRIBE?

Before delving further, it is worth clarifying what is meant by tribes and tribalism. The notion of "tribe" has long been controversial among social scientists, in general, and students of North African and Libyan politics, in particular.[3] There has been much aversion against using a notion seen as closely associated with colonial rule and analysis. The process through which colonial administrators created or cemented tribal leaders or even whole tribes has been analyzed in detail by academics, with some even going as far as dismissing tribes as an invention of colonial powers.[4] Today, the use of the term "tribe" is being criticized as suggesting premodern, unchanging social structures, and is sometimes dismissed in favor of notions that lack normative connotations such as "neo-tribal associations," which refer to the way the networks in question transcend lineage and common descent.[5]

In contrast to such neologisms, this volume prefers the standard usage of "tribe" in the Libyan case, for two main reasons. First, Libyans themselves habitually use the notion of *qabila*, for which "tribe" is the best translation. Dismissing the widespread local usage of the notion of "tribe" to analyze the Libyan reality is akin to the kind of cultural condescension that critics of the term see as being inherent in its use by Western commentators. Second, the notion does not necessarily imply an age-old, unchanging social structure. In Libya, as elsewhere, tribes have always evolved along with changing economic or military conditions and as a result of their interaction with states. The same is true today. The fact that tribal networks are not exclusively based on lineage is not new either. Nor is there any doubt that Libyan genealogies enter the realm of the mythical as one moves further away from a given individual or the present time. What matters is that common origin—perceived or real—is invoked as a key bond among a group of individuals that conceive themselves as being united in some form of solidarity.[6] This is the—loose—definition of "tribe" applied here and throughout this volume. The key questions are how politicians use tribal loyalty as a mobilizing tool and to what political effect.

That said, the notion admittedly remains vague, and in the Libyan case the tribe can serve to describe a wide range of forms of social and political organization. In Cyrenaica, tribal elders can resolve murder cases by resorting to customary law ('*urf*), whereas in the Tripolitanian coastal plain, tribal figures would be entrusted with minor disputes only (if at all). The extent to which Libyan tribal leaders wield authority varies from one community and sheikh to another. Generally, however, tribal elders have a mediating function, as opposed to an executive one, and their authority is rarely unrivalled or uncontested within their tribe or even within their tribal sub-section—as Emrys Peters already observed during the 1940s.[7]

In this chapter and the next one by Henry Smith, the term "tribal politics" is also applied to the Tubu and Tuareg. Both are non-Arab ethnic groups that have historically featured highly inegalitarian social structures, within which tribes and clans were positioned at different levels in the hierarchy[8]—though the authority of tribal leaders differs strongly between the two. Our understanding of how the social and political functions of tribal institutions vary across Libya remains sketchy, since little academic research has been conducted on these issues since the 1970s.

A TRIBAL CIVIL WAR? TRIBAL POLITICS DURING THE REVOLUTION

From the beginning, the divisions of the civil war clearly had a tribal, in addition to a regional and city-specific, dimension. In Benghazi and Misrata, support for the revolution drew on long-heeded feelings of neglect and marginalization by the regime, including among both cities' once-powerful bourgeoisie. But across parts of Cyrenaica and much of Jabal Nafusa, the tribe was a key locus of political mobilization during the first weeks of the uprisings. In some cases, tribal leaders played a leading role in calling on their communities to join the uprisings—such as al-Tahir al-Jadi' of Zintan, who sided with the revolution as early as 16 February 2011,[9] or Shaykh Faraj al-Zwai, a Zwai leader, who went on television on 19 February threatening to cut off oil production from the tribe's area unless regime repression ended.[10] Such statements reflected prior closed-door consultations with key figures in their tribe, including officials in the regime. In other cases, tribal leaders and senior officials were driven to join the revolution by pressure from their communities, after youth had taken to the streets and regime repression had begun. The defections from Qadhafi's security apparatus of two leading representatives of the Obeidat of Cyrenaica—commander of the Tobruk military region Suleiman Mahmoud and Interior Minister Abdul-Fattah Yunis, who defected on 20 and 22 February, respectively—are a case in point.

From early on, tribal loyalties helped ensure that the entire north-east and much of Jabal Nafusa sided with the revolution, and that the regime was unable to reconquer these areas. In the first weeks of the revolt, the two larger Arab tribes and towns in the Jabal, Zintan and Rajban, rose up alongside the predominantly Berber towns, quelling fears that the regime could exploit tribal rifts in the area.[11]

In the Jabal, some towns are synonymous with tribes or considered to be inhabited by members of one tribe, such as Zintan, Rajban, Jadu, and Awlad Mahmud. In other Jabal Nafusa towns, such as Yifran, Kabaw, and Kikla, the population is structured into smaller subtribal groups closely tied to each other, including through common institutions such as regular meetings of tribal elders. In March 2011, liberated Jabal Nafusa towns founded a common council whose representatives were predominantly tribal leaders (see map 2).[12]

Among those communities that sought to stay on the sidelines of the war, or that supported the regime, tribal loyalties and tribal elders played an equally important role. Of particular significance were the tribes whose members formed the backbone of the regime's security apparatus—most significantly, the Warfalla (with their stronghold in Bani Walid), the Maqarha (centered in Wadi al-Shati, which is a region of Fezzan with its main town being Brak), and Qadhadhifa (in both Sirte and Fezzan).[13] Immediately after 17 February, Warfalla elders adopted a supposedly neutral but functionally proregime position, refraining from supporting the revolution but preventing the arrest of youth who staged small antiregime protests in Bani Walid in early March. Shaping that stance was the experience of regime repression following a failed coup attempt by Warfalla officers in 1993. George Joffé has illustrated in Chapter 1 that since that fateful incident, the Warfalla senior leadership never again lent its full support to Qadhafi and although it sought accommodation with the regime, it also developed its own independent capabilities.

In the 1993 coup, the tribe's position within the regime had suffered, but at the same time, Warfalla leaders had resented the failure of other tribes and cities to come to their rescue as the regime executed suspects, occupied the town, and leveled the homes of officers involved in the coup attempt. Increasingly, however, Warfalla tribal figures became the focus of intense lobbying from both sides. The regime sent key officials from the tribe, like Saleh Ibrahim or Omran Boukraa, to woo tribal elders with offers of cash and cars. Leading Warfalla representatives in the revolutionary camp, such as Muhammad Bashir and Mahmud Abdul-Aziz al-Warfalli, held secret meetings with tribal elders in Austria and Turkey, seeking to win them over to the revolution.[14] The bloody repression of an uprising by Warfalla revolutionaries in Bani Walid on 28 May 2011 marked the end of these efforts, and signaled the regime's victory in the battle for tribal elders' allegiance. Together with Sirte, Bani Walid remained one of the regime's last bastions until October 2011, reflecting the fact that a significant portion of loyalist forces were from the Warfalla. The city suffered severely during its capture by revolutionary brigades, laying the basis for the subsequent conflicts between the Warfalla establishment and the revolutionary camp.

Similar behind-the-scenes negotiations took place among other constituencies that did not join the revolution. A senior Tuareg tribal leader, Afnayt al-Kuni, tried in vain to convince the commander of the Maghawir brigade in Ubari, Ali Kanna, to join the uprisings.[15] Despite these entreaties, the Maghawir brigade—recruited from Malian and Nigerien Tuareg—refused to side with the rebels. Outpowered by the Maghawir, other Tuareg tribal leaders decided against taking a stance in the conflict, although Afnayt's younger brother Musa al-Kuni defected from his position as Libyan consul to Mali in March 2011, to join the NTC. As a result, following the regime's demise, the Tuareg tribal establishment suffered a significant loss of influence, both in Libya's southwest and at the national level.

The positioning of tribes vis-à-vis the conflict also became an important element in the propaganda war between the regime and the revolutionary camp. In the first two weeks, dozens of statements were issued on the Internet in the names of tribes declaring their support for the revolution. Contrary to videos showing known representatives of tribes from liberated areas in the Nafusa Mountains and Cyrenaica, most of these statements remained anonymous, and many may have been fake or not unanimously supported by tribal leaders.[16] Nevertheless, the fact that these declarations referred to the positions of tribes rather than any other social category is significant. Each side sought to use tribal loyalties to mobilize support, with the regime and the NTC organizing rival conferences purportedly featuring representatives of the country's leading tribes.[17] French philosopher and prorevolution activist Bernard Henri-Lévy also organized a reunion of tribal leaders directed primarily at public opinion in the West, where the media was increasingly wondering about the strength of Qadhafi's tribal support base.[18] Qadhafi appeared repeatedly on television with tribal leaders pledging their allegiance to him: for example, on 11 May 2011 with figures from Cyrenaican tribes or on 7 June with purported Tuareg leaders. In the latter case, the figures attending the meeting were not identified and had their faces almost completely covered, with some even wearing sunglasses.[19]

As the regime became increasingly embattled, it focused its efforts on tribes that were most critical to its survival, such as the Warfalla. Qadhafi himself, as well as his leading propagandist Yusif Shakir, appeared in several televised meetings targeted specifically at mobilizing Warfalla support.[20] Shakir continued calling on tribes considered to be pillars of the regime—including the Warfalla, Tarhouna, and Warshafana—even beyond the fall of Sirte and Bani Walid, from his Syrian exile.[21]

Local Tribal Politics during the Civil War

While the political and military leadership of each side sought to rally support on a tribal basis, the bottom-up mobilization of tribal identities and institutions was even more important. This was part of a wider pattern whereby local communities mobilized and organized to defend themselves as well as to establish order as state institutions broke down. In Misrata, mobilization into revolutionary brigades occurred on the basis of neighborhoods or extended families; in Benghazi and northeastern towns—such as Darna, Bayda, or Tobruk—brigades organized on the basis of individual towns, with some brigades displaying Islamist ideological tendencies varying from moderate to jihadist.[22] In Jabal Nafusa, brigades formed on the basis of individual towns as well, but as outlined above, these also featured a tightly knit tribal fabric. If brigades proudly displayed their local origin on pickup trucks, or later covered the walls of Tripoli with graffiti such as *Thuwwar Jadu* or *Thuwwar Rajban* (Revolutionaries of Jadu/Rajban), this carried a tribal undertone, and in many cases could be understood as reference to the tribe and the town at the same time. Much emphasis has been laid on the rise of a supratribal *Amazigh* movement that provided a basis for common political activism in the Berber towns of the Jabal, as well as Zuwara and other *Amazigh* enclaves.[23] Nevertheless, allegiance to individual towns and tribes remained strong even among the *Amazigh*, as the pattern of mobilization into local brigades demonstrates. It continued to define politics in the transitional period.

   Local tribal rifts also emerged in the Jabal between prorevolutionary towns on the one hand, and the Mashashiyya and Asabi'a tribes on the other hand; the latter were accused of having joined the regime's forces or allowing them to use their towns as a basis for attacks on the Jabal. When Zintani brigades seized Mashashiyya areas in June 2011, they forcibly expelled the Mashashiyya population of al-Awiniya and Zawiyyat al-Baqul and destroyed homes, preventing local families from returning even after the war.[24] In the case of the Mashashiyya, the rift with Zintan occurred against a historical background of conflicts over land that had raged in the late nineteenth and early twentieth centuries.[25] Tensions had persisted throughout the Qadhafi era due to regime policies to attribute land claimed by Zintan and Berber towns to the Mashashiyya. This allowed the regime to mobilize the Mashashiyya, playing on fears that they would lose out from a victory of the revolutionary towns in the Jabal.[26] However, traditional patterns of tribal alliances (*saff/sufuf*) and historical conflicts were no consistent guide for the rifts in the Jabal: the tribal civil wars of 1915 and 1920 had seen the Asabi'a and Mahamid side with Zintan and Rajban against the Berber towns and the Mashashiyya.[27] Accounts of local conflicts during and after the uprisings that emphasize the "enduring" legacy of historical tribal rifts therefore provide only part of the explanation.

   In the south, where Tubu and Zwai had initially cooperated in the liberation of Kufra in late February 2011, tribal rifts became increasingly pronounced in the revolutionary camp during the postconflict period. Tribal and military leaders agreed to establish a joint force from Tubu, Zwai, and Awlad Suleiman to liberate the south, which however remained largely inactive in the Benghazi and Ajdabiyya areas until July 2011.[28] By the time revolutionary brigades began entering the Fezzan, starting with the liberation of Murzuq by Tubu brigades on August 17, militias organized along tribal lines had emerged.

Leading the Tubu brigades were Barka Wardagu, who during the 1990s had led a rebel group fighting against the government of Niger, and Issa Abdul-Majid Mansour, who in 2007 had founded and led the Tubu Front for the Salvation of Libya (TFSL) against the Qadhafi regime.[29] The military and local councils that emerged in Kufra were headed and dominated by Zwai, excluding the Tubu. In Murzuq, Wardagu set his brigade up as the local military council. Tubu, Zwai, and Awlad Suleiman brigades integrated former members of the regime's security apparatus from their respective communities, including—in the case of the Awlad Suleiman—contingents of the brigades that had fought the revolutionary forces. In Sabha, several neighborhoods fell to revolutionary forces in mid-September without any resistance, while others saw intense fighting. This was due to the fact that these districts had a different social fabric, with Qardha dominated by local families of sedentary origin (*al-ahali*) and the Hasawna tribe, while areas such as Manshiya or Hay al-Fatih—as well as the regime brigades garrisoned in Sabha—were dominated by the Qadhadhifa and Maqarha.[30] Searches for suspects from the Qadhadhifa repeatedly triggered clashes in Manshiya in the following months, such as in June 2012.

In sum, for many communities of the hinterland, the civil war had deep local and tribal significance, in addition to its obvious national dimension. For tribes heavily represented in the regime's security apparatus, the political and physical survival of their communities was perceived to be at stake in the war. At the same time, to interpret the conflict as a tribal civil war would mean reducing it solely to its local dimension, which was prevalent in the hinterland, while ignoring its urban, ideological, and national dimensions, which were dominant in the big coastal cities and also at play in the hinterland.

Tribal politics was not only manifest in the conflicts of the civil war; it was also critical to the establishment of local order. The collapse of state authority triggered the emergence of local institutions, and the rise of tribal notables as key local power brokers in many areas. In Cyrenaica, councils of tribal, religious, and urban notables (*Majalis Hukama'*) emerged soon after the local town councils, which were formed in February and March 2011.[31] In some cases—such as in Tobruk—meetings of tribal leaders trumped the town councils as forums for local decision making. Tribal leaders who had already played a leading role in the region's politics under the regime ensured a high degree of continuity between the prerevolutionary and revolutionary orders.[32] In Zintan, tribal elders in March established a *Shura* (advisory) council that appointed the local council and liaised with the military council, a model that was replicated in other towns in the Jabal. Figures with tribal prestige assumed leadership positions inside the NTC and at the local level, and sometimes combined formal with informal and tribal with political and military authority. Prominent examples are Anwar Fekini (mentioned in Chapter 4), whose family had historically led the Rajban, and who during the war returned to the Jabal from exile to lead the town's defense; or Abdul-Majid Saif al-Nasr, whose family—the historical leaders of the Awlad Suleiman—had traditionally sought to dominate the Fezzan until their forced exile under Qadhafi in the early 1970s.[33] Abdul-Majid Saif al-Nasr became an NTC member who after the fall of Tripoli first headed the city's Supreme Security Committee, and later coordinated the Awlad Suleiman militias in Sabha.

PERVASIVE CONFLICTS, ELUSIVE RECONCILIATION: TRIBES IN THE TRANSITIONAL PERIOD

After the fall of Sirte and Bani Walid in October 2011 (see map 4), tribal politics acquired even greater significance for conflict dynamics and initiatives for conflict resolution. Top-down and bottom-up mobilization along tribal lines during the war meant that many postwar rifts developed between neighboring tribes. The lack of progress on the judicial prosecution of crimes committed during and after the civil war meant that rifts between groups deepened, as dynamics related to solidarity (*'asabiyya*) took hold within these groups. At the same time, tribal leaders increasingly stepped into the void left by the weak transitional government to establish councils of elders and lead reconciliation efforts. Tribal politics also had a wider, historical dimension. For many protagonists of the transitional period, at stake was the establishment of a new balance of power that would see the rise of the cities and tribes that were the primary protagonists of the revolution, and the defeat of the tribal alliance that had constituted the backbone of the regime.

In the immediate postconflict period, several conflicts erupted along tribal lines, or between tribes and towns. In November 2011, fighting broke out between a brigade from Zawiyya and fighters from the Warshafana tribe, following attempts by Zawiyyan *thuwwar* to collect weapons in Warshafana areas and arrest members of the tribe suspected of having participated in the regime's brigades during the war. Initial clashes caused other Warshafana to mobilize and fighting lasted for three days. The Zawiyya Military Council was quick to denounce its adversaries as remnants of former regime brigades, reinforced by "fighters from Bani Walid and Sabha."[34]

Between the Asabi'a (the name describes both a tribe and a town) and brigades from the town of Gharyan, as well as between the Mashashiyya and the Zintan military council, truces had been reached during the last months of the war. These involved the disarmament of the Asabi'a and the Mashashiyya—both considered supporters of the former regime by their adversaries. However, the truces were repeatedly violated and broke down when fighting erupted between Zintan and the Mashashiyya in December 2011—provoked by killings of Mashashiyya suspects by Zintan brigades—and between the Asabi'a and Gharyan in January 2012, over demands by Gharyan for Asabi'a suspects to be handed over. The heavy fighting that followed involved the shelling of Asabi'a and Mashashiyya villages by Zintani brigades, while in the town of Mizda, militias from the Quntrar tribe allied themselves with Zintan against the Mashashiyya.[35]

Resentment among these communities continued to grow, as demonstrated by a statement from Mashashiyya elders demanding the right of their displaced families to return and rejecting the handover of suspects before the reestablishment of a neutral judicial system.[36] Fighting erupted again in June 2012, when Zintani militias shelled the Mashashiyya towns of Shaqiqa and Wamis, and clashes broke out in Mizda between the Quntrar and Mashashiyya, causing several thousand civilians to flee. The fighting had been triggered by the killing of two Zintanis by a Mashashiyya militia, but Zintan's demand for the handover of suspects was still the key underlying issue.[37]

The divisions and crimes of the civil war, and group solidarity in the face of external threats, were the key drivers of armed conflicts along tribal lines in the postwar period. However, rivalries over the distribution of spoils and local power also played a role. In April 2012, fighting flared between brigades from the city of Zuwara (whose *Amazigh* identity emerged as a key mobilizing factor during and after the uprisings) and armed groups from the Nawail and Safaat tribes, in the towns of Rijdalain and Jumail. The conflict partly reflected rifts going back to the civil war. Qadhafi's prime minister Baghdadi al-Mahmoudi, a leading Nawail figure, had ensured that the tribe predominantly sided with the regime, whereas Zuwara had suffered heavily under a regime clampdown. Zuwaran political and military figures continued to accuse their neighbours of counterrevolutionary activity after the war. Cases of torture and killings on both sides were the immediate triggers for the fighting.[38] Rivalries over the control of the Abu Kammash petrochemical complex, as well as the Ras Jdeir border crossing and smuggling routes across the Tunisian border, added another dimension to the conflict.[39] These rivalries, in turn, were partly rooted in a historical background of feuding over land rights between the Nawail and the Berber tribes from Zuwara during the nineteenth and early twentieth centuries.

Meanwhile, the conflicts in Sabha and Kufra were more obvious examples of struggles for local hegemony and control over lucrative smuggling routes (see Chapter 6 by Henry Smith, which delves further into the tribal nature of these conflicts). In neither case was fighting triggered explicitly by disputes going back to the civil war. Its origins were simultaneously a product of dynamics unique to post-Qadhafi Libya or to historic ethnic tensions. In Kufra, for example, the legacy of intercommunal conflict in 2008 and racial prejudice in the new Libya loomed large and trumped the fact that both Tubu and Zwai had fought *on the same side* against Qadhafi.

Demands for Justice and the Limits of Tribal Reconciliation Initiatives

Heavy fighting along tribal and ethnic lines, as it was raging in Jabal Nafusa, the Jafara plain, and southern Libya, was conspicuously absent from Cyrenaica in the postwar period. The obvious reason was that Cyrenaica had been wholly liberated early on and, apart from the Ajdabiyya-Ras Lanuf area and the Awjila and Jalu oases, had seen no fighting during the civil war. Consequently, the war by and large had not triggered local conflicts between towns or tribes in the region.

The main exception was the tensions over the killing of General Abdul-Fattah Yunis al-Obeidi, chief-of-staff of the defected army units and the NTC's first defense minister. Yunis was killed on 28 July 2011 while returning to Benghazi following the summons of a three-member panel of judges tasked by the NTC and its executive committee to investigate him. Yunis's family and Obeidat leaders mobilized immediately following the assassination, blaming senior figures in the NTC and threatening to take justice into their own hands.[40]

Like many of the conflicts along tribal lines in western Libya, the mobilization of Obeidat 'asabiyya was closely related to the failure of judicial investigations into the crimes committed during the civil war.

After Qadhafi's fall, the Obeidat increased pressure on the NTC, as the probe into Yunis's murder failed to progress. In November 2011, members of the Obeidat established a permanent sit-in opposite the Tibesti Hotel in Benghazi to protest against the NTC's failure to arrest and prosecute the suspects. They also briefly closed down the main road between Benghazi and the Egyptian border, and threatened to block oil exports from Tobruk.[41]

Yunis's assassination clearly caused the Obeidat establishment to unite and demand justice. Contrary to the conflicts in western and southern Libya, however, their adversary was not another community, but a list of suspects that included senior officials, judges, and Islamist militants from various tribes, including members of the Obeidat themselves. The issue therefore could not be addressed within a tribal framework, but had to be dealt with through the justice system. However, this failed; by July 2012, only one out of 17 suspects named by the prosecution had been arrested. Starting as early as January 2012, repeated attempts were made on the life of Jum'a al-Jazwi al-Obeidi—a judge who had headed the three-member panel—as well as his son and brother. In June 2012, al-Jazwi was finally killed, shortly after the relevant court had decided to widen the probe to include senior officials.[42]

The inability of the NTC and its government to end local conflicts and prosecute crimes committed during and after the civil war, due to the absence of a functional security apparatus and judicial system, caused tribal leaders to play an increasingly prominent role in conflict resolution. The impetus for this development came both from the grassroots and from the NTC itself. As outlined above, tribal leaders had been organizing in liberated areas since the beginning of the uprisings, setting up formal or informal councils that played a preeminent role in managing local affairs in some Cyrenaican and Jabal Nafusa towns. After the war, *Majalis Hukama'* were set up in many towns. The NTC and its government, conscious of their own impotence, explicitly promoted conflict-resolution strategies based on tribal customs, and led by tribal elders and religious scholars.

As early as September 2011, NTC chairman Mustafa Abdul-Jalil helped form a national reconciliation committee (*Lajnat al-Musalaha al-Wataniyya*) including tribal and religious leaders. The committee intervened in every major conflict from the November 2011 Zawiyya-Warshafana clashes onward. The transitional authorities also supported the foundation of a national council of tribal notables, *Majlis Hukama' Libya*, which was appointed by representatives of local *Majalis* in March 2012.[43] The reconciliation committee formed earlier was reshuffled and placed under the authority of this national council. In addition, tribal elders also mediated on their own initiative between warring parties, as in Kufra or in the Zintan-Mashashiya conflict.

The mixed record of these initiatives exposed the limits to the authority of tribal leaders and institutions. Without a neutral and effective army to enforce cease-fire agreements, and without the prosecution of suspects through the state justice system, many deals reached by tribal elders quickly collapsed. In Ghadames, six agreements struck by Tuareg tribal elders and Ghadamsi notables between September 2011 and June 2012 successively broke down in the absence of a neutral security presence.[44] In Kufra, where the intervening Libya Shield Force—a militia force under the nominal control of the army chief of staff [45]—was biased against the Tubu, none of the numerous mediation initiatives succeeded in bringing about a lasting agreement. In the Zuwara-Rijdalain conflict, the transitional government failed to heed the reconciliation committee's calls for the prosecution of suspects and the restoration of state control over the Abu Kammash industrial zone.[46] In sum, the government's lack of authority allowed tribal leaders to assume an increasingly prominent role—but at the same time, tribal figures could not consolidate their newfound influence because state institutions were too weak to provide the necessary backing.

Bani Walid, the Warfalla, and the Tribal Balance of Power

Nowhere was the role of tribal loyalties and leaders stronger—and nowhere were the political rifts that developed along tribal lines of greater national importance—than in the case of the Warfalla and their stronghold of Bani Walid. Following the city's capture after lengthy negotiations and heavy fighting in October 2011 (map 4), Warfalla revolutionaries established a local council that exercised a tenuous control over the city. Leading the revolutionary camp was Muhammad Bashir, who had participated in the 1993 coup attempt by Warfalla officers, but had managed to escape execution.

In November 2011, Bashir's 28 May Brigade, named after the protesters who were killed in Bani Walid on 28 May 2011, drew the ire of the Warfalla establishment by arresting former Qadhafi regime security officials and other suspects, while drawing on revolutionary brigades from the Tripoli suburbs of Souq al-Jum'a and Tajoura for military backing. Tensions came to a head when the 1993 Warfalla Martyrs' Brigade (a loyalist outfit), led by Salem al-Wair—another participant in the 1993 coup attempt—clashed with the revolutionary brigades in late November 2011, killing a dozen *thuwwar* from Souq al-Jum'a.[47]

The 28 May Brigade and its local council were eventually forced out of Bani Walid in January 2012 by al-Wair's militia. In a bid to mobilize external support, Warfalla revolutionaries were quick to portray the development as a takeover by former regime loyalists, who allegedly had raised Qadhafi's green flag in the town. In reality, the revolutionary camp had been unable to gain broad support in the town; resentment of the destruction and pillaging suffered during its capture was running high, and the Warfalla establishment was ostracized in the new order as a pillar of the ancien régime. The rift between revolutionaries and counterrevolutionaries also partly overlapped with tribal divides within the Warfalla, with many former senior officials and backers of the 1993 Brigade coming from the Sadat subsection, while many revolutionary leaders and victims of the 28 May crackdown were drawn from the Jumamla.[48]

In the place of the local council, tribal elders formed a "social council of the Warfalla tribes" to oversee affairs in the town—a move that marked the Warfalla establishment's distance from the new political order. While the NTC refused to recognize the new entity as the legitimate local authority in Bani Walid, the social council reciprocated by omitting any reference to the NTC and the revolution; contrary to the red-black-and-green flag adopted by all local councils, the social council's logo was light green. The council in January 2012 told defense minister Usama al-Juwaili that it rejected the handover of Warfalla suspects to NTC authorities for trial and would repel any attempts by outside forces to enter Bani Walid. Backed by the 1993 Brigade, the council successfully insisted on this position despite heavy external pressure, including repeated blockades of the town by revolutionary brigades from Misrata and Tripoli. In May 2012, it also emerged victorious in a standoff with Zlitan revolutionaries over prisoners held by both sides—winning the release of dozens of Warfalla tribesmen held in Zlitan.[49]

At the time of writing in the middle of 2012, Bani Walid continued to be effectively outside the new political order, although the social council allowed the 7 July 2012 elections to be held in Bani Walid. Moreover, the dispute with the NTC and the exiled Bani Walid local council over the handover of suspects remained deadlocked. Whether the social council would have been able to impose a surrender of suspects on the 1993 Brigade is doubtful, and therefore the degree of authority wielded by tribal leaders in Bani Walid remains unclear, despite the fact that their political leadership was obvious.

The Warfalla's rejection of the new order had a wider significance because of the tribe's political weight and its historical leadership in Libyan tribal alliances (*Sufuf*). The Warfalla establishment began rallying support from other tribes reputed to have been pillars of the former regime and alienated by the NTC. In June 2012, Warfalla leaders sought to build something akin to an "alliance of the losers of the uprisings" by hosting the second forum of Libyan tribes in Bani Walid, which included representatives of the Qadhadhifa, Warshafana, Maqarha, Hasawna, Tarhouna, Nawail, Safaat, Asabi'a, and Mashashiyya, among others.

Leaving aside the question of how representative the figures attending the meeting were among their communities, these tribes clearly shared vital interests: their political influence had suffered in the new political order, they were in continual conflict with revolutionary forces, and they faced demands for the handover of suspects. The Bani Walid forum and a subsequent meeting in Wadi al-Shati called for the release of imprisoned members of their tribes in the absence of a neutral justice system, and the withdrawal of "illegal militias" from their tribes' areas. Their final statements made no reference to the 17 February revolution or the NTC. Instead, they stressed the historic bonds linking the tribes, with strong tribes promising to support weaker communities.[50]

Factual evidence supports the claims of historic ties linking these tribes only to a certain extent. The Qadhadhifa had indeed been aligned with the Warfalla since the nineteenth century, whereas their alliance with the Maqarha was clearly a product of the Qadhafi regime's policies. But the historical imaginary was significant in that it referred to a perception of the revolution as a major shift in the tribal balance of power: away from the alliance led by the Warfalla, Qadhadhifa, and Maqarha; toward the tribes of Cyrenaica and the Jabal, as well as the city of Misrata. This perception was widely shared, both among tribes who saw themselves as politically ascendant and those who felt sidelined by the NTC, its government, and the revolutionary brigades.[51] The coalition spearheaded by the Warfalla underlined the ambition of these tribes' leaders to regain their lost influence and the potential for counterrevolutionary tribal forces to pose a challenge to the new order.

Coastal Cities and the Tribal Hinterland in the New Political Order

The rise of tribal politics and conflicts along tribal lines during and after the civil war was not consistent across Libya. In the big coastal cities—Zawiyya, greater Tripoli, Misrata, and Benghazi—the tribal dimension was much less pronounced. Tribal politics was particularly important only in the hinterland and on the whole its proponents were socially and politically conservative forces. As such, tribal politics formed a counterweight to the revolutionary militias and the national political forces in the new order.

Social and cultural conservatism has long been inherent in Libyan tribal politics. Women are absent from meetings of tribal leaders, and their emphasis on seniority mostly excludes the younger generation that led the uprisings.[52] This "political conservatism" ranged from the outright counterrevolutionary stance promoted by the Warfalla and their allies, to attempts by Qadhafi-era tribal elites to ensure their political survival while ostensibly accepting the new order. The *Majalis Hukama'* and informal forums of tribal elders of the transitional period could—at least to some extent—be seen as successor institutions to the Popular Social Leadership (PSL) established by Qadhafi in the 1990s (for more on the re-tribalization of Libya and the PSL's institutionalization of tribal power see Chapter 1). The tribal leaders of the transitional period had in many cases been members of the PSL. The approach taken in Sirte—where *thuwwar* elected their local *Majlis Hukama'* to avoid a return of Qadhafi-era figures—remained the exception.[53]

Tribal political forces were also conservative in that they were uninterested in the emergence of national political camps along ideological lines. Instead, tribal politics was by definition local or regional, and focused on the access of individual constituencies to political power and public resources at the national level. One example was the lobbying by Cyrenaican tribal leaders from the Awaqir and Magharba for representation in the cabinet of Prime Minister Abdul-Rahman al-Kib, as well as their protests when they failed to win ministerial posts.[54] Another was the initiative for federalism and regional autonomy in Cyrenaica. Initially, its key proponents were tribal leaders. Later, army officers from Cyrenaican tribes joined the movement.

From April 2011 onward, tribal figures began agitating for a federalist structure that would grant Cyrenaica a degree of autonomy from central government.[55] This culminated in the single-handed declaration of regional autonomy by the 6 March 2012 Barqa Conference—seen by many as an attempt by parts by the Cyrenaican tribal establishment to grab power. The movement's figurehead Ahmad Zubair al-Sanussi—a member of the royal family that ruled Libya from 1951 to 1969—had been imprisoned for most of the Qadhafi era. Other key players, however, had held senior positions under Qadhafi. Leading Obeidat figure al-Tayyib al-Sharif, for example, had headed the Tobruk PSL.[56]

The Barqa Conference's move was immediately rejected by local councils across Cyrenaica, some of the most powerful revolutionary brigades in the region, as well as by ideologically based national forces such as the Muslim Brotherhood. The federalist initiative failed to make much headway thereafter, although army officers loyal to the Barqa military council rallied to the initiative, disgruntled by their marginalization in the new security sector institutions controlled by militia leaders. The attempts by federalist activists to forcibly obstruct the elections or block road traffic at Barqa's supposed borders further eroded support for the federalist project in Cyrenaica. In sum, conservative tribal forces in Cyrenaica represented a counterweight against—but could not overcome—the region's new urban, civil, and cosmopolitan political forces.

Positing a strict dichotomy between conservative tribal forces and revolutionary urban politics is, of course, an oversimplification. Among the exceptions are the towns and tribes of the Jabal Nafusa, who were among the staunchest proponents of the revolutionary camp. They also forced the NTC to accept that each Jabal town should send one representative to the National Congress—except Zintan, which had two seats—and that no party lists could field candidates in the Jabal. Parochial politics coincided with a prorevolutionary stance in the Jabal, the common denominator being the advance of individual town tribes' influence at the national level.

At first sight, the results of the elections to the National Congress in July 2012 appear to contradict this picture of parochial politics in the hinterland and revolutionary politics in the big coastal cities. Among the party lists, Mahmoud Jibril's National Forces Alliance (NFA) came first in 16 out of 20 voting districts, suggesting a broad majority for Jibril's list across Libya. Of the four districts where the NFA did not win, only Ubari and Wadi al-Shati fit into the hinterland category. Nevertheless, lists that ran or won in only one district, and often represented particular tribal constituencies, gained their seats mostly in the interior of the country, such as in Ubari, Wadi al-Shati, Sirte, Jufra, and Sabha. In contrast, the Muslim Brotherhood's Justice and Construction Party mostly won its seats in the coastal cities. Moreover, the NFA and other national lists took the tribal factor into account when choosing their candidates in hinterland constituencies, and some of their candidates courted elders at tribal meetings.[57] Jum'a al-Sayih, a winning independent candidate from Nasiriyya affiliated with the NFA, based his electoral strategy on the mathematics of Warshafana subclans, focusing on the support of the demographically strongest sections.[58] Such calculations were even more pertinent for candidates running for independent seats, which made up 120 out of 200 Congress seats, against 80 for party lists. Particularly in the hinterland, independent candidates often ran, and won, as the representatives of their tribe or tribal section. (The results and implications of the GNC elections are discussed in greater depth in Chapters 2 and 7.)

CONCLUSIONS

In many respects, the rise of political mobilization, organization, and conflict along tribal lines was symptomatic of a broader development that characterized the uprisings and their aftermath: the primacy of local interests and loyalties, as well as the emergence of local power centers—councils and militias—as key players on the political and military scene. In coastal cities such as Misrata, Zawiyya, and Zuwara, this development manifested itself in the creation of a cohesive urban political fabric, with militias and politicians defending these cities' perceived interests at the regional and national levels. In Jabal Nafusa, Cyrenaica, and Fezzan, tribal rifts and loyalties defined the evolution of local politics. Many conflicts that erupted along tribal lines during the transitional period related to the issues surrounding justice for crimes committed during and after the civil war. As such, there was nothing specifically tribal about these conflicts, other than the fact that group loyalty (*'asabiyya*) caused communities to unite along tribal lines over such disputes.

However, this chapter's analysis also highlights a major divide in Libyan politics during and after the war: the split between conservative tribal forces in the hinterland and revolutionary or urban political forces in the coastal cities. This divide represented an important aspect of the conflict between revolutionary and counterrevolutionary forces that played out between Bani Walid and the revolutionary brigades largely from Misrata and Tripoli. It also manifested itself in the 7 July 2012 elections. The tension between conservative tribal politics in the hinterland and revolutionary or ideological politics in the coastal cities is likely to define Libya for years to come.

NOTES

1. This chapter uses the terms "revolution," "civil war," and "uprisings" to capture different dimensions of the events unfolding in Libya from February to October 2011. The use of the term "revolution" is based on the recognition that the uprisings led to the total collapse of the former

political order, making necessary the establishment of an entirely new one. Since the latter was the professed aim of the majority of antiregime forces, the chapter refers to these forces as "revolutionaries" or the "pro-revolutionary camp," thereby adopting the term *thuwwar* used in Arabic. The use of the term "revolution" follows Charles Tilly's definition of a revolutionary situation: "1. The appearance of contenders, or coalitions of contenders, advancing exclusive competing claims to control the state, or some segment of it; 2. Commitment to those claims by a significant segment of the citizenry; 3. Incapacity or unwillingness of rulers to suppress the alternative coalition and/or commitment to its claims." Charles Tilly, *European Revolutions, 1492–1992* (Oxford: Blackwell, 1993), 10. The term "civil war" is the subject of frequent scholarly and political controversy; the use of the term in this chapter follows one of the most widely used definitions, that of the Correlates of War Project: "(1) military action internal to the metropole of the state system member; (2) the active participation of the national government; (3) effective resistance by both sides; and (4) a total of at least 1,000 battle-deaths during each year of the war." Meredith Reid Markees, "The COW Typology of War: Defining and Categorizing Wars," undated paper, http://www.correlatesofwar.org.

2. John Davis, *Libyan Politics: Tribe and Revolution* (London: I. B. Tauris, 1987); Moncef Ouannes, *Militaires, Élites et Modernisation dans la Libye Contemporaine* (Paris: L'Harmattan, 2009); Hanspeter Mattes, "Formal and Informal Authority in Libya since 1969," in *Libya since 1969: Qadhafi's Revolution Revisited*, edited by Dirk Vandewalle (Basingstoke: Palgrave Macmillan, 2008), 55–81; Ali Dolamari, "Le tribalisme libyen: un critère géopolitique," *Outre-Terre* 23 (2009): 123–25; Moncef Djaziri, "Tribus et État dans le système politique libyen," *Outre-Terre* 23 (2009): 127–34.

3. Jacques Berque, "Qu'est-ce qu'une tribu nord-africaine?," in *Eventail de l'Histoire Vivante: Hommages à Lucien Febvre* (Paris: Armand Collin, 1953), 260–71.

4. Jean-Loup Amselle and Elikia M'Bokolo, eds., *Au Cœur de l'Ethnie: Tribalisme et l'Etat en Afrique* (Paris: La Découverte, 1985).

5. Thomas Hüsken, "Die neotribale Wettbewerbsordnung im Grenzgebiet von Ägypten und Libyen," *Sociologus* 2 (2009): 117–43; and "Politische Kultur und die Revolution in der Kyrenaika," in *Libyen: Hintergründe, Analysen, Berichte,* edited by Fritz Edlinger (Vienna: Promedia, 2011), 47–69. Hüsken also emphasizes the innovative nature of "neo-tribal" interaction with the state, which produces "hybrid" forms of governance, and runs counter to the conventional equation of tribal politics with traditionalism.

6. Yazid Ben Hounet, "La tribu comme champ social semi-autonome," *L'Homme* 194 (2010): 57–74; Mounira Charrad, "Central and Local Patrimonialism: State-Building in Kin-Based Societies," *Annals of the American Society of Political and Social Science* 636 (2011): 49–68.

7. Emrys L. Peters, "The Power of Shaykhs," in *The Bedouin of Cyrenaica: Studies in Personal and Corporate Power* (Cambridge: Cambridge University Press, 1990), 112–37.

8. Monique Brandily, "Les inégalités dans la société du Tibesti," in *Gens du Roc et du Sable: Les Toubou*, edited by Catherine Baroin (Paris: Editions du CNRS, 1988), 37–71.

9. Interviews, members of the local and *shura* councils, Zintan, November 23, 2012; see also al-Tahir's public speech in Zintan, posted on the internet on February 19, 2011, http://youtu.be/xLOJWm4yo2c.

10. "Libyan Tribe Threatens to Cut Off Oil Exports Soon," *Reuters*, February 20, 2011.

11. "Bayyan Ahali Qabilat al-Rajban," Video dated February 24, 2011, posted online on December 4, 2011, http://youtu.be/wbFGgTAQijE.

12. "Bayyan Majlis Mudun Jabal Nafusa al-Mutaharrara," Video posted online on March 26, 2011, http://youtu.be/GSD3H9aV5c4.

13. Hanspeter Mattes, *Challenges to Security Sector Governance in the Middle East: The Libyan Case*, Geneva Centre for the Democratic Control of Armed Forces Working Papers 144 (Geneva, August 2004).

14. Interview, Dr. Mahmoud Abdelaziz al-Warfalli, Tripoli, June 9, 2012.

15. Interview, Tuareg tribal leaders, Tripoli, June 2012.

16. See, for example, "Tarhouna: tu'lin qaba'il Tarhouna taayyudha al-kamel lil-thawra al-shaabiya," *Libya al-Yawm*, February 21, 2011, http://www.libya-alyoum.com/news/index.php?id=21&textid=1775; or "Bayyan Qabilat Magharba," *Libya al-Yawm*, February 21, 2011, http://www.libyaalyoum.com/news/index.php?id=21&textid=1780.

17. Coverage of tribal forum, Libyan state TV, May 6, 2011; "Gadhafi Stages Event to Show Libyan Tribal Unity," *Wall Street Journal*, May 6, 2011; "al-multaqa al-awwal li-qabail al-junub w-l-wasat bil-mintaqa al-sharqiya bi-benghazi," *Brnieq*, May 23, 2011, http://www.brnieq.com/news/?p=38630.

18. "Toutes les tribus de Libye n'en font qu'une," *La Règle du Jeu*, April 27, 2011, http://laregledujeu.org/2011/04/27/5465/toutes-les-tribus-de-libye-nen-font-quune/.

19. Libyan state television, May 11 and June 7, 2011.

20. Coverage of the Forum of Warfalla tribes by Libyan state TV, July 9, 2011; Televised speech by Qadhafi to the Warfalla, July 21, 2011.

21. See, for example, Shakir's message to Bani Walid, posted online on January 23, 2012, http://youtu.be/gewBrtrIDgA, or Shakir's message dated June 4, 2012, http://youtu.be/HRWjzk14hwU.

22. International Crisis Group, *Holding Libya Together: Security Challenges After Qadhafi*, Middle East/North Africa Report 115 (Brussels, December 14, 2011).

23. Salem Chaker and Masin Ferkal, "Berbères de Libye: un paramètre méconnu, une irruption politique inattendue," *Politique Africaine* 125 (March 2012): 105–26.

24. "Ahali Gharyan: ma hadath fil-Asabi'a khiyana yunafi al-akhlaq al-insaniya," *Quryna*, September 13, 2011, http://qurynanew.com /?p=11785; "Libya: Opposition Forces Should Protect Civilians and Hospitals," *Human Rights Watch*, July 13, 2011, http://www.hrw .org/news/2011/07/13/libya-opposition-forces-should-protect-civilians -and-hospitals.

25. Ali Abdullatif Ahmida, *The Making of Modern Libya: State Formation, Colonization, and Resistance* (New York: SUNY 2009), 130–32.

26. Interviews, members of the local and *shura* councils, Zintan, 23 November 2012.

27. Ahmida, *The Making of Modern Libya*.

28. Interviews, Tubu and Zuwayya representatives, Tripoli and Benghazi, June 2–6, 2012.

29. "Ra'is al-majlis al-askari li-madinat Murzuq: fulul al-Qadhafi harra-bat al-asliha ila al-Jazair w Mali w-l-Nijer ba'ad tahrir Libya," *Quryna*, December 26, 2011, http://www.qurynanew.com/24914.

30. Interviews, Maqarha and Hasawna representatives, Tripoli, June 2–9, 2012; "Qabilat al-Qadhadfa bi-Sabha tusallim aslihatiha lil-thawwar," *Quryna*, October 2, 2011, http://qurynanew.com/?p=14633.

31. Interview, Amal Obeidi, Benghazi, June 7, 2012.

32. Hüsken, "Politische Kultur," 57–59.

33. Angelo Del Boca, *Mohammed Fekini and the Fight to Free Libya* (Palgrave: New York, 2011); Dennis D. Cordell, "The Awlad Sulayman of Libya and Chad: Power and Adaptation in the Sahara and Sahel," *Canadian Journal of African Studies* 19, no. 2 (1985): 319–43.

34. "Bouras yufannid musanadat ahali Warshafana did thuwwar al-Zawiyya," *Quryna*, November 14, 2011, www.qurynanew.com/20110; "Masa'i lil-musalaha bain muqatilin al-Zawiyya w Warshafana," *Quryna*, November 14, 2011, http://www.qurynanew.com/20066.

35. "Muqtal ithnein w asr 'ashara fi hujum 'ala mintaqat Umm al-Baqr qurb al-Shaqiqa," *Quryna*, December 16, 2011, http://www.qurynanew .com/23968; "Juweili yazur al-Asabi'a li-tuhdiat al-a'wda'," *Quryna*, January 14, 2012, http://www.qurynanew.com/27297; "Al-mahallian Gharyan w-l-Asabi'a yuwadihan asbab al-ishkaliyat w-l-ahdath al-waqi'a bayn al-Janibayn," *Quryna*, January 14, 2012, http://www.qurynanew .com/27227.

36. "Qaba'il al-Mashashiya yu'akkid iltihamha ma'a thawrat sab'atashar Febrayer w tamassukha bi-wahdat al-turab al-Libi," *Libya al-Yawm*, March 26, 2012, http://www.libya-alyoum.com/news/index.php?id=21& textid=9097.

37. "Muqtal thalath'ashar w jurh thalatha w thalathin akhirin khilal qisf 'ala mintaqat al-Shaqiqa w-l-Mane' yuakkid tadakhul al-jaysh," *Quryna*, June 14, 2012, http://www.qurynanew.com/36565; "Senior Qaddafi Commander Reported Captured in Ongoing Nafusa Mountain Clashes," *Libya Herald*, June 14, 2012 (online; article no longer accessible);

172   Wolfram Lacher

"Several Thousand Displaced in Jebel Nafusa: ICRC Claim," *Libya Herald*, June 21, 2012 (online; article no longer accessible).

38. "Tasaulat haul i'tidaat azlam al-maqbur 'ala thuwwar Zuwara," *Al-Watan al-Libiya*, April 13, 2012, http://alwatanlibya.com/more.php?newsid=21300&catid=23.

39. "Bayyan jam'iyat muthaqqifin Zuwara, muhamum wa muhamiyat wa qudha wa atba fi dakhil wa kharij Libya," April 8, 2012, http://www.libyaalmostakbal.net/news/clicked/21158; "'Ummal masna' Abu Kammash ya'tasimun amam al-wuzara bi-sabab tardihim min qabl musallihin min Zuwara," *Quryna*, December 3, 2011, http://www.qurynanew.com/22612.

40. David Kirkpatrick, "Killers of Libyan Rebel General Were among His Own Forces," *New York Times*, July 30, 2011; "Younes' Tribe Warns Rebels over Probe," *Reuters*, August 2, 2011.

41. Interview, Obeidat leader, Benghazi, November 24, 2011; Khaled Moheir, "Qabila Libiya yuhaddid bi ighlaq mina nafti," *al-Jazeera.net*, November 19, 2011, http://aljazeera.net/news/pages/c6f54482-7639-4a65-a066-56d7e80904c3.

42. "Court Reopens Investigation into Yunis Killing," *Libya Herald*, June 1, 2012 (online; article no longer accessible); "Benghazi Official Linked to Yunis Killing Assassinated," *Libya Herald*, June 21, 2012 (online; article not accessible anymore).

43. "Tawasul a'mal al-ijtima' al-ta'asisi li-majlis hukama' Libya bi-madinat Surman: wakil wuzarat al-'adl Khalifa Ashur yad'u li-wahdat al-saff bayn abna' al-watan al-wahid," *al-Watan al-Libiya*, March 19, 2012, http://tinyurl.com/dyu744a.

44. Interview, members of Tuareg negotiation committee for Ghadames, Tripoli, June 2012.

45. See International Crisis Group, *Divided We Stand: Libya's Enduring Conflicts*, Middle East/North Africa Report 130, Brussels, September 14, 2012.

46. "Ijtima' tar'i li-fid al-niza' bayn Zuwara w Rijdalain w Jumail," *Quryna*, April 4, 2012, http://www.qurynanew.com/32527; "Lajnat al-musalaha al-wataniyatutalibbi-taf'ildawral-jayshal-wataniwta'zizshir'iyatal-dawla," *Irassa*, May 8, 2012, http://www.irassa.com/modules/publisher/item.php?itemid=2021.

47. "Bani Walid tutalib bi-i'adat tahrirha," *Irassa*, November 26, 2011, http://www.irassa.com/modules/publisher/item.php?itemid=1422.

48. Interview, Dr. Mahmoud Abdelaziz al-Warfalli, Tripoli, June 9, 2012.

49. Telephone Interview, Mustafa Fetouri, May 22, 2012.

50. *Al-bayyan al-khitami li-multaqa al-qabail al-Libiya fi Bani Walid*, Bani Walid, June 6, 2012; *Bayyan al-multaqa al-thalith lil-qabail al-Libiya*, Wadi al-Shate', June 17, 2012, unpublished documents.

51. Interviews, Hasawna, Warfalla, Maqarha, Zintan and Yifran representatives, Tripoli, November 2011 and June 2012.

52. Hüsken, "Politische Kultur," 64; Interview, Amal Obeidi, Benghazi, June 7, 2012.

53. "Tashkil lajnat li-ikhtiyar adhuiyat majlis hukama Sirt," *Press Solidarity*, June 12, 2012, http://presssolidarity.net/20635/.

54. "Mu'akkidan annaha tash'ur bil-iqsa' wal-tahmish…ahad a'yan qabilat al-Awaqir: sanadkhul al-intikhabat wa nuqaddim ashkhasan wa nantakhibhum," *al-Manara*, December 29, 2011, http://tinyurl.com/cjfo3q2.

55. "Taharrukat qibliya muqalqa sharqi Libya," *Al-Jazeera*, April 10, 2011, http://www.aljazeera.net/NR/EXERES/CAEEACC4–5691–4952 -A6E8-F48F57D2349C.htm; "Rafd taqsim Libya ila fidiraliyat," *Al-Jazeera*, July 21, 2011, http://www.aljazeera.net/NR/exeres/6C403781 -A193–45F8-A392–2A900CB1CD4E.htm.

56. "Al-Haj al-Sharif ahad a'yan al-Obeidat ihdharu radab wa quwa Barqa," Video posted online May 14, 2012, www.youtube.com/watch?v=pLkniy _WxUk.

57. Al-Sanusi Bsikri, "Intikhabat al-mu'tamar al-watani al-Libi wa khiyarat al-kutal al-siyasiya al-faiza," July 23, 2012, http://studies.aljazeera.net /ResourceGallery/media/Documents/2012/7/24/2012724105183 48734Libyan National elections.pdf.

58. Interviews, Warshafana representatives and electoral candidates, Tripoli, June, 2012.

6

THE SOUTH

Henry Smith

To most analysts, the main fighting of the 2011 Libyan uprisings was waged over a thin strip of Mediterranean coastline, with events in Libya's "south"—that is its vast Saharan interior—seemingly tangential to the outcome of the civil war. Consequently, despite the intense media and academic focus on the uprisings from February 2011 onward, much of Libya remained terra incognita; unlike the maps in this volume, most media maps depicting the rebel and pro-Qadhafi controlled areas tended to focus entirely on the littoral region—a physical representation of the widely held view that because events in Libya's Sahara were geographically peripheral and involved different tribes and ethnic groups that they were somehow less politically significant to the course of the uprisings or to the country's postconflict stability. Overlooking the south was in some respects inevitable due to the paucity of accurate, timely information available to mainstream media. However, similar to the dynamics at play in the north, the separate and disparate uprisings in Libya's south demonstrated their own localized sociopolitical and tribal dynamics, very similar to those described by Wolfram Lacher in Chapter 5.

The relationships between Libya's Tubu and Tuareg ethnic minorities and the Arab and *Amazigh* (Berber) populations—with whom they tend not to intermarry—were not only *decisive* in shaping the Saharan uprisings but also *divisive* for the trajectory of post-Qadhafi Libya. The nature of the fissures evident in the southern uprisings owed much to the legacy of Qadhafi-era policies. Yet, they also drew upon older cleavages, which challenged the new Libyan authorities' abilities to create an inclusive political system after Qadhafi's fall. The failure to recognize Libya's heterogeneity and to institutionalize minority representation and rights risked perpetuating longer-term

instability and insecurity in Libya, in general, and across the broader
Saharan region, in specific. The early indications were not positive;
violence in Libya's south was worse in 2012 than during the 2011
uprisings.

This chapter begins by demonstrating the centrality of "Arab-ness"
to Qadhafi's construction of Libyan identity. It builds on the discussions of the historical and contemporary role of tribes in Chapters 2 and
5 to investigate Qadhafi's relationships with Libya's non-Arab Saharan
minorities—the Tuareg and the Tubu.[1] The uprisings in the Saharan
towns of Kufra, Sabha, and Ghadames are then explored showing the
decisive importance of these relationships in shaping the nature and
course of the 2011 uprisings in the south and also, equally importantly,
how they fostered intercommunal violence in 2011–2012.

BUILDING AN ARAB STATE

Qadhafi couched Libyan identity strictly in terms of its "Arab-ness."
As with most postindependence regimes in North Africa during the
mid-twentieth century, pan-Arabism, and anticolonialism were key
elements of Qadhafi's interpretation of Libyan identity. Qadhafi's
Revolutionary Command Council affirmed the Arab nature of the
1969 revolution in the Constitutional Proclamation that created the
Libyan Arab Republic. Libya's Arab character was restated in 1977
when Qadhafi proclaimed his *jamahiriyya* system in Sabha. The name
of the country was changed from the Libyan Arab Republic to the
Great Socialist People's Libyan Arab Jamahiriyya.[2] Notwithstanding
the occasional tactical concession, Qadhafi's insistence on the Arab
and anticolonial character of the state, which he at times linked to one
another, continued until the collapse of his system in 2011.[3] Qadhafi
ignored Libya's ethnic, cultural, and linguistic heterogeneity, granting no official recognition to its three largest ethnic minorities—the
Amazigh (or Berber), the Tuareg, and the Tubu. His *jamahiriyya*
system also fostered myriad inconsistencies about the legal position
of significant numbers of sub-Saharan African economic migrants.

In the mid-2000s, Qadhafi adopted a relatively conciliatory stance
toward Libya's *Amazigh* population, becoming the first North African
leader to meet publically a delegation of international *Amazigh* activists. However, by early 2007 this position was reversed, with Qadhafi
linking challenges to his claim of Libya's Arab homogeneity to overt
colonial interference, "[we] in North Africa are Arabs, and North Africa
is 100 percent Arab.... The fact that France and Western colonialism

say to them [i.e. the Berbers] 'you are not Arabs'—whoever accepts this will bear [the] responsibility."[4] Saif al-Islam's efforts to champion the *Amazigh* cause during the peak of his public prominence in the mid-2000s were also undone as his power was progressively curtailed by the establishment's hardliners as the decade wore on.

Despite their marginalization by Qadhafi, Libya's *Amazigh* did not exhibit particularly acrimonious personal relationships with the broader Libyan Arab population, with which there is a significant but unquantifiable degree of intermarriage. However, Qadhafi's repressive policies toward them led to the Nafusa Mountains—the Libyan *Amazigh*'s main population center—emerging as one of the most effective arenas of antiregime opposition during the uprisings, with *Amazigh* (and Arab) militias assaulting Tripoli in August from the northwest (see map 3).

MINORITIES IN THE SOUTH: TUAREG AND TUBU

The Qadhafi regime's relationships with the Tubu and the Tuareg were less consistent than its repressive approach toward the *Amazigh* population. The treatment of these darker-skinned ethnic minorities in part reflected Qadhafi's aspiration to regional leadership, since both minority groups were intermittently manipulated for the purposes of foreign policy. In addition, particularly in the case of the Tuareg (both Libyan and non-Libyan), Qadhafi used these minorities to populate his security forces from the 1980s onward. Qadhafi's policy was motivated by a variety of considerations: preventing development of an alternative power base to his own; foreign policy pursuits in the Sahara and asserting his role as a continent-wide power player; balancing competing domestic constituencies; and—most notably with the Tuareg—populating his security forces.

The Tuareg are indigenous inhabitants of the Sahara, yet also share cultural and linguistic ties to the *Amazigh* population—from whom they nonetheless are ethnically distinct. Traditionally nomadic pastoralists, they occupy a vast swath of the Sahara and Sahel, stretching from Libya, through northern Niger, southern Algeria, northern Mali, and into Burkina Faso. The largest number, estimated at almost a million (out of two to three million across the region), live in northern Mali, where they declared the separatist republic of *Azawad* in April 2012. Although the Tuareg live and work throughout Libya, they are predominantly found in Fezzan (southwestern Libya), particularly in the oasis towns of Ghadames, Sabha, Ubari, and Ghat. They have traditionally moved with relative ease across Libya's modern-day southern borders, and have family and tribal ties in neighboring states, participating in regional trade and smuggling.

The Tubu are also autochthonous inhabitants of Libya's Sahara, particularly in the region around the southeastern oasis towns of Kufra, Rabiana, and Buzayma, and also in the southwestern Fezzani towns of Sabha, Murzuq, and al-Qatrun. They are connected to sub-Saharan populations ethnically and linguistically and hence are totally distinct from the rest of the Libyan population; however, like the Tuareg, they have cross-border ethnic and family links into Chad, Niger, and Sudan and have been also traditionally involved in regional trade and smuggling.

KUFRA

Approximately 1,000 miles from the Mediterranean, the southeastern town of Kufra is built around a series of oases near the Chadian, Egyptian, and Sudanese borders. Its significant sub-Saharan African influence distinguishes Kufra's atmosphere from Libya's Mediterranean population centers. The town serves as a regional agricultural hub and as a nexus for legal and illegal trade networks.[5] Collaboration between the Arab Zwai and Tubu meant Kufra was the first of the major Saharan towns to be wrested from loyalist control, with the last attack by Qadhafi forces occurring in May 2011.

As a marginalized minority under Qadhafi, the Tubu played a central role in the Kufra uprising. They were instrumental in stemming cross-border supplies to loyalist forces, with a prominent Tubu leader, Issa Abdul-Majid Mansour, appointed by the National Transitional Council (NTC) to supervise Libya's southeastern border security. Mansour had been head of the Tubu Front for the Salvation of Libya (TFSL), an organization formed in 2007 to promote the rights of Libya's Tubu.

The cooperation and relative peace between the Tubu and Zwai that prevailed during the uprising was short-lived as violence erupted in Kufra in February 2012, causing in excess of one hundred deaths. The conflict saw the two communities militarize their respective districts in Kufra, with Tubu neighborhoods subject to mortar fire in the following months.[6] Despite the initial spark for violence being relatively minor—the death of a Tubu taxi driver—the severe escalation reflected significant underlying antagonisms between the two communities, which pre-dated the 2011 uprisings. These antagonisms—usually centering on competition over scarce resources (both legal and illicit) and the Tubu's comparative political and economic marginalization—were long-standing. They had previously boiled over in 2008 when the Tubu demonstrated in Kufra in response to the government stripping some of their members' Libyan nationality. On that occasion, violence occurred between the Tubu and the Zwai—who were perceived as beneficiaries of the regime's measures. The government responded through a violent but effective crackdown against the Tubu.[7]

The Zwai trace their origins to the area around the northern oasis town of Jalu in the Sirte Basin. However, over the past two centuries, the tribe expanded its geographical reach becoming dominant in Kufra in the eighteenth century and forming an alliance with the Sanussi Sufi Order in the nineteenth century. The Zwai became the principal landowners in the oasis, monopolizing the limited agricultural cultivation area—a source of tension with the Tubu. Although the last head of the General People's Congress, Muhammad Abdul-Qasim al-Zwai, was a Zwai, they were not one of the Arab tribes that traditionally formed the backbone of Qadhafi's security forces, as discussed below. However, they were clearly politically and economically dominant over the Tubu, which was partly facilitated by the policies of the former regime.

The Tubu population has grown in recent decades but accurate, official statistics do not exist; aid agencies estimate the Tubu population of Kufra at around 4,000 out of 50,000.[8] The growth is primarily a result of immigration from Chad's Tibesti region due to the superior economic conditions in Libya. Qadhafi also sought to entice Chadian Tubu to work in Libya's oil industry during the 1980s conflict with Chad as an attempt to stake his claim to Tubu areas in Chad's part of the Aouzou Strip. The Tubu had been integral to Qadhafi's claim to the mineral-rich border region, which led to conflict between the two states in the 1980s, and during which he encouraged Tubu migration to Libya. Qadhafi also supported the National Liberation Front of Chad (better known as FROLINAT), a Chadian independence movement that counted many Tubu as members. However, rather than genuine support, Qadhafi's actions were merely manipulations of the Tubu for foreign policy purposes.

This dynamic is made clear by the fact that Qadhafi never supported the Tubu domestically. He began to strip some Tubu of their Libyan passports from 2007 onward. Tubu were subject to evictions, arbitrary arrest, detentions, and official refusals to renew their Libyan identification documents.[9] This meant poor access to employment opportunities and social welfare. It served as fuel for the aforementioned violence around Kufra in 2008. It was followed by another wave of forced evictions and denials of nationality in 2009.

Competition to control smuggling networks was also a source of antagonism—one which had a key role in driving violence in Libya's border regions after the 2011 uprisings. Libya's extensive system of blanket price subsidies meant that goods—particularly fuel and food— could command higher prices in neighboring states. The transnational connections maintained by the Tubu allowed them to prosper, but the Zwai are understood to have been the principal profiteers from illicit trade networks under Qadhafi—collecting tariffs on petroleum, and food products heading south, while human trafficking networks, drugs, and contraband consumer products, particularly cigarettes headed north. Since the uprisings began, weapons have slotted seamlessly into these networks. With this in mind, it is perhaps unsurprising that criticism from elements of the Zwai toward Issa Abdul-Majid Mansur often drew on perceptions that he was profiteering from his newfound influence as an NTC representative tasked with controlling the borders.[10]

Aside from political and commercial competition, Arab resentment toward the Tubu also built on discriminatory attitudes toward blacks. In keeping with widespread Libyan perceptions of African migrants before the uprisings, the Tubu—even those of Libyan nationality— were routinely regarded mistrustfully by the Arab population. While traveling through the Rebiana Sand Sea to the west of Kufra in 2010, the author's mandatory security escort regularly referred to the Tubu as "*klifty*," colloquial Libyan Arabic for "thieves." Although nothing was offered to substantiate the claim, the inability of some of our Libyan travel partners to sleep when camping in and around Kufra suggested that they genuinely believed their accusations![11]

In the aftermath of the February 2012 violence in Kufra, transitional government figures, militia leaders, and Arab residents of Kufra—in a manner comparable to that of the former regime—accused Kufra's Tubu of having external sponsors: specifically, receiving logistical and military support from Chadian and Sudanese Tubu.[12] Although little evidence was provided to substantiate the claim, it played into existing sensitivities and paranoia about foreign interference in Libya's affairs, as well as discriminatory attitudes among Libya's Arab majority toward Africans and dark-skinned Libyans. In such an atmosphere, accusations of this nature by the Arab Zwai also served to discredit their political and commercial competitors, regardless of the accusations' validity. Indeed, post-Qadhafi Libya's fragmented but Arab-dominated security services appeared to display a discriminatory attitude toward the Tubu. The Libya Shield Force—ostensibly under the Ministry of Defense but comprising different regional militias—was accused of intervening on the side of the Zwai in April and June 2012, rather than positioning itself with the neutrality of a national army.[13]

SABHA

Similarly to Kufra, Sabha occupies a traditionally strategic position on trans-Saharan trade networks, with routes flowing west through Ubari and Ghat toward Algeria and south through Qatrun and Murzuq toward Niger. Sabha was originally three oases—Jedid, Qarda, and Hejara—that were consolidated into one settlement in the twentieth century. Today, the unified town has a population of around 200,000 people. It became the administrative capital of the Fezzan region after independence, and it played a formative role in Qadhafi's prerevolutionary development as he met many of his prominent co-conspirators while attending high school there. It also served as the site of Qadhafi's 1977 proclamation of the Socialist People's Libyan Arab Jamahiriyya.[14]

Sabha was not wrested from loyalist control until mid-September 2011 (map 4). However, unlike in the other towns that held out after Tripoli's seizure in August 2011—Bani Walid and Sirte—there was little intense fighting. Murzuq and Qatrun to the south had already been seized by a mix of Tubu (some from Kufra) and Arab militias.[15] The remainder of the southwest, including the towns of Ubari and Ghat, was seized swiftly and fairly uneventfully after Sabha.

Many of Qadhafi's security officials, and their associated tribes, have their roots in Sabha and the surrounding Fezzan region, which largely accounts for the lack of a decisive uprising until the latter stages of the conflict. Masud Abdul-Hafiz was Qadhafi's military chief in Sabha and a fellow member of the Qadhadhifa tribe. The Qadhadhifa, together with the more numerous Maqarha based in Wadi al-Shati (the province around Brak), formed the bedrock of Qadhafi's tribal support base and were well-represented in his security forces.[16] Abdullah al-Senussi, though born in Chad, hails from a portion of the Maqarha based to the north of Sabha.

Other notable tribes from the region, such as the Awlad Suleiman and the Hasawna, were comparatively—though not entirely—marginalized under Qadhafi in favor of the Qadhadhifa and Maqarha. Sabha's short-lived uprising in early June 2011—quelled by loyalist forces—was confined to a district of the city in which the Awlad Suleiman is dominant. However, the lack of significant violence in Sabha during 2011 suggests that power shifts between tribes in the city were less severe than in other towns and regions, where pro- and anti-Qadhafi divides were more pronounced (see Chapter 5). Indeed, elements of the Awlad Suleiman were thought to have had roles in Qadhafi's security apparatus, suggesting a degree of collaboration with the regime, although much less extensive than that of the Qadhadhifa and Maqarha.

Before the Qadhafi era, the Awlad Suleiman had been ascendant in the Fezzan region during the Ottoman Empire, colonial rule, and the monarchy. Abdel-Jalil Saif al-Nasr, who headed the tribe at the time, led the resistance against the Ottoman Empire in the early 1800s.[17] Although the Ottomans were ultimately successful, Saif al-Nasr, whose jihad predated Omar al-Mukhtar's resistance by over 100 years, later became a heroic figure of resistance for Libyan nationalists. With this in mind, it is unsurprising that it was some of the Awlad Suleiman who instigated the attempted June 2011 uprising in Sabha.

This tribal inversion, with tribes powerful under the monarchy and the Ottomans regaining their ascendancy during the uprisings, was characteristic of developments throughout Libya. This marginalization of once-dominant tribes took place across Libya under Qadhafi, and following the 2011 uprisings there was in some respects a partial restoration of the pre-1969 order, aspects of this dynamic have been treated in Chapters 1, 2, and 5. This meant the reassertion of greater Awlad Suleiman influence in Sabha, with the tribe taking control of the local military council after the conflict. It also meant a reversal of fortunes for the Saif al-Nasr family: Abdul-Majid and Mansour Saif al-Nasr were appointed during the uprisings as the NTC member for Sabha and the ambassador to France, respectively. Their father, Ghaith Saif al-Nasr, had served as the governor of the Fezzan region under the monarchy and was hence highly connected to France, which maintained bases and a postcolonial presence in the area.[18]

The violence in Sabha after the 2011 uprisings was primarily between the Awlad Suleiman, the Abu Saif, and the Tubu. The initial spark for the violence remains disputed, but the death of an Abu Saif member at the hands of Tubu carjackers on 26 March appears to have been the cause, with an ensuing reconciliation meeting ending in a firefight.[19] In the five days of fighting that followed, the Tubu district of Sabha called Tayuri, which is also home to some Tuareg, was fired on by the Awlad Suleiman and other Arab communities using tanks and Katyusha rockets, and 140 of the predominantly Tubu inhabitants were killed.[20]

The violence between these ethnic groups was driven by a variety of political and economic concerns, some of which predate the Qadhafi period. The role of the uprisings in briefly transcending old antagonism is revealed by the fact that Mansour Saif al-Nasr issued a statement on *Al-Jazeera* on 22 March 2011 with Musa al-Kuni, who later became the Tuareg's representative on the NTC, and Barka Wardagu, a Tubu leader, to call for their constituencies to unite against Qadhafi.[21]

The roots of the antagonisms between the Tubu and the Awlad Suleiman in Sabha were similar to those in Kufra: struggles for political dominance and control over legal and illicit regional trade. Sabha's role as a nexus of trans-Saharan trade and smuggling routes in the southwest is similar to that of Kufra in the southeast, with the export of subsidized fuel, food, and weapons. Also familiar are the connected accusations that the Tubu are non-Libyans, recipients of foreign backing, and malefactors seeking to undermine Libya's national integrity. Muhammad Shahhat, a member of the local council in Sabha and an Awlad Suleiman member, said, "Not all the Tubu are Libyan. Libyans are welcome here, but outsiders are not. There are rumors around that Tubu have their nation in the south of Libya. We are afraid of a situation similar to what is happening in Mali where the Tuareg are trying to establish their country. The Tubu are not just a tribe, they are a nation."[22]

Although it is credible that the Tubu relied on transnational links to Chad and Niger to secure logistical support, this is secondary to the widely held perception among Libya's broader population that they were reliant on external aid, and by extension, that the Tubu as a group are detrimental to Libya's national cohesion. The response from elements of the Tubu to the violence in Sabha served to fuel suspicions. Mansour resurrected the TFSL, which had been temporarily disbanded after the 2011 uprisings, claiming that he sought to prevent the ethnic cleansing of the Tubu, and furthermore, "...if the need arises, we will demand international intervention and seek to establish a state like South Sudan."[23] Although the comment probably contained an element of political opportunism and the Tubu lack a demographic majority in any major town (perhaps with the exception of Murzuq), the ability and willingness of individuals to make such assertions indicated the fragility of Libya's core in relation to its peripheries.

However, in the aftermath of the 2011 uprisings, it was unclear if any single individual could claim to speak on behalf of Libya's Tubu, especially given the lack of exposure of the community—and indeed all of Libya—to participatory politics. Although Mansour's comments received media attention and he had been an advocate of Tubu rights

before and after the 2011 uprisings, it was unclear whether he had a
meaningful constituency among Libya's Tubu that could grant him a
legitimate mandate to speak on their behalf. The failure to institutionalize minority rights in Libya's reconstituted political system risked
perpetuating the uncertainty over minority representation. This risked
increasing support for secessionism, despite the practical obstacles to
achieving it.

TUAREG AND THE SECURITY FORCES

Similar charges—of being non-Libyan foreign-backed agents with
an impulse for secession—were leveled against Libya's Tuareg population. This attitude among Libya's Arab population reflected the
Tuareg's transnational kinship ties and sub-Saharan origins, but also,
in the context of the 2011 uprisings, the accusation and perception
that the Tuareg had enrolled as mercenaries for Qadhafi.

Unlike the Tubu, the Tuareg were integrated into Qadhafi's political system and security apparatus. At the outset of the 2011 uprisings,
Libya's consul to Mali, Musa al-Kuni, a Tuareg, who then defected in
March 2011 and became a member of the NTC. The governors of the
provinces (*sha'abiyat*) of Ghat and Wadi al-Hayat were also Tuareg;
the former governor of Ghat, Amid Hussain al-Kuni, was accused of
recruiting mercenaries and placed under UN sanctions.[24]

Tuareg were integrated into Libya's security forces from the 1980s
onwards when Qadhafi formed his Islamic Legion. When this project
failed, Tuareg were integrated into the regime's leading security bat-
talions, such as the Khamis Brigade, which led the worst of the Qadhafi
regime's brutal repression during the 2011 uprisings.[25] However, the
extent to which these Tuareg were Libyan is unclear; a significant
Malian and Nigerian component is known to have been present in the
Maghawir brigade based in southwest Libya. Its leader General Ali
Kana fled to Niger in early September 2011.[26]

The role of Tuareg in the Qadhafi regime—and the recruitment
of Tuareg fighters from Libya and neighboring states—led to charge
that the Tuareg *as a community* were "loyalists." However, this is a
reductionist view that belies the complexities of their relationship with
the Qadhafi regime. As others have noted, "[since] the mid 1970s,
the relationship between Gaddafi [*sic*] and the Tuareg has been one of
mutual opportunism rather than shared ideals or common destiny."[27]
As with the Tubu, the Tuareg suffered political disenfranchisement
and socioeconomic marginalization.

Another similarity was Qadhafi's use of the Tuareg as a foreign policy tool, attempting to manipulate them to exert influence in the Sahara region. Qadhafi attempted to mediate various Tuareg rebellions in Mali and Niger, but faced stiff competition from Algeria—his chief competitors for regional influence. Consequently, while Qadhafi clearly put stock in his positive relations with the Tuareg as a prop for his regional influence and claims for pan-African leadership, their official status in Libyan political and commercial life remained marginal. They also suffered uncertainty regarding their claims to Libyan nationality. The lack of national identity documents deprived certain Tuareg of access to social services in a manner comparable to the Tubu.

However, popular perceptions of the Tuareg's role as loyalists and mercenaries are now clearly engrained in elements of the broader Libyan population. These allegations have proven socially divisive, particularly in the northern Saharan town of Ghadames, where there was arguably much substance behind such claims. It is unlikely that the popular identification of the Tuareg as mercenaries for Qadhafi will change anytime soon.

GHADAMES

Ghadames is located in the border region with Algeria and Tunisia. It is much smaller than either Kufra or Sabha with a population of only around 10,000 people. Its traditional role as a trans-Saharan trading post has bestowed it with two UNESCO World Heritage Sites. The more nomadic Tuareg had coexisted for centuries with the broader Arab and Berber population in the sleepy oasis, with Tuareg providing security for caravans heading to and from the Mediterranean.[28]

Although the Arab population of Ghadames rose up in February 2011 against the Qadhafi regime, elements of the local Tuareg population served as the regime's local enforcers, suppressing demonstrators until July and August 2011, when they were either ousted from the town or recognized Qadhafi's imminent defeat and withdrew. Tuareg property in Ghadames was bulldozed or set alight in retaliation, while more was confiscated or stolen. A number of Tuareg were also imprisoned in the town. Many Tuareg from Ghadames and further afield fled to neighboring Algeria at the Debdeb border crossing in fear of further reprisal attacks.[29] Others moved east to the far smaller Libyan town of Derj, with calls for an independent Tuareg town in a location known as Alwaal, which was allegedly promised to Libya's Tuareg by King Idriss ten days before the 1969 revolution.[30]

The retaliatory violence gave rise to a spate of kidnappings of Ghadamsi residents (and at least one foreigner) by young Tuareg men in September 2011.[31] Despite numerous attempts at reconciliation mediated by the interim authorities and traditional community leaders, intermittent periods of violence flared around Ghadames between Tuareg and Arab militias, and forces linked to the state. Although not on the scale of the violence in Kufra and Sabha, it reflected clear and comparable antagonisms between communities that both predated and resulted from the 2011 uprisings. The government's inability to manage the issue led to al-Kuni's resignation from the NTC in response to a bout of violence in May 2012, ostensibly in condemnation of the authorities' treatment of the Tuareg.[32]

In a situation comparable to that of the Tubu, it is unclear who had the mandate to speak on behalf of Libya's Tuareg, notwithstanding the presence of a Tuareg member on the NTC. Although Musa al-Kuni partly adopted this role, it is unclear whether, in the absence of elections and well-developed civil society, he actually had a mandate to speak on behalf of Libya's Tuareg. The failure to protect minority rights in Libya's new political system risks perpetuating this uncertainty and encouraging support for Tuareg independence. Al-Kuni downplayed the secessionist tendencies of Libya's Tuareg, but in late May 2012 he acknowledged the potential for it to emerge if communal relationships failed to be reconciled.[33]

CONCLUSION

In exploring the relationships between Libya's Tubu and Tuareg minorities and the broader Arab and *Amazigh* populations in Libya's south, this chapter has demonstrated that the uprisings in Kufra, Sabha, and Ghadames were each uniquely shaped by specific local sociopolitical dynamics. Although from 1969 to 2010, the Qadhafi regime prevented the outbreak of significant intercommunal violence by repressing the non-Arab population, its constructions of Libyan identity failed to recognize Libya's rich ethnic, linguistic, and cultural heterogeneity.

Libya's interim rulers had a rare opportunity in mid-2012 as the transition period was ending, to engage Libya's diversity and attempt to reconcile intercommunal tensions. However, the weakness of the "center" as seen in the state's lack of institutional capacity and the security forces' fragmentation hamstrung those who sought to seize the opportunity to connect Libya's diverse communities. Although the Tuareg and the Tubu were able to participate in July's elections to the General National Congress (GNC)—albeit in Kufra only after intervention by the Libyan Shield Forces—their disputed claims to nationality are likely to remain unresolved during Libya's constitutional drafting process.

Reconciling relationships damaged by decades of mistrust and antagonism, and exploited by Qadhafi, will be challenging and may have few political champions, given the sensitivities that destructive communal violence has fostered. Participation in politics and Libya's emerging civil society will give the Tuareg and the Tubu opportunities to appoint individuals with mandates to represent them and engage in reconciliation and dialogue on their behalf.

Practical reasons abound for the recognition of minority rights in the south. Intercommunal violence may not single-handedly be able to derail Libya's transition to a more democratic state, but it will certainly curtail socioeconomic development. Some of Libya's oil-producing regions and critical infrastructure are exposed to the violence stemming from the issues discussed in this chapter, which stunts the return of expatriate workers (and tourists) to the south. Disenfranchised minorities with transnational ties risk leading to secessionist bids and providing regional Islamist militant networks, with more receptive audiences and logistical hubs. These factors will not only challenge the reconstitution of the Libyan state but also damage attempts to improve relationships with other regional states. Although Libya's south may be geographically peripheral, the integration of its people into Libyan political life is of central importance for post-Qadhafi Libya.

NOTES

1. For this analysis, the Tuareg and the Tubu will be treated as tribes, not withstanding that their social structures differ from that of Arab tribes in Libya.

2. For further reading on the nature of the *Jamahiriyya system*, please consult Chapter 1; Dirk Vandewalle, *A Modern History of Libya* (Cambridge: Cambridge University Press, 2006); Hanspeter Mattes, "Formal and Informal Authority in Libya since 1969," in Dirk Vandewalle, *Libya since 1969: Qadhafi's Revolution Revisited* (New York: Palgrave Macmillan, 2008); Alison Pargeter, *Libya: The Rise and Fall of Qaddafi* (London: Yale University Press, 2012).

3. For the centrality of anticolonial rhetoric to Qadhafi's foreign policy, see: Alison Pargeter, "The Libyan-Swiss Crisis: A Lesson in Libyan Foreign Policy," *The International Spectator: Italian Journal of International Affairs* 45, no. 3 (2010).

4. The Middle East Media Research Institute, "In Overture to Iran, Qaddafi Declares North Africa Shi'ite and Calls for Establishment of New Fatimid State," Special Dispatch No.1535 (April 2007); Bruce Maddy-Weitzman, *The Berber Identity Movement and the Challenge to North African States* (Austin: University of Texas Press, 2011), 139–43.

5. The World Food Program (WFP) had an office in Kufra that used to distribute humanitarian supplies to Chad and Sudan. However, the office closed during the 2011 conflict, and as of August 2012 the convoys from Kufra had not been restarted.

6. For further details on the violence in Kufra in 2012, see: Jamestown Foundation, *The Battle for Kufra Oasis and the Ongoing War in Libya*, February 2012, http://www.unhcr.org/refworld/docid/4f4b5a502. html; Nicholas Pelham, "Is Libya Cracking Up?" *The New York Review of Books*, June 21, 2012, http://www.nybooks.com/articles/archives /2012/jun/21/libya-cracking/?pagination=false.

7. International Crisis Group, *Divided We Stand: Libya's Enduring Conflicts*, Middle East/North Africa Report 130, Brussels, September 14, 2012, 6–7.

8. Rebecca Murray, "Peace Lost in the Libyan Desert," *Inter Press Service*, April 28, 2012, http://www.ipsnews.net/2012/04/peace-lost-in-the -libyan-desert/

9. United Nations' General Assembly Human Rights Council, "Summary prepared by the Office of the High Commissioner for Human Rights in accordance with paragraph 15 (c) of the annex to Human Rights Council Resolution 5/1—Libyan Arab Jamahiriya," November 1–12, 2010, http://lib.ohchr.org/HRBodies/UPR/Documents/Session9/LY /A_HRC_WG.6_9_LBY_3_Libya.pdf

10. Murray, "Peace Lost in the Libyan Desert."

11. The Tubu were also associated by European explorers with thievery; for examples see Justin Marozzi, *South from Barbary* (London: Flamingo, 2002), 209–11.

12. Imed Lamloum, "Libya Ethnic Conflict Risks Spilling Over Borders," *Agence France-Presse*, March 22, 2012.

13. Dominique Soguel, "12 Killed in South Libya Violence: Tribal Leader," *Agence France Presse*, April 21, 2012; Nicholas Pelham, "Libya's Restive Revolutionaries," *Middle East Research and Information Project*, June 1, 2012, http://merip.org/mero/mero060112.

14. Pargeter, "Libyan-Swiss Crisis," 49–50.

15. "Libya: Toubou Rebels Engage in Battle against Gaddafi," *Ennahar Online*, August 20, 2011, http://www.ennaharonline.com/en/inter national/7088.html; Andrew Beatty "Tribal Call for Help from Libya's Obscure Desert Front," *Agence France Presse*, July 22, 2011, www .afp.com; "Libya Rebels Claim Capture of Sahara Desert Post," *Agence France Presse*, August 25, 2011, www.afp.com.

16. Hanspeter Mattes, "Formal and Informal Authority in Libya since 1969" in *Libya since 1969*; Mattes, *Challenges to Security Sector Governance in*

the Middle East: The Libyan Case, Geneva Centre for the Democratic Control of Armed Forces Working Papers, no. 144, August 2004. The positions held under Qadhafi by those that escaped in September 2011 to Libya's southern neighbors are instructive, for example, Ali Khana was chief of the armed forces in Ubari, and Mahammed Abdul-Karim was commander of the military in Murzuq.

17. Vandewalle, *A Modern History of Libya,* 18.

18. Wolfram Lacher, "Families, Tribes and Cities in the Libyan Revolution," *Middle East Policy* 4 (Winter 2011): 140–54, http://www.mepc.org /journal/middle-east-policy-archives/families-tribes-and-cities-libyan -revolution.

19. International Crisis Group, *Divided We Stand: Libya's Enduring Conflicts,* Middle East/North Africa Report 130, Brussels, September 14, 2012, 7

20. "Libya: Uneasy Calm in Sebha after Clashes," *Integrated Regional Information Networks (IRIN),* May 14, 2012, http://www.unhcr.org /refworld/docid/4fb22af12.html.

21. *Al-Jazeera TV,* March 22, 2011.

22. "Libya: Uneasy Calm."

23. *Al-Jazeera TV,* March 24, 2012.

24. United Nations Security Council Resolution 1973 (2011), http://www .un.org/ga/search/view_doc.asp?symbol=S/RES/1973(2011).

25. Peter Gwin, "Former Qaddafi Mercenaries Describe Fighting in Libyan War," *The Atlantic,* August 31, 2011, http://www.theatlantic.com /international/archive/2011/08/former-qaddafi-mercenaries-describe -fighting-in-libyan-war/244356/?single_page=true.

26. "Libya Conflict: Gaddafi General 'Flees to Niger,'" *BBC,* September 9, 2011, http://www.bbc.co.uk/news/world-africa-14853369.

27. Andy Morgan, "The Causes of the Uprising in Northern Mali," *Think Africa Press,* February 6, 2012, http://thinkafricapress.com/mali/causes -uprising-northern-mali-tuareg.

28. See Marozzi, *South from Barbary.*

29. Anonymous, "Libyan Tuaregs Flee to Algeria: Government Official," *Agence France Presse,* August 31, 2011, www.afp.com.

30. Marcus Rhinelander, "Distrust in Ghadames as Tuareg Dream of New City," *Libya Herald,* April 7, 2012, http://www.libyaherald.com/distru st-in-ghadames-as-tuareg-dream-of-a-new-city/.

31. Justin Marozzi, "This Is It: A Bullet to My Head and a Desert Grave," *The Times,* September 18, 2011, http://www.thesundaytimes.co.uk/sto /newsreview/features/article777763.ece.

32. "Koni Resigns from NTC over Tuareg Treatment in Ghadames: Report," *Libya Herald,* May 22, 2012, http://www.libyaherald.com /2012/05/22/konu-resigns-from-ntc-over-tuareg-treatment-in-ghadames -report/.

33. *Al-Jazeera TV,* Doha, Qatar, Arabic Broadcast at 21:30 GMT on March 24, 2012.

7

ISLAMISTS

Noman Benotman, Jason Pack,
and James Brandon

INTRODUCTION

To the untrained eye, Libyan "Islamists"[1] appeared to function as a coherent group playing a coordinated role throughout the entire 2011 uprisings. In reality, however, there was no unified Islamist movement in Libya, but rather multiple competing factions which pursued entirely disconnected policies. Frequently at cross purposes to one another, Islamists cannot be described as catalysts for the revolution. Nonetheless, they became increasingly prominent as the military action against Qadhafi wore on; their power crested in the aftermath of the fall of Tripoli, when Islamists associated with the Libyan Islamic Fighting Group (LIFG) appeared to be in control of the newly liberated capital. Yet, after that moment, the actual power of both the most theologically radical and the most militarily significant Islamist groups precipitously waned. These groups—epitomized by the Salafists and the LIFG, respectively—suffered a great defeat at the ballot box during the 7 July 2012 elections, while the more "moderate" Islamists, such as that of the Brotherhood, successfully integrated themselves into the larger Libyan political framework, albeit with a lackluster performance at the ballot box.

Simultaneous to an apparent "decline" of the Islamists as political actors in their own right,[2] all the main political currents inside Libya—from the so-called Liberals, to regional militiamen, to Western-trained technocrats—came to absorb aspects of a moderate Islamist rhetoric, such that all strands of Islamism except that of the Salafists were no longer on the fringes of Libyan political life. This process of accommodation was bidirectional. After the revolution, as non-Islamist actors adopted moderate Islamist rhetoric, most Islamist actors also competed to rapidly enter the mainstream political consensus, accepting the democratic transition process as laid out by the NTC. The changing role of Islam in the Libyan political process as a result of the uprisings has been treated in detail in Chapter 2. Therefore, this chapter is not so much concerned with the role of Islam in Libyan society or even Islamist rhetoric in post-Qadhafi Libya, but rather with the role Islamists played as political, social, and military agents during the uprisings and in their aftermath (see note 1).

This approach reveals that Islamists (rather than Islam or any kind of vague and diffuse Islamic rhetoric) were important but not preponderant actors in the Libyan revolution. We can certainly refer to separate discrete "uprisings" taking place among different Islamist currents as part of the larger tapestry of the 2011 uprisings. Yet, it bears repeating that the precise contours of the Islamists' multifaceted roles have been heretofore obscured by Western and Arab media.

To disentangle fact from fiction, it is also necessary to understand why Islamists received such disproportionate media prominence during the revolution (at the expense of tribal, regional, technocratic, and civil society actors who were actually more important in toppling Qadhafi), why their role was so misrepresented, and why disparate Islamist groups were frequently portrayed as a monolith. Firstly, from the start of the uprisings, Colonel Qadhafi himself promoted the idea that Islamists and non-Libyan jihadists were the central players in the revolt and that they acted in unison.[3] Secondly, many Libyan Islamists sought to depict themselves as the key drivers of anti-Qadhafi activity. Thirdly, this self-representation was accepted without much factual basis and even cleverly reinforced by particular media outlets, such as the Qatari-owned *Al-Jazeera*, which had a vested interest in portraying Islamists as a central unified force in the uprisings. For example, their coverage exaggerated the military importance of the Islamist Tripoli Military Council, turning its leader Abdul-Hakim Bilhajj into an international media figure, while militarily more relevant non-Islamist commanders from Misrata, Zintan, and Souq al-Jum'a were not given airtime and, hence, remained unknown. Lastly, Western media frequently sensationalized the Libyan revolution by scaremongering about the role of a unified Islamist movement as potential "hijackers" of the popular uprisings, which had supposedly begun among the non-Islamist and tech-savvy youth. These four factors—as well as the clear influence of Islamists in post-Qadhafi Libya—help explain why Islamists were often mistakenly referred to as the preeminent force during the revolution.

Putting these four misunderstandings aside, in reality, Islamists played a more complex, and often much murkier, part. The aim of this chapter is to trace the role played by the main currents of Islamist actors in Libya during the 2011 uprisings, and then to show how their position in post-Qadhafi Libya derives from their revolutionary role. In so doing, it will be shown that each Islamist current acted in accordance with its own unique political, ideological, and social tendencies, as well as its unique positioning under Qadhafi.

To more accurately describe the role of Islamists in recent Libyan history, this chapter will proceed chronologically by giving a brief history of four key Islamist movements that sought to oppose Qadhafi from the 1970s onward: *Hizb al-Tahrir*, the Muslim Brotherhood, Wahhabi-influenced Salafists, and the Libyan Islamic Fighting Group (LIFG). It will be explained how and why the first group was quickly crushed, while the others negotiated with the regime, securing their survival in return for abandoning violent opposition. Importantly, as will be shown, the co-optation of the Brotherhood and the LIFG—which accelerated from 2006 onward—meant that at the start of the uprisings, the main currents of Islamism inside Libya were suffering from organizational disarray and were actually lending tacit support to the Qadhafi regime, which explains their often initially sluggish response to the revolution.

Therefore, as in Egypt and Tunisia, Islamists did not catalyze the Libyan uprisings, although they gradually came to assume an undeniably important role. Although not demonstrable, it is a reasonable assumption that the uprisings would have successfully overthrown Qadhafi without any Islamist participation. The multifaceted Islamist role transpired in more complex ways than is usually imagined, with sharp distinctions among the three main *organized* groups present at the time: the LIFG's impact was primarily on the battlefield, the Muslim Brotherhood's on Libyan society and the political process, and that of the Salafists focused on fostering and enforcing their social and religious doctrines.

Islamists in Libya Prior to the 2011 Uprisings

The role of Islamists and the use of Islamic references by a wide range of actors in the 2011 Libyan uprisings can be partly explained by the religious, social, and political environment in Libya prior to the uprisings. Islam had been adopted as a legitimizing tool both by the Qadhafi regime and by a wide range of opposition forces throughout recent decades. The role of Islam within the Libyan social fabric and in legitimating rule in Libya as well as the importance of Islamic rhetoric for mobilization against Qadhafi have been treated at length in Chapter 2. Therefore, this section seeks to present the different forms of the Islamist challenge to Qadhafi and their evolution over time— along the way uncovering how these developments explain the eventual role that Islamists played in the uprisings and their aftermath.

Upon taking power in 1969, the new Revolutionary Command Council's espoused Nasserist slogans and made references to the traditional Ba'thist slogan of "Unity, Socialism, and Freedom." However, Qadhafi quickly augmented these secular constructions with his own idiosyncratic religious and political beliefs.[4] These combined Nasserite pan-Arabism with third world internationalism and Qadhafi's own distinct religious conceptions.[5]

The consequences of this hybrid, Islamically tinged socialist philosophy became evident soon after Qadhafi's seizure of power when the Revolutionary Command Council banned alcohol, gambling, and prostitution—all of which had been legal under King Idriss. At the same time, Qadhafi attacked forms of Islam and certain Islamic actors that he felt could pose a political threat.[6] In May 1975, he banned Libya's ulama from commenting on politics and abolished the position of Grand Mufti. In 1980, Shaykh al-Bishti, the outspoken imam of Jami'a al-Qasr, a prominent mosque in Tripoli, was arrested in his mosque and then murdered.[7] Likewise, in 1984, Qadhafi ordered the destruction of the tomb of Sayyid Muhammad ibn Ali al-Sanussi, the founder of the Sanussi Order—a powerful symbol of King Idriss al-Sanussi's regime and of opposition to Qadhafi.[8]

Hizb al-Tahrir in Libya

While Qadhafi sought to eliminate political threats from Libya's traditional religious establishment and to present himself as an "Islamic" leader, he also faced a considerable challenge from Islamist organizations which were able to exploit the country's lack of institutions or of a credible religious leadership. One of the most prominent early Islamist challenges to Qadhafi came from *Hizb al-Tahrir* (The Party of Liberation) a global organization of Palestinian origin that aimed to create a caliphate through primarily nonviolent means.[9] Although the group's operations in Libya were never large, during the 1970s, *Hizb al-Tahrir* (HT) was well-organized, determined, and firmly convinced of the righteousness of its message. Having initially sought to follow its usual strategy of radicalizing high-ranking military officers with the hopes of fostering a bloodless pro-HT coup, in September 1978, the party sent emissaries to meet Qadhafi in an attempt to convince him to reject his *Green Book* and to adopt HT's ideology instead. According to an official account by HT, during a four-hour face-to-face meeting, the party's delegates delivered a comprehensive criticism of Qadhafi's ideology. They gave him a specially produced communiqué which called on him to "abandon your *Green Book*...[and] to hand over to us the authority so as to declare the establishment of the Khilafah."[10]

Unfortunately for HT, but quite predictably, this open challenge had the opposite of the intended effect. The meeting convinced Qadhafi that the group posed a direct ideological and political threat. As HT later related, "After the distribution of the communiqué, Gadaffi [*sic*] ordered his henchmen to publicly hang the members of *Hizb al-Tahrir* in their university campuses."[11] This marked the start of a renewed struggle between the group and Qadhafi—marked by the murder of Libyan HT members abroad. Most notably, Mohammed Ramadan, a prominent BBC Arabic employee and HT member, was killed outside London's Regents Park Mosque in 1980.[12] Unsurprisingly, HT's Libyan followers, principally urban academics and intellectuals, were no match for the Libyan state, and soon *Hizb al-Tahrir* ceased to have any viable presence inside Libya.

HT's brief threat to Qadhafi affected how all subsequent Islamist challengers would behave. They learned from its mistake of confronting the regime too quickly. Subsequent Islamist movements would gradually build their organizations (whether militarily or socially) before presenting a direct challenge to Qadhafi. They also learned the value of clandestine networks, frequently adopting Leninist-style cell structures. Additionally, the HT episode caused Islamist actors to mistrust non-Islamist forces and avoid collaboration even on shared goals. During the 2011 uprisings, one could interpret the Islamists' insistence on maintaining completely separate command structures rather than interfacing with other anti-Qadhafi forces as an indirect consequence of the HT episode.

The Muslim Brotherhood

Following in the footsteps of his hero Gamal Abdul-Nasser, Qadhafi also identified the Muslim Brotherhood as a key threat, both organizationally and ideologically. Unlike many regional leaders, Qadhafi spoke out against the Muslim Brotherhood directly and even denounced Sayyid Qutb, their intellectual lodestar. This was accompanied by security operations against high-level Brotherhood members in Libya. Since the Brotherhood operated a top-down system, the elimination of its leaders effectively meant a reduction of its operational capabilities in Libya, although it failed to eliminate their adherents.

Nevertheless, the ideas of the Muslim Brotherhood continued to flow into Libya, particularly through the influx of Palestinian and Egyptian teachers and university professors, many of whom were members of the Brotherhood. For example, Dr. Muhammad Morsi, a lifelong Muslim Brotherhood member and now the president of Egypt, worked as a professor at Al-Fateh (now Tripoli) University in Tripoli between 1982 and 1985.[13] Some of these foreign Brotherhood activists were arrested and others executed. Yet, the regime was unable to entirely stop the flow of Brotherhood literature into the country.

Additionally, Libyans studying abroad—mostly on graduate courses in engineering and science in the West—were easily recruited into the Brotherhood overseas. This was a result of the Brotherhood's clever policy since the early 1960s of using university Islamic societies and prayer rooms, particularly in the United Kingdom and the United States, as vehicles for recruiting visiting Muslim students. However, these efforts actually led to the transient formation of an independent Libyan Muslim Brotherhood grouping, which first rejected the international Brotherhood's Egypt-based leadership and later was eradicated by Qadhafi:

> By the late 1970s a number of Libyans in the UK and US had decided that they wanted to set up their own Libyan Ikhwani [i.e. Brotherhood] organisation. They included Ashur Shamis [later co-founder of the National Front for the Salvation of Libya (NFSL)] and Mohamed al-Magrief [later first President of the Libyan General National Congress]…in 1984 [after putting down organizational roots in Libya] the group [in coordination with the (NFSL)] launched a disastrous attack on Colonel Qadhafi's Bab al-Aziziya barracks in Tripoli, which finished it off as a credible force.[14]

Therefore the "independent" Libyan Brotherhood group acted like *Hizb al-Tahrir* and suffered the same consequences. On the other hand, remaining Brotherhood figures inside Libya adopted a gradual social approach while deciding to operate in a clandestine fashion with strong connections to Brotherhood currents throughout the Arab World.

In addition to this process, from the mid-1990s onward, the influence of the international Brotherhood's ideas increased drastically inside Libya, partly as a result of Qatar's promotion of the group's ideology via *Al-Jazeera* and partly because of the increasing popularity of well-known Muslim Brotherhood websites, often linked to Yusuf al-Qaradawi.[15] Some analysts have asserted that during the 1980s and 1990s the Brotherhood developed a range of underground cells ready to spring into action to overthrow the Qadhafi regime, yet this cannot be proven.[16]

From 2005, however, the Muslim Brotherhood had changed tack and developed a working relationship with the regime, by vocally praising Saif al-Islam's reformist efforts and exchanging active opposition for its new role of tacitly policing Libyan Islam on behalf of the state. For instance, Imad al-Banani, the exiled former leader of the Libyan Muslim Brotherhood, had by the time of the 2011 uprisings reconciled with Saif and returned to live in Libya.[17] Likewise, by early 2011, Ali Sallabi, the Muslim Brotherhood–influenced and Doha-based cleric, had become involved with the Qadhafis, notably working with them to persuade the LIFG to abandon violence and recognize the regime. Sallabi was also a board member of the Qadhafi International Charitable Foundation; he had also been appointed as "Islamic advisor" to the committee formed by Saif al-Islam to develop a reformist constitution as part of his *Libya al-Ghad* pledge.[18] Paradoxically, this position had given Sallabi a significant public profile and Islamic legitimacy in Libya, where he had previously been unknown. Similarly, international elements of the Brotherhood had begun accepting money from the Qadhafi family in return for not criticizing it, with Libya, for instance, funding the influential UK-based, pro-Brotherhood TV channel *al-Hiwar*, run by prominent Hamas supporter Azzam al-Tamimi.

Wahhabism and Salafism in Libya

Throughout the 1970s, Qadhafi also faced a rising challenge from a loosely organized Saudi-inspired Wahhabi movement.[19] Unlike *Hizb al-Tahrir* or the Muslim Brotherhood—both organizations with clear ambitions to directly take political power in Libya—Wahhabism posed a subtler, longer-term threat to Qadhafi. Essentially, adherence to Wahhabi doctrines necessitated the rejection of Qadhafi's rule as "un-Islamic" and his idiosyncratic form of Islam as heretical.

Qadhafi saw the Saudi government's global sponsorship of Wahhabism—and the broader current with which it is associated, Salafism[20]—as a direct threat to his domestic and international ambitions. Increasing Saudi regional influence directly challenged Qadhafi's plans to combat religious conservatism in Libya and to push his anti-colonial agenda in Africa and the Middle East. Saudi Arabia was a pro-Western power that supported the US and the Middle Eastern status quo while denouncing socialism as atheistic. Moreover, the Saudi religious establishment—doubtless partly at the behest of the monarchy—directly spoke against Qadhafi. For instance, Saudi Arabia's Council of Senior Ulama issued a fatwa against him in 1980,[21] and King Khalid labeled him "a spearhead against Islam."[22] Additionally, the Saudi program of overseas proselytizing also threatened Qadhafi's ambitions, with Saudi charitable largesse in places like Africa directly undermining his own political-religious outreach through the World Islamic Call (*Da'wa*) Society.

Unlike the Muslim Brotherhood and *Hizb al-Tahrir*, the spread of Wahhabism manifested itself less through political activism than through cultural and social changes. Accordingly, beards and Saudi-style white *thawb* and *ghutra* for men, and hijab and conservative comportment for women, became increasingly common in Libya during the late 1980s and 1990s, including in professional environments and in previously Westernized university campuses. Demands for greater official recognition of religion followed. For example, students demanded more space in universities to be allocated for prayers and mosques, and began attending *fajr* prayers en masse.[23]

Some Wahhabi practices led to considerable social tensions. One example was the trend for followers of *al-Sahwa al-Islamiyya*—the Saudi-led "Islamic Awakening" movement that was tied to world Salafism—to attempt to prohibit the use of traditional Islamic prayer beads (*misbahah*), which they regarded as a religious innovation (*bid'a*).[24] When this movement spread to Libya, young men confiscated prayer beads from older men and destroyed them. In the tense political climate of Qadhafi's Libya, such activities often developed into an unspoken contest over social space, control over expressions of Islam, and acceptable standards of public behavior. Indeed, as in other countries such as Egypt, the spread of Salafism ultimately entailed an indirect dispute over the legitimacy of an "Arab Nationalist regime" to govern. For instance, the Salafis asserted that only they possessed the right to enforce "correct" behavior and determine legitimate governance, a clear challenge to the government, even if a more subtle one than that posed by HT or the Brotherhood.

In response to the rising visibility of Wahhabism and the renegade Salafist Mohamed Fahkih's suicidal 1989 jihad against the Qadhafi regime,[25] the Libyan authorities launched campaigns against beards and hijabs, which were seen as symbols of Saudi influence and of the rejection of Qadhafi's "modernizing" ideology; this led to the imprisonment of bearded men and the expulsion of women in *niqab* from universities.[26]

However, since suicidal militants like Fahkih were rare and Salafism was largely a leaderless social movement, inspired more by changes in worldwide Islamic practice and by global social trends than by charismatic local figures, it often escaped government control. In addition, the overt repression of displays of religious piety could not easily be reconciled with Qadhafi's own very public commitment to Islam, which he identified as a form of anti-Western resistance.[27] Qadhafi's attempts to control Salafism/Wahhabism were therefore less effective than his campaigns against more direct political threats. In short, the mosque became the one place in Libyan society where the Qadhafi regime could not crush all dissent or eliminate preexisting social networks.

In parallel to this indirect social resistance to the regime and the status quo, overtly subversive activities also took place, inspired both by the mainstream *Sahwa* movement and by more confrontational preachers in Libya and abroad. For example, cassettes of Wahhabi speakers were circulated among students; these typically called for Muslim societies to be entirely re-aligned upon Saudi-influenced "Islamic" principles. Abdul-Aziz bin Baz, Muhammad al-Albani, and Muhammad ibn al-Uthaymin were the most popular, followed by Alexandrian Salafis, particularly, Muhammad Ismail al-Muqaddam. Travel to Saudi Arabia also gave Libyans the chance to witness evolving trends in Islamic practice—from which they were normally cut off due to the Qadhafi's blackout censorship of foreign media, books, and newspapers. This included, for example, the growing pan-Arab movement to support and arm the Afghan resistance following the 1979 Soviet invasion.

Rising support for Wahhabism, Salafism, the Saudi *Sahwa* movement, and certain forms of passive resistance to the regime, coincided with an increase in overt antiregime activism in Libyan universities, even though university campuses were under the direct control of key regime enforcers from Libya's Revolutionary Committees Movement (for more on their role in imposing Qadhafi doctrine on the populace, consult Chapter 1). During the mid-1970s, campus tensions escalated, with both Islamist and communist ideas abounding, leading to a quasi-uprising in January 1976 at the University of Benghazi in which several students were killed. This was followed by a broader purge of opposition activists from Libyan universities in April 1976. On the first anniversary of the 1976 events, two students previously imprisoned over the unrest were executed in Benghazi's main square. This effectively ended overt opposition to the regime at Libyan campuses during this period.

By the early 1980s, these trends were beginning to have important consequences. The weakening of Libya's traditional religious institutions had created a leadership vacuum. Furthermore, secular political groups had also been destroyed along with democrats, liberals, nationalist, socialists, communists, and independent trade unions; they were all virtually wiped out. Despite these purges, the Muslim Brotherhood and HT still had political ambitions in Libya but had been drastically weakened by the late-1970s and were unable to operate openly. *Sahwa*-inspired movements were popular in the 1980s and were more difficult for the regime to repress because passive opposition to the regime, religiously expressed, could not easily be disentangled from increased Islamic piety, which the Qadhafi regime itself favored and actively promoted, making such grassroots evangelism (*da'wa*) almost impossible to eradicate.

With all forms of civil society activity utterly dominated by pro-Qadhafi bodies and in the absence of effective opposition within Libya, it was perhaps unsurprising that Libyan opposition activists would begin to look outside the country and to more radical ideologies for solutions. As they spread in the 1970s and 80s, Wahhabism and the *Sahwa* prepared their adherents to absorb the larger corpus of Salafist thought from the late 1980s onward. This process was facilitated by the rise of Salafi-jihadism in Egypt and by the Soviet invasion of Afghanistan, with dramatic consequences. This, too, went hand-in-hand with the decline of non-Islamist forms of political opposition across the Arab world, with communist, socialist and secular democratic movements either being crushed, dismissed as Western innovations, or seeking forms of accommodation with various incumbent regimes, a process which progressively left Islamism as the most credible remaining form of opposition.

The Libyan Islamic Fighting Group

From the early 1980s, hundreds of young Libyan men frustrated by the lack of political, economic, and social opportunities in Libya, traveled to Afghanistan to fight the Soviet occupation. These young men were usually highly idealistic: fighting in the path of God (*Sabil Allah*) by helping a fellow Muslim people fight a war of self-defense against a colonialist, and explicitly atheistic invader, as well as answering the call to install an Islamic form of governance.[28] Following the Soviet retreat from the country in 1989, a number of Libyan jihadists formed the *Saraya al-Mujahidin* (Mujahidin Brigades) later to be renamed Libyan Islamic Fighting Group (LIFG), which aimed to depose Qadhafi and establish an Islamic state in Libya through force.[29] Although many of its members returned to Libya, it maintained training centers and outposts abroad. The LIFG, both in an official capacity and through its individual members, made common cause with a range of other revolutionary groups, ranging from quasi-nationalist groups, such as Laskhar-e-Taiba of Pakistan, to global pan-Islamic groups, such as al-Qaeda.

Throughout the 1990s, the LIFG was strongest in areas that were traditionally opposed to Qadhafi—such as the whole Eastern part of the country (Cyrenaica). There it tapped into Islamist and Salafist networks that had escaped Qadhafi's repression at the end of the 1980s. Until 1995, it remained largely hidden from the regime's security services as it grew in strength and prepared itself to overthrow Qadhafi.

However due to a tactical error, the LIFG was forced into battle before it was ready. After a Benghazi cell was randomly discovered in 1995, the regime brutally repressed not only suspected Islamists but all of Cyrenaica. This provoked the LIFG into waging a low-scale guerrilla war—leading to the declaration of a state of emergency and military rule throughout all of eastern Libya. LIFG members assassinated senior security officials and even attempted to assassinate Qadhafi, throwing a grenade at his motorcade when he visited the desert town of Brak in Wadi Shati. For its part, the regime used air strikes and rocket launchers to bomb LIFG hideouts while giving the Revolutionary Committees Movement free-rein to engage in collective punishment against the towns where the fighters came from.[30]

By the late 1990s, the LIFG had failed to achieve its goals and had been ejected from its bases in Cyrenaica, as well as in Pakistan and the Sudan. Nonetheless, it remained committed to the principle of revolutionary jihad, yet similarly to other jihadist movements the group was beginning to reassess its strategy. In 1997, the Egyptian group *al-Gama'a al-Islamiyya*—one of the earliest Salafi groups to adopt jihadist violence—unilaterally launched "The Initiative for Stopping Violence" (*mubadarat waqf al-'unf*) from prison. This was swiftly and publicly rejected by other Arab jihadist groups.[31] The LIFG published a *fatwa* (decree) by Abdul-Mundar al-Sa'adi in the LIFG's *al-Fajr* monthly magazine denouncing the initiative as Islamically impermissible because it involved the recognition of an apostate regime and the concomitant abandonment of jihad against the Egyptian state, which the LIFG understood as *fard al-'ayn*—an individual duty for all Muslims.[32] Later in 1999, when the Egyptian government officially responded to *al-Gama'a*'s initiative, the LIFG again issued another official statement rejecting the initiative.[33] The rejection of the Egyptian nonviolence initiative reflected concern within jihadist circles—including within the LIFG—that the initiative would undermine global jihadist ideology and especially its belief in physical jihad as the sole viable instrument of change in the Middle East and North Africa. The LIFG held firmly to this conclusion partly because of the failure of the MB, HT, and Libyan followers of the *Sahwa* movement to achieve any meaningful results through more gradualist approaches.

Despite taking a hard line on *al-Gama'a al-Islamiyya*'s antijihad sentiment in the years that followed, the LIFG repeatedly rejected Osama bin Laden's direct requests to both assist al-Qaeda's global campaign and to merge the group into al-Qaeda, as Ayman al-Zawahiri's Egyptian *al-Jihad* group had done. Rather, the LIFG remained focused on its sole goal of overthrowing Colonel Qadhafi and establishing an Islamic state in Libya. Prior to the 9/11 attacks, LIFG leaders told bin Laden that any al-Qaeda attack on the United States from Afghanistan would be Islamically illegitimate, given the lack of express permission from Mullah Omar, the head of the Islamic Emirate of Afghanistan, whom LIFG members generally held in high regard.[34] Following the US-led attack on Afghanistan in late 2001, the LIFG ordered all its members to leave Afghanistan. Within the LIFG, this was regarded as a grave setback; the leadership had been in the process of using Afghanistan to rebuild the movement while also establishing a network of training camps in the country and enjoying a good working relationship with Mullah Omar. After the US invasion, the LIFG's leaders and followers scattered to Iran, Pakistan, and remote areas in Afghanistan, as well as even further afield to China and Indonesia.

Saif al-Islam al-Qadhafi and the LIFG Reconciliation Program

One unexpected result of 9/11 was to facilitate the first contact between the LIFG and Saif al-Islam Qadhafi. In the aftermath of the attacks, Saif al-Islam arranged—with the help of the United States and Pakistan—the transport of many Arabs and their families from Afghanistan to Libya. Although all evacuated Arabs went through security checks, Saif al-Islam's NGO (The Qadhafi International Charitable Foundation) also assisted jihadists, both from the LIFG and from other groups, to leave Afghanistan. This initiative by the Qadhafi Foundation was controversial within the LIFG as it was seen as "pro-Western," while at the same time it did impress some of its jihadist beneficiaries who began to question some of their negative perceptions of the regime.[35]

These events took place at a time when the LIFG's position was weak and while Qadhafi was in the process of stabilizing his regime by portraying himself as an ally of the West, which was uniquely well positioned to provide counterterrorism assistance.[36] This new Libyan alliance with the West had a direct impact on the LIFG. The LIFG's activities in the West became much more difficult, the group was added to various terrorist lists, and many members were arrested and imprisoned in the United Kingdom, a country that—along with Taliban-ruled Afghanistan—had provided the group with its main safe haven. The group was also weaker financially, as its fundraising activities were curtailed by a wide range of post-9/11 international initiatives. In 2004, the LIFG's most important figures, Abdul-Hakim Bilhajj and Abu Mundir al-Saadi, were arrested and rendered to Tripoli.[37] Bilhajj is currently pursuing legal proceedings against the British government and its officials—particularly former British foreign secretary Jack Straw and former head of MI6, the respected Arabist and Libya expert Sir Mark Allen, for their involvement in his supposedly illegal rendition to Libya. Other more junior LIFG figures were also affected by this new closeness with the West, for instance, Khalid Sharif, who was detained in Bagram airbase in Afghanistan for two years, and Sufian Bin Gumo, known in the media as "Bin Laden's driver," who was imprisoned in Guantanamo Bay.

Simultaneously, however, internal developments in Libya opened new opportunities to the group. From approximately 2005 onward, Saif al-Islam Qadhafi began to emerge as the leading reformer within the regime, perhaps as part of a strategy to outflank his brothers in the struggle for succession. He sought to restore Libya's relations with the West while gradually introducing economic reforms that he hoped would modernize Libya and attract foreign direct investment, while also perpetuating the Qadhafi family's dominance. Additionally, he knew he could rely on certain global business interests to support him against his brothers. It appears that as part of this "reform program," Saif attempted to mitigate the regime's ongoing crackdown on Islamists and to turn these "pardoned Islamists" into strategic assets in his quest for the succession.[38] Paradoxically, Saif looked to both extreme ends of the Libyan political spectrum, jihadists and Western-educated secular elites, to support him against his brother Mu'tasim Billah, who sought to attain power by protecting the interests of the powerful security services, Qadhafi-aligned tribesmen, the Revolutionary Committees Movement, and mid-level bureaucrats scared of change.

In 2007, as part of his wider "reform" process, Saif initiated a reconciliation process with the LIFG's members in prison. This led to the release of more than 1000 Islamists of whom over 200 were LIFG members. The LIFG's imprisoned leaders also began work on a book of refutations (*muraja'at*), the first draft of which was completed in August 2009. It sought to prove that violent jihad was actually at odds with orthodox Islamic theology by using traditional exegetical practices of the sacred texts. The publication of this *dirasaat al-tashihiyya fi mafaahim al-jihad wal-hisba wal-hukum 'ala al-nas* (Corrective Studies in the Concepts of Jihad, Hisba, and Judgment of People) in March 2010, facilitated the group's formal public renunciation of jihadist revolutionary violence. This renunciation occasioned the release of the imprisoned LIFG *shura* (advisory) council members, Abdul-Hakim Bilhajj (aka Abdullah Sadiq), Sami Saadi (aka Abdul-Mundir al-Sa'adi), and the group's deputy leader Khalid Sharif (Abu Hazim). Others sympathetic to the cause, but who were not members of the LIFG, such as Salafists, were also released in waves, overseen by Abdullah Senussi, the onetime head of Libya's ruthless internal security service. Senussi was one of Colonel Qadhafi's most trusted confidants, his brother-in-law, and a prominent Maqarha tribesman. He is also widely accused of the Abu Salim prison massacre.[39]

Senussi and other security types were often in disagreement with Qadhafi's closest confidants over the releases. In March 2010, the then head of internal security Tuhami Khalid strongly opposed the release of Bilhajj, Al-Sa'adi, and Abu Hazim. He was overruled by the Qadhafi family. Similarly, the security services opposed the publication of the LIFG's *muraja'at*, which they believed would increase the group's profile and enhance the status of its leaders as religious scholars. In the long term they were correct, while the political benefits accrued by the Qadhafi family were only short term.

An unintended consequence of the LIFG reconciliation program was to make the "LIFG brand" well known in Libya and to turn its leaders into household names.[40] Prior to the reconciliation program, many Libyans did not know the name of the LIFG or its leaders—they often referred to the group as *Al-Sunna* ("the people of tradition," a comment on the seemingly excessive religiosity of its members).[41] The process of familiarizing Libyans with the LIFG and its leaders was further boosted through the pan-Arab media such as *Al-Jazeera*, *al-Hiwar*, and *al-Hayat*, which covered the group extensively, including running multiple interviews with key former members, as did Western outlets such as *CNN*.[42] The overall effect was to present the LIFG as a viable opposition force, one with which the Qadhafi regime was negotiating and seeking to make an accommodation, something that had been unheard of in Libya. Although other opposition groups such as the NFSL were already well known, the unprecedented "reconciliation" gave the LIFG instant credibility at a critical moment when the regime was initiating reforms, and a transition period was potentially around the corner as Qadhafi aged.

Following the releases, the LIFG also gained the freedom to operate abroad, which it had been denied in the wake of 9/11. For example, the European security services judged that the LIFG no longer posed a threat to European national security. This led to a relaxation of restrictions, enabling the group's members to unfreeze accounts and to travel and communicate more freely. This also enabled the group to reestablish communications with its scattered members, allowing, for instance, LIFG members outside Libya to phone colleagues inside Libya to discuss the group's activities, particularly in the context of the reconciliation process, a degree of freedom that had never been granted to a group like the NFSL. Although such calls were still subject to monitoring by the security services and no controversial issues could be discussed, these conversations nonetheless helped the group to regain some of its old cohesion and to reestablish personal links, even if the group remained short of money and with low membership numbers.[43]

These positive developments for the group were offset by the mysterious death in prison of Ibn al-Shaykh al-Libi (not to be confused with Abu al-Yahya al-Libi who was higher up in the same organization) in May 2009. Ibn al-Shaykh al-Libi was a senior al-Qaeda leader who had been arrested in Pakistan and was then tortured and interrogated in various Arab countries before being rendered to Libya. Although he had never been part of the LIFG and had not been part of the reconciliation process, his death—purportedly by suicide—in Abu Salim prison revived old tensions and suspicions between Islamists and the security services. Senior LIFG members believed the security services may have killed him to try to derail the reconciliation process—which they were known to oppose but could only indirectly sabotage for risk of being accused of countermanding the Qadhafis' wishes. Ibn al-Shaykh al-Libi's death served to remind LIFG members and other Islamists of the security services' capability for brutality and extrajudicial killing, thus undermining their loyalty to the regime and the reconciliation.

Furthermore, parts of the LIFG in the United Kingdom and Switzerland had by this time become semi-independent of the main organization in Libya. Despite their respect for the group's leadership, these branches continued to regard the Qadhafi regime as an apostate government and rejected all Saif's initiatives. By 2009, they had formed the Libyan Islamic Movement for Change (*al-haraka al-islamiyya al-libiyya lil-taghayr*), which operated mainly in exile (and would later during the uprisings become the successor organization of the whole LIFG and emerge as a political force in post-Qadhafi Libya.) The creation of this movement was opposed by LIFG leaders inside Libya, including Abdul-Hakim Bilhajj, who feared it would jeopardize the whole reconciliation process. This demonstrated that the reconciliation program was not universally supported, even within the broader LIFG itself, and that the group's members were continually confronted with the possibility of returning to an oppositional stance against the regime.

Despite the tensions caused by al-Libi's death and the differences of opinion present within the LIFG, the group's fortunes continued to improve in February 2011. The final wave of prescheduled releases of LIFG prisoners occurred on 16 February 2011, which included senior LIFG members, such as Abdul-Wahhab al-Qaid (aka Abu Idris)—the older brother of Abu Yahya al-Libi who was also a *shura* council LIFG member and had been in prison since 1996. Following this wave of releases, only a few nonaligned Islamists and jihadists remained in Libya's prisons, together with lower-level political prisoners, such as members of the public who had made antiregime statements—on blogs or Facebook for example.[44]

On 15 February 2011, the eve of the final LIFG release, a spontaneous uprising had broken out in Benghazi. The timing of this snowballing revolt was highly fortuitous for the LIFG, even though the group remained low in membership and effectively bankrupt. First, the revolt occurred when all LIFG members were out of prison and hence available to take up arms, as well as freeing the group to act without fearing reprisals against their imprisoned colleagues. Second, due to the reconciliation program from 2007 onward, the organization and its leaders were known to the Libyan people, and the group had begun reestablishing its old organization and communication networks both in Libya and abroad. Third, the LIFG refutations, widely publicized on media outlets such as *CNN*, had succeeded in finally disassociating the LIFG from al-Qaeda and particularly from al-Qaeda's vision of global jihad. This global recognition allowed for the group to become a legitimate political interlocutor with foreign governments such as Qatar. This unique combination of factors would prove to be critical in the months ahead.

THE 2011 UPRISINGS

In the weeks before the uprisings began, various Facebook groups were set up to call for a Libyan revolution, in emulation of the Egyptian and

Tunisian revolutions. Some groups called for an uprising in downtown Benghazi on 17 February to commemorate the five-year anniversary of the anti-cartoon protests.[45] In the face of this threat, the Libyan regime was uncertain how to respond, torn between employing its traditional tactics involving massive use of repressive force or alternatively adopting a novel and more conciliatory approach in line with Saif al-Islam's reformist orientation and tendency to co-opt opposition.

On 15 February, however, Libya's internal security service arrested Fathi Terbil, a prominent pro-transparency activist and Benghazi lawyer who had lost three brothers in the Abu Salim prison massacre in 1996. Since 2010, he had arranged peaceful weekly demonstrations in the main street of Benghazi where relatives of the victims of the Abu Salim massacre publicly demanded justice.[46] These weekly gatherings—unimaginable a decade earlier—had largely been allowed to unfold unhindered, powerful evidence of the impact of the gradual political liberalization in Libya advocated by Saif al-Islam and a necessary consequence of Libya's increasing openness to the world through trade, satellite TV, and the Internet. However, in the context of heightened expectations caused by the "Arab Spring" in Libya's neighbors, the security services thought they could stem potential dissent by preemptively arresting Terbil for conducting his standard weekly demonstration.

Like Hosni Mubarak instructing his loyalists to shoot into the crowd in Cairo's Tahrir Square to "disperse" the demonstrators, this move immediately backfired, partly due to the new organization opportunities offered by social media, the Internet, and cell phones.[47] Within hours, hundreds of ordinary Libyans began spontaneously marching in front of the security headquarters in Benghazi, demanding Terbil's immediate release. In an attempt to contain the protests, the security forces then arrested Idris al-Mismari, a leading intellectual and pro-democracy activist. Coincidentally, his arrest was broadcast live on *Al-Jazeera* as he was being interviewed on his cell phone at the time.[48] This further miscalculation by the security services led to even larger demonstrations, notably those led by Abdul-Hafiz Ghuqah, a local lawyer. Events escalated rapidly with security forces in Benghazi using antiaircraft weapons against protesters, dashing any hopes that political reform and peaceful compromise might prevail. In response, demonstrators surrounded and captured local government buildings, a trend that quickly spread to other Cyrenaican cities such as Darna, Tobruk, and Shahat. By 22 and 23 February, most cities in Eastern Libya were freed from regime control, with other disconnected uprisings occurring in Misrata, Zawiyya, Zuwara, and in the Nafusa Mountains. The revolution, at that point, had no "Islamist" aspect to it. Its rallying cries concerned political freedom, regional, and historical grievances—and to a lesser extent, transparency, democracy, rule of law, and freedom of speech. These were the themes one would expect from a protest movement led by human rights lawyers, unemployed youths, civil society activists, and the scions of Cyrenaica, a once powerful but now disadvantaged region.

Initially, Libyan Islamist organizations were caught off guard by the uprisings. They had been weakened by years of repression and had, to a certain extent, been co-opted by the regime. The Muslim Brotherhood, for instance, as so often in its history in other countries, had put its own institutional ambitions ahead of any principles it claimed to hold. In particular, it had reached an accommodation with the government (described above) that saw its own influence within Libya enhanced and a steady stream of Qadhafi money flow into its international operations, effectively gaining special privileges for the movement while doing nothing to advance wider political liberalization or Islamist legislation. As the Brotherhood had become used to legitimizing the regime and enjoying the privileges of accommodation, it would have been in a difficult position if it were to suddenly change course again and back armed opposition to the regime.

Similar problems affected other Islamist groups and figures, including the LIFG. In 2009, for instance, Abdul-Hakim Bilhajj, an LIFG *shura* council member, had written a public letter to Colonel Qadhafi apologizing for his previous acts.[49] Likewise, the Libyan Salafist movement had continued to reject involvement in quotidian politics on the basis that it could lead to disorder (*fitna*); this position, rather than being neutral, in fact favored the Qadhafian status quo. As a result, these groups—despite their perceived status as part of the opposition—had actually accommodated themselves to the Qadhafi regime over the course of the 2000s. The subservience of these groups to the regime was made even more necessary because of their acute lack of both funds and a strong base of members. By the start of 2011, the LIFG had only around 200 active members, many of them abroad. The Libyan Muslim Brotherhood faced similar problems: its entire leadership was based abroad with its official membership not exceeding 300.

In the early days of the rebellion, Islamists pragmatically feared that if the uprisings were defeated, their penalty for betraying the regime would be death. They could not "rebel lightly." In contradistinction, the young "Facebook generation" that flocked to the rebellion largely lacked personal experience of prior regime repression, torture, and prison sentences, and had often come of age during the period of Saif's liberalizing reforms. Moreover, unlike Islamist leaders, many of the most prominent civil society and human rights activists were plugged into international networks that would make it more per-ilous—but not necessarily impossible—for the regime to summarily execute them, giving them courage to pursue the revolt.

Hence, in the early days of the uprising in Benghazi, the first lead-ers to emerge were not Islamists but were instead veteran non-Islamist opposition figures like Terbil and Ghuqah. These figures were joined by senior reformists from within the Qadhafi regime like Mahmoud Jibril, Ali Issawi, and Mustafa Abdul-Jalil. Most of these early figures were educated and Cyrenaican in background and a larger number had origins in Benghazi itself—highlighting that the rebellion sought to redress regional grievances. None, however, were Islamists or had any links to Islamists groups, with only Abdul-Jalil potentially holding any sympathy for the Islamist's agenda.

Similarly, while Benghazi was liberating itself with dizzying speed, partner uprisings outside the cities were frequently led by tribal leaders, while in Misrata neighborhood leaders responded to hearing the news of the Benghazi uprising by holding a meeting and collectively decid-ing to launch their own movement. In Tripoli too, spontaneous antire-gime protests broke out on 20 February. In response to Saif al-Islam's bellicose and condescending speech of that evening, they occupied what was then called Green Square in central Tripoli. They seized it as, similar to Tahrir Square in Egypt, it was a key symbol of the regime's claim to legitimacy. Simultaneously, other entirely independent upris-ings with their own local leaderships broke out in Zawiya (40 km west of Tripoli) and in the Nafusa Mountains in western Libya—where local *imazighen* (Berbers) and the Arab tribe of Zintan united against Qadhafi. There was also an "uprising" in Qadhafi's diplomatic service. When Abdul-Rahman Shalgam—Libya's ex-foreign minister, who was then its permanent representative at the United Nations—announced his support for the rebellion on 26 February 2011, a wave of mass defection spread across Libyan embassies around the world.

Gradually, as the scale of the revolt became apparent, the Islamist groups, which were initially caught on their heels, were forced to react. The Libyan uprisings were not unique in being initiated by non-Islamist actors; the same was true of their sister revolutions in Tunisia, Egypt, and even, Syria. However, in Libya, just like in her neighbors, despite being slow off the starting block, the organized Islamist movements quickly sought to take advantage of this new environment.

The Organized Islamist Response

Darna, the Myth of an Islamic Amirate, and the Reality of Freelance Jihadists

At the very start of the uprisings, Darna, 250 km east of Benghazi, was among the first towns to be liberated. By 20 February, the spontaneous uprising there had completely cleared the city of regime officials. The Qadhafi government repeatedly referred to the establishment of an "Islamic Amirate of Darna" hoping to scare Western governments by exaggerating the presence of anti-Western jihadist forces in the liberated areas of eastern Libya.[50] This propaganda ploy by the Qadhafi regime led many media outlets and counterterrorism analysts to refer erroneously to the formation of an overtly al-Qaeda aligned force called the Darna Brigades and to state that the primary military and political leaders of the 2011 uprisings throughout eastern Libya were linked to al-Qaeda.[51] It was easy for Qadhafi to encourage ill-informed analysts to proclaim that the whole revolutionary movement was merely an Islamist-dominated uprising centered on Benghazi, Bayda, and Darna. However, even the man referred to by the regime as the self-appointed "Amir" of Darna, former Guantanamo inmate Abdul-Hakim al-Hasadi, later publicly stated that the allegation was a fabrication by Qadhafi's propaganda machine.[52]

By February 2011, the Libyan city of Darna had been well known in counterterrorism circles as one of the world centers of "spontaneous" jihadism. According to the so-called Sinjar Records, a captured al-Qaeda list of foreign fighters in Iraq, more foreign jihadists traveled to Iraq from Darna than any other city in the world.[53] In the early 1990s, the LIFG also found people from Darna to be unusually receptive to jihadist propaganda and they recruited more individuals from Darna than from any similar-sized city in Libya.

On the face of the matter, it is unclear why people from Darna would be particularly susceptible to jihadism, as Darna is a relatively prosperous and laidback seaside town, which until the 1990s enjoyed a reputation of being among the least conservative areas in Libya. Close to the Egyptian border, it has historically benefited from wealth-producing trade linkages with the eastern Arab World. However, Alison Pargeter has hinted that the prominence of Darna in global jihadi recruitment may be a product of its unique role in the anti-Italian jihad in the 1920s, combined with the deliberate underdevelopment of the town by Qadhafi.[54] Similarly, Charles Levinson, who visited Darna at the start of the 2011 uprisings, has pointed that "the first uprising against Col. Gadhafi's [sic] rule took place in Darna in 1970, less than a year after he seized power. [Also] the city proudly boasts that the first political prisoner killed by the Gadhafi regime was a Darna native."[55] From 2001 to 2010, many Darnans, and other Libyans, traveled to Iraq and Afghanistan to engage in jihad. On their return, several hundred were arrested by the Libyan security services and were imprisoned. This usually led to their families and friends adopting moderate jihadist opinions in solidarity with their relatives and in opposition to the Libyan government.

Although it is true that in Darna and elsewhere men who had fought in Iraq and Afghanistan flocked to the cause of the uprisings, their role was the subject of deliberate misinformation by the Qadhafi regime, which was later dramatized by the international media. The majority of ex-jihadis chose to fight within organized political and military structures and hence were unable to exert a coherent influence on the political course of the uprisings. It follows that this chapter confines its analysis to identifiable *organized jihadist groups* rather than lone Islamist individuals or their lone brigades, as it is impossible to accurately assess the military role of such "freelancers" during the fighting. We believe that their military contribution may have been significant, yet their lack of organization meant that after the fall of Qadhafi, they were arguably underrepresented in town councils and in the July 2012 national elections. They lacked the organizational know-how to transition from fighting to providing social assistance. They did not attempt to form coherent political parties and use the electoral mechanism to seek power as other Islamist movements did. This is not to say that these groups were not of tremendous political importance for Libya's future. These now battle-hardened freelancers represented a pool of potential recruits for foreign and domestic extremist groups, including al-Qaeda.

The LIFG and the Uprisings

As the revolutionary intent of the uprisings and the existential threat they posed became clear to the Qadhafi regime by late February, its first reaction was to cement what it saw as its "alliance" with the LIFG. In the last week of February, two leading members of the LIFG, al-Sa'adi and Abu Hazim were summoned by Saif al-Islam and Sa'adi Qadhafi. At the meeting, the two Qadhafi sons asked for the LIFG's direct support to defend the regime by calming down the protesters and helping the regime recover a modicum of religious legitimacy. The LIFG leaders told the Qadhafi brothers that, for all intents and purposes, the LIFG no longer existed as a coherent command structure; consequently, it would be difficult for them to help. Following the meeting, Sami al-Saadi and Abu Hazim remained in Tripoli and attempted to conceal their whereabouts—however, both were subsequently arrested.[56] In response, other LIFG leaders and members quickly fled Tripoli.

A core group of former LIFG members formed around Abdul-Hakim Bilhajj, who cleverly escaped from Tripoli to Misrata on 15 February 2011. In Misrata, Bilhajj began to contact other LIFG members, including those based in the United Kingdom. This core group accepted the agenda of the Libyan Islamic Movement for Change (LIMC), which has been discussed above. The main current of the LIFG had previously refused involvement with the LIMC because of its stance against the reconciliation process, but following the dramatic changes in the political landscape of mid-February, Bilhajj and his circle decided to support the uprisings under the banner of the LIMC. In late April 2011, Abdul-Wahhab Al-Qaid (aka Abu Idris, currently a GNC member, and elder brother of Abu Yahya al-Libi) and other prominent LIFG members relocated to the al-Hawari district on the outskirts of Benghazi. With help from local Islamists, they established a prominent Islamist military camp. This gave the new grouping operational independence and freedom of movement, recruitment, and supply, relative to other parts of the revolution.

In this way, the LIFG—now rebranded as the LIMC—constituted its own separate uprising with a command and control structure entirely separate from the NTC or the locally based militias in whose territory it operated. Although the NTC would have been powerless to stop this development, they actually encouraged it because many of the former LIFG members had combat experience in Afghanistan and Iraq. Most other rebel fighters lacked any formal military training—their driving up and down the coastal road in pickup trucks and shooting into the air was making only a small contribution to the key battles between Ajdabiyya and Ras Lanuf being waged by former army officers and battle-hardened Islamists.[57]

Once firmly established in Benghazi, LIMC leaders Abdul-Hakim Bilhajj, Anis Sharif, and Abdul-Ghaffar organized the creation of LIMC offices in Egypt and Tunisia.[58] This facilitated the movements of people, funds, and arms. Qatar was another important hub for the LIMC. The group's presence in the emirate was facilitated by Ali Sallabi, the Libyan Brotherhood–leaning cleric who had facilitated the LIFG's refutations as mentioned earlier. As a result of this coordination, Qatar became a major channel for the group to receive foreign funds.[59] Moreover, according to some members of the NTC, Qatar was instrumental in seeking a greater military role for the Islamists. According to Abdul-Maajid Mlegta—one of the seven people who ran the NTC's operations room at a July 2011 meeting in Djerba of the NTC, Bilhajj, two Qatari officials, and others—the Qataris requested that Bilhajj be the head of the NTC's military affairs and the chief distributor of all Qatari-supplied weapons. Unsurprisingly, this out-landish request was rejected by the NTC.[60]

One of the most important acts by LIFG members was the forma-tion of the Omar Mukhtar Brigade in March 2011. It was the brain-child of Abdul-Mun'im al-Madhuni, an LIFG *shura* council member who had fled to Iran from Afghanistan after 9/11 and stayed there until the start of the uprisings, at which point the LIFG office in Egypt arranged for his return to Libya.[61] The ranks of the Omar Mukhtar Brigade contained former LIFG members and other assorted jihad-ists, as well as non-Islamist Libyans seeking hard-core military training. This openness to, and training of, non-Islamist recruits improved the LIFG's reputation, and allowed the LIMC to exert influence over the Brigade's fighters.

The choice of Omar Mukhtar as a symbol was also a propaganda coup, symbolizing the new, purportedly more moderate LIMC ide-ology. Omar Mukhtar was a nationalist figure and a member of the Sanussi Sufi Order, which is sometimes viewed as heterodox by jihadis and Salafists. This choice of figurehead showed that the LIFG had become less antagonistic toward both traditional Libyan religiosity and mainstream nationalism. Omar Mukhtar's image and the flag of the Sanussi Monarchy (both pictured on this volume's cover) became the overarching symbols of both the uprisings and the Libyan people.

The actions of these members rapidly helped the LIFG grow in stature among ordinary Libyans. Front line revolutionary fighters and the political leaders of the uprisings came to understand and value the tactical capacity that LIFG fighters added to the rebel's haphazard arsenal. For example, Mustafa Abdul-Jalil met with Abdul-Mun'im al-Madhuni several times in Benghazi—presumably to consult his military opinion on the situation.[62]

From April to August as offensive operations on the coastal road leading from Benghazi to Sirte stagnated, the LIMC made the wise strategic decision to focus their efforts in the Nafusa Mountains, estab-lishing a military camp in Ninud, an *Amazigh* city near the Tunisian border, and one in Rajban, closer to Tripoli. During this period, ex-LIFG members in the Nafusa Mountains established good relations with Mahdi al-Hurrati, a well-known Libyan Islamist living in Ireland who had in March established the "Tripoli Brigade" in the Nafusa

Mountains, recruiting revolutionaries with roots in Tripoli, who were able to get to the mountains for training.

At its peak, this group reached 1,500 fighters (Al-Hurrati's claim of 8,000 is not credible), many recruited from western Europe and North America. The Tripoli Brigade later joined the military structure under the leadership of Bilhajj. The NTC's optimistic appraisal of the LIMC's military capacity for both offensive operations and postliberation security operations, based largely on exaggerated claims made by the Tripoli Brigade, such as that they were spearheading the spontaneous people's uprising inside Tripoli, led Mustafa Abdul-Jalil to issue an executive order appointing Bilhajj as the head of the Tripoli Military Council, created shortly before the fall of Tripoli on 20 August. Mahdi al-Hurrati, who occupied a more military role, was appointed as his deputy. In reality, Bilhajj and Hurrati were still in the Nafusa Mountains while groups from Misrata were actually leading the charge on Tripoli (see map 2), but the impression created by the media savvy "Tripoli Brigade" swayed Abdul-Jalil to this course of action. This erroneous impression was perpetuated when media outlets such as *Al-Jazeera* intentionally slanted their coverage to the role of LIFG fighters in the capture of Tripoli, ignoring the actual preponderance of Misratan fighters in the last battles against elite Qadhafi troops in Bab al-Aziziyya and elsewhere. Capitalizing on this "perception of success" and the ensuing increase of Qatari backing, the LIMC chose to base their operations in the capital after its conquest in a bid to establish themselves as its political (as well as security) authorities.

The prominent role seized by Bilhajj and al-Hurrati as leaders of the anti-Qadhafi movement was not only due to their skillful propaganda, aided and abetted by *Al-Jazeera*, but also due to the LIFG's genuine military abilities. For instance, guided by their Afghanistan experiences, they set up fast-track training programs that could prepare volunteer fighters for the frontlines in a single day—without even insisting that new recruits had to sign up to the group's ideology. Moreover, the NTC leadership felt that the LIFG had moved on from its origins in jihadism; this was partly due to the widespread publicity surrounding the *muraja'at* and partially a result of the reformulated LIMC's intense public commitment to abandoning any particularist agenda in the quest to overthrow Qadhafi.

On 17 April 2011, the LIFG took part in a secret conference in Istanbul between different Libyan Islamists, organized by Ali Sallabi in an attempt to establish an umbrella group unifying competing factions, provisionally titled *al-Jabha al-Islamiyya* (The Islamic Front). This initially took place without the knowledge of the NTC and was later seen by them as a Qatari-led attempt to prepare a united Islamist movement poised to capitalize on the opportunities inherent in the political fragmentation of postrevolutionary Libya.

In reality, the LIFG accepted the political leadership of the NTC, but it, along with other Islamist groups, strongly opposed the NTC's first chief of staff, Abdul-Fattah Yunis, and attempts by high-level defectors from the Libyan military like him or returned exiles like Khalifa Hiftar to take control of its armed brigades. They accused Yunis of participation in Qadhafi's mid-1990s crackdown on Islamists (especially in eastern Libya around Darna). Moreover, they proclaimed him a traitor for maintaining communications with the Qadhafi's regime during the current uprisings and delaying the rebel assault on Brega in the days immediately after the enforcement of the no-fly zone had tipped the military situation in favor of the rebels (for more on this, consult Chapter 4). In response to these Islamist-led accusations, the NTC formed a four-person investigative committee to look into these allegations. However, this process was overtaken by Yunis's abduction, torture, and murder on 28 July—purportedly by Islamists from the Abu Ubaida ibn al-Jarrah Brigade. Abdul-Jalil later said that accusations against Yunis were false and declared him a national hero. On 29 November 2011, a court in Benghazi charged 18 Islamists with his murder, and the Abu Ubaida ibn al-Jarrah Brigade was disbanded by the NTC.[63] Much controversy still surrounds this episode. (It is treated in greater detail in Chapter 5, which alludes to its tribal dimensions. In the Introduction, Jason Pack refers to it as a turning point leading to the fragmentation of the NTC, assuring that the new Libya would not emerge with a coherent, united "center," but would in fact remain dominated by the many disconnected peripheries.)

After the overthrow of the Qadhafi regime and the capture of Tripoli, the LIFG/LIMC split from the emerging Islamic Front coalition advocated by Qatar, while also itself starting to internally fragment. Sami al-Saadi, the LIFG's spiritual mentor and onetime leader, set up his *al-Tajama al-Umma al-Wasat* (The Moderate Umma Coalition) to take part in the July 2012 elections. Most LIMC leaders joined al-Saadi, including Abu Wahhabi al-Qaid, Mufta al-Dawaghi (aka Abdul-Ghaffar), and Ismail Kumuka, while Bilhajj established his *Hizb al-Watan* (Homeland Party), claiming to be one of the heroes of the uprisings capable of leading the Libyan people. Yet within months of the fall of Tripoli, Bilhajj suffered a dramatic electoral defeat in the parliamentary elections: in spite of running a lavish and high-profile campaign and Bilhajj's decision to be a candidate in the Souq al-Jum'a area of Tripoli, which should have been highly favorable to his message, he was personally defeated, and his party failed to gain a single seat. In Chapter 2, Youssef Sawani attributes the Homeland Party's spectacular failure to perceptions that it was a front for Qatar. As a result of his electoral failure and the need to present himself as being relevant, Bilhajj shifted his focus from Libyan politics to concentrate on sending jihadists to northern Syria to battle Assad.[64]

To accurately capture the LIFG's military contribution to the uprisings, it must be remembered that the Islamists' true military might never matched that of the regionally or tribally based militias of Zintan or Misrata, which came to dominate key locations in the capital like the international airport, hospitals, and key road interchanges. While observers outside Libya were dependent for their information on the international media, which enjoyed holding press conferences with bearded veterans of the anti-Soviet jihad and of Qadhafi's prisons, Libyan voters could appreciate the actual contributions of the various forces on the ground to toppling Qadhafi, as well as the decisive nature of the NATO intervention, which had been facilitated by the diplomacy of the "liberals" within the NTC, like Mahmoud Jibril.

Indeed, the greatest successes of the LIFG during the uprisings derived from their ability to adapt their ideology and external presentation to the novel circumstances, as well as their highly effective courtship of Qatar. For instance, their former emphasis on establishing an Islamic state was dropped in favor of an emphasis on the nation (*al-watan*), while their military capacity—and hence political influence—was effectively multiplied by Qatari arms supplies. This process was, to some extent, facilitated by the LIFG's prior ideological gymnastics, in the form of the 2009 recantation. They also adopted the political aims shared by many Libyan fighters, stating that they fought to establish democracy and transparency in Libya. This was crucial to gaining the trust and support of the international community. Yet, when it came to postrevolution politics, the LIMC was largely outgunned and outclassed. Even their fruitful relationship with Doha became damaging, as they were easily painted as little more than stooges of the Qatari monarchy.

The Muslim Brotherhood

On 15 February 2011, the Libyan Muslim Brotherhood's leadership held a *shura* council meeting at an undisclosed international location to discuss issues arising from the Arab Spring in general and Libya in particular, in light of growing Facebook agitation calling for an uprising in Benghazi two days hence. The aim of the meeting was to plan a response and decide upon what role—if any—the Brotherhood should play. After minimal discussion, the attendees decided to support the uprising without reservations, principally because they calculated that the uprising was likely to gain traction given the Arab Spring climate, even though abandoning their profitable alliance with the Qadhafi family would damage them in the short term. In this way, the Brotherhood showcased their superior strategic understanding relative to all other Islamist currents as well as their ability to take coherent action quickly.[65]

Following the full outbreak of the revolution a few days later, the leadership of the Libyan Muslim Brotherhood consequently ordered their cadres abroad to prepare themselves for an immediate return to Libya. They also ordered their members in Libya—particularly those released from prison during the Brotherhood's 2005–6 rapprochement with the regime—to play a social and political role in the uprisings.[66] The Muslim Brotherhood therefore quickly became engaged in events both inside and outside Libya, notably becoming deeply involved in the early conversations that sought to bring together a range of groups into an umbrella organization that led to the creation of the NTC.

At the same time, the Brotherhood rapidly established a range of media and aid organizations to operate in Libya, creating media outlets such as *Sabil Rahid*, *Shabab Libya*, and *Libya Lion* to get their message out to the public.[67] They also created an organization, *Al-Nada* (the Call), that forged financial links between governmental and nongovernmental organizations in Libya and the GCC countries arranging for aid convoys from Egypt and Tunisia. *Al-Nada* soon became the Muslim Brotherhood's key vehicle for reintroducing themselves to Libyan society, a version of their long-standing tactic—used widely in Palestine, Egypt, and elsewhere—of using social work as a political vehicle.[68]

Al-Nada also began to work with independent charities that had been established throughout Libya, particularly in the eastern part of the country. *Al-Nada*'s support for these local charities quickly enabled the Brotherhood to build strong local links with emerging political and social forces throughout the country that would give them social and political relevance in a post-Qadhafi Libya, in which the state was eviscerated and local nonstate actors were king. Unsurprisingly, this pattern is similar to the role of other Brotherhood affiliates operating in areas with a lack of state authority, notably in Gaza with Hamas.

Brotherhood members also began organizing a series of events and training workshops around the liberated areas of Libya, partly with the help of the United Nations and other international organizations, on a range of issues related to human development and civil society.

The Muslim Brotherhood therefore quickly began applying the lessons they had learnt in countries such as Egypt, Jordan, Palestine, and Morocco, on how to gradually build support via grassroots social work and the use of international funding for political purposes.[69] This hands-on approach rapidly began to overturn prior distrust among the Libyan people caused by the Brotherhood's opposition to the overthrowing of Qadhafi in the 2005–10 period.[70]

At the same time, the Libyan Brotherhood also acquired high-level political influence in the NTC, gaining around 12 to 15 council seats—or nearly a fifth of the total. Some Brothers achieved cabinet positions in the Jibril and al-Kib governments. Dr. Abdullah Shamia, a well-known and widely respected professor of economics at Benghazi University, who had been imprisoned under Qadhafi, became the economy minister. Salim al-Shaykhi, a Manchester-based imam, became the NTC's minster of religious affairs (*awqaf*); he was also nominated for the highly sensitive role of interrogating General Abdul-Fattah Yunis to investigate the veracity of the claims against him.[71] Some Brotherhood NTC members later managed to maintain this influence in the first postrevolutionary government. The head of the Libyan Muslim Brotherhood's Shura Council, Manchester-based Dr. Alamin Bilhajj (no relation to Abdul-Hakim Bilhajj but rather a former professor of engineering at Tripoli University), was appointed as head of the committee charged with writing the rules and regulations that would govern the July 2012 Libyan elections. Nasser al-Manaa, a UK-based Brotherhood member, became the official spokesman for the GNC.

Although the Brotherhood did not prioritize military activities, a few self-identified members organized their own brigades to fight on the ground. Fawzi Bu Katif, a petroleum engineer and Muslim Brotherhood member who spent nearly two decades in Qadhafi's prisons, became the leader of the well-known 17 February Brigade in Benghazi—an umbrella outfit linking together the major Islamist but non-Salafi militias in Cyrenaica. As his influence grew, he was briefly appointed deputy minister of defense under the NTC, prior to the declaration of liberation. The Brotherhood also established a brigade to be responsible for security in Benghazi and surrounding cities under Fawzi Qadhafi (no relation to either Muammar Qadhafi or Fawzi Bu Katif). At the same time, however, their operations during the revolution remained focused on rebuilding their organization and jockeying for power within the NTC rather than on fighting Qadhafi's forces.

On 21 November 2011, the Brotherhood held elections to choose a new leadership, electing Bashir al-Kibti, who had spent 33 years in exile in the United States, as general supervisor of the group. This was a clear step toward reorganizing the group in order to best take advantage of the political dynamics in post-Qadhafi Libya. It led directly to the Brotherhood's later establishment of a political party *al-Adala wa al-Bina'a* (Justice and Construction Party), which they described as a national political party "based on Islamic references." Although this party was soundly defeated in the 7 July elections, its leader, Muhammad Sawan, was still one of the most important figures in Libya, capable of forging a coalition to block Mahmoud Jibril's attempts to secure higher office for himself or for other liberal-minded technocrats aligned with his National Forces Alliance. In short, the Brotherhood first rooted themselves in the local political life of Libya's disenfranchised communities and later became spoilers at the national level, willing to block political progress if it was in their organization's interests.

Therefore, while the LIFG concentrated on winning influence through their actions on the battlefields and through training fighters, the Brotherhood concentrated on building influence at the grassroots level while also conducting extensive political maneuverings in anticipation of the post-Qadhafi era. It could even be said that the militias attached to Brotherhood figures like Fawzi Bu Katif were always political movements "posing" as armed militias—rarely did they engage loyalist forces or suffer battlefield losses. The LIMC, by contrast, was primarily a group of highly trained and motivated fighters, instrumental in fighting loyalist forces in the Nafusa Mountains, the capture of Tripoli, and elsewhere, who only later attempted unsuccessfully to morph into a political party.

The Brotherhood's use of the revolutionary period to deepen its roots in Libyan society, following the model it had carefully honed in Jordan, Palestine, and Egypt, must largely account for its relative success in the struggle for power in post-Qadhafi Libya, while the LIFG's military focus and reluctance even to indoctrinate volunteers at its training camps for its relative failure. Moreover, while the LIFG lost many of their most experienced figures in the fight against Qadhafi, the Brotherhood suffered no such losses.

Salafis in the Uprisings

Prior to the 2011 uprising, there was a significant Salafi presence in Libya, particularly in Tripoli and the Green Mountain region (south and east of Benghazi). However, the movement was never unified and lacked a formal structure. As discussed above, Salafism was usually organized at a local level with no national organization or leadership. Indeed, most of the intellectual leaders of the Libyan Salafi movement were non-Libyan Arab thinkers based in Egypt, Saudi Arabia, and Yemen.

Initially, Salafis in Libya responded to the uprising much more hesitantly than the Brotherhood and the LIFG. In many cases, their first public reaction was to announce that the uprising against the government was *haram* (forbidden), because it would lead to *fitna* (discord). This mirrored their previous stance of avoiding confrontation with the Qadhafi regime and defending their stance in theological terms. Potentially they also adopted this position because they knew that non-Islamists were at the forefront of the Benghazi uprising, making supporting the revolution—to their minds—both theologically and practically problematic.

Local Salafi leaders, particularly in Tripoli, were also encouraged by the regime to give speeches in mosques and on national television against the rebellion. Abu Hudaifa, one of the most learned Libyan Salafis who had studied in Saudi Arabia during the late 1980s, appeared on Libya's national television, *Jumhurriya TV*, to denounce the rebels for causing *fitna* and for opening the country to Western invasion.[72] Similarly, the government encouraged Salafists to appeal for *fatwas* from abroad that would denounce the rebellion, particularly from Saudi Arabia.

This approach was undermined when Shaykh al-Haydan of Saudi Arabia effectively reflecting sentiment within the Saudi state, decreed that the Saudi *ulama* could not support the Qadhafi regime as it was no longer Islamically legitimate.[73] As a result, during the early days of the uprisings, some Salafists—but only in the liberated eastern areas of Libya—publically critiqued the Qadhafi regime and disagreed with the pronouncement of the revolution as *haram*. Yet these developments by themselves were not initially enough to cause a widespread abandonment of the Salafis' traditional quietist approach by those still in Qadhafi-controlled areas.[74] Additionally, in those early days as LIFG members and some Brotherhood activists flocked to the frontlines between Ajdabiyya and Ras Lanuf, the Salafists remained absent.

As February turned into March and the no-fly zone guaranteed that Cyrenaica was and would remain firmly in rebel control, the Salafis abandoned their earlier stance, joining the rebellion and taking up arms, just as most Egyptian Salafists only openly began opposing Mubarak once the battle against him had been effectively won. Their military role in the uprisings remained relatively minor, but they came to prominence in the media in the wake of Salafi attacks on gravestones and Sufi shrines, which they held to be forbidden by Islam. In a notable incident in Zlitan, Salafis attacked the shrine of Abdul-Salam al-Asmar, one of the most revered saints in the country, leading to major tensions within the rebel forces.[75]

On the cultural front, following the example of the Brotherhood (but not that of the LIFG), many Salafis chose to concentrate on grassroots activism, particularly through taking control of mosques and setting up NGOs. For the first time in Libya, genuinely popular Salafi leaders also began to emerge, such as Shaykh Issa al-Ghadari, who had studied in Saudi Arabia in the 1980s. The Salafists' relations with other Islamist parties remained tense, however, particularly between Tripoli Salafists and the LIFG's Abdul-Hakim Bilhajj, whom they saw as a potential rival competing for the same constituencies.[76]

After the fall of the regime, the Salafists debated whether to establish a political party to participate in the 7 July 2012 elections. Although most agreed on this course of action, they were not able to establish an effective party and campaigning organization in time, due to a lack of a cohesive organization and democratic know-how. Nonetheless, there are competing estimates as to how many Salafists are in the GNC as part of party lists or as individual candidates. Some sources state that there are no overt Salafists in the GNC. On the other hand, Mary Fitzgerald of the *Irish Times* has asserted that 25 GNC members have Salafist tendencies and that they have entered the Congress primarily as individual candidates and in rare occasions as members of the party lists. She also claims that they are organized into various "parliamentary Salafist groupings."[77] The difficulty in verifying these assertions suggests that Salafists remain primarily in the shadows as a cultural force that lacks a defined hierarchy like the LIFG or Brotherhood. As such assessing their political power is well-nigh impossible.

CONCLUSION

As can be seen, the various responses to the 2011 Libyan uprisings by Islamists actors—including the Muslim Brotherhood, the LIFG, and the Salafists—have substantially shaped the contours of post-Qadhafi Libya and the trajectory of the groups themselves. The Brotherhood's focus on social networks and rebuilding their grassroots organization clearly set them on course to play a key role as a mainstream social and political force in post-Qadhafi Libya. On the other hand, the LIFG's focus on purely military activities helps explain why they quickly faded from prominence in the war's aftermath—lacking a clear base of support or coherent political agenda. This dichotomy is actually not surprising because the LIFG was founded to overthrow Qadhafi and never articulated any other policy agenda, while the Brotherhood has been preparing itself to provide social services and even governance in Egypt, Gaza, and other Arab countries for decades.

Among the extremist Islamists, the Salafists responded slowly to both the uprisings and to the opportunities offered by the democratic process. This helps explain their relative lack of visibility at the political level post-Qadhafi. They rooted themselves in radical mosques and in the lives of the undereducated and radicalized youth—exactly the segment that they had monopolized prior to the uprisings. Meanwhile, ill-defined freelance jihadist groups—which may have sprung from the "freelance" Islamist actors—grew in prominence immediately after the transition phase ended.

The killing of the US Ambassador J. Christopher Stevens on 11 September 2012 by a terrorist attack on the US mission in Benghazi brought to prominence the role of fringe jihadist militias. In the aftermath of that attack, the headquarters of a number of implicated Islamist militias were stormed, including Ansar al-Sharia, a militia which had threatened to withdraw its security provisions from Benghazi. These widespread popular displays of anti-Islamist militia feeling demonstrate that the Islamist militants on the fringes of the new political structure do not have extensive popular support, nor are they capable of rooting themselves in mainstream political life.[78] Ansar al-Sharia and other freelance jihadists have eschewed both the media and formal political processes. As a result, their role in the struggle for post-Qadhafi Libya remains unclear. Given events in Mali and the terrorist attack on gas installations at In Amenas, Algeria, it appears that freelance jihadists have figured out how to utilize Libya's ungoverned spaces to recruit, train, and project power throughout North Africa. Inside Libya, they are likely to remain spoilers to the more established political forces—able to derail progress toward national reconciliation and infrastructure building, but not to contribute anything meaningful to the political debate.

Further research into other factors—such as recruitment numbers, infiltration of Islamists into the security services especially the Supreme Security Committee, the use of the media, and Qatari attempts to empower Islamists at the expense of secularists within the central government—is needed to present a deeper more nuanced picture of the role of Islamists, especially the freelance jihadists, during the uprisings and their aftermath. One productive avenue for research would relate to the implications of Islamists transcending previous doctrinal rigidity and suddenly discovering theological flexibility. Study of *fatwas* and *khutaba*s (religious sermons) would be an interesting way to grapple with the theological innovations required for groups like

the LIFG to acquiesce to NATO airstrikes and their cooperation with
non-Muslim military forces. A mere decade earlier, the LIFG was at
war with NATO in Afghanistan and the United States in Iraq. It had
also maintained that all non-Muslim military forces on—or interventions in—Muslim lands were forbidden.

While the shape of post-Qadhafi Libya remains unclear and the ultimate roles of Islamist groups remain uncertain, it is clear that as in Egypt
and Tunisia, Islamists did not instigate the Libyan uprisings. Moreover,
although Libyan Islamists gradually came to assume an undeniably
important role in the uprisings, their political position post-Qadhafi is
arguably weaker and more disunited than their Islamist counterparts in
Egypt and Tunisia. Likewise, the multifaceted Islamist role in the revolution was more complex than was depicted by the media at the time,
with Islamist groups rarely directly cooperating and more often following starkly different agendas. All groups showed themselves adept at
reexamining their ideologies and adapting them pragmatically to changing circumstances so as to remain relevant in the new circumstances.

In the aftermath of the uprisings, much in Libya remains uncertain and it seems no exaggeration to say that the country's future will
be defined to a great extent by how these groups—along with liberal
and nationalist groups—continue to adapt and change their ideologies,
goals, and tactics relative to the problems confronting Libya. If the
LIFG and Brotherhood members continue their quest to enter mainstream Libyan politics, it appears likely that they will reach out to more
liberal actors like the National Force's Alliance against the destabilizing
role of the Salafists and freelance jihadists.

NOTES

1. This chapter is concerned with Islamist actors and not Islamism.
   Furthermore, many non-Islamist actors in Libya's political life espouse
   Islamist positions for reasons of political expediency or actual convic-
   tion. For coherent definitions of "Islamists" and "Islamism," consult
   the works of John Esposito, Olivier Roy, James Piscatori, and especially
   Gilles Kepel, *Jihad: The Trail of Political Islam*, translated by Anthony
   Roberts (London : I. B. Tauris, 2003).
2. Islamist forces fragmented and lost power from the fall of Qadhafi to the
   handover of power to the General National Council 9 months later, yet
   this does not preclude Islamists from reemerging as powerful or even
   dominant political and military actors in Libya's future.
3. See, for example, "Gaddafi Dismisses Protest Reports, Blames Al-Qaeda,"
   Reuters, March 2, 2011, http://af.reuters.com/article/libyaNews/idAF
   WEB284220110302.

4. Mahmoud Ayoub, *Islam and the Third Universal Theory: The Religious Thought of Muammar al-Qadhdhafi* (London: Routledge, 1991)

5. Dirk Vandewalle, *A History of Modern Libya*, 2nd edition (Cambridge, Cambridge University Press, 2012), 78–80.

6. For more on Qadhafi's construction of a hegemonic discourse and Islamist attempts to counter it, see Alia Brahimi, "Islamic Radicalisation in Libya," in *Islamist Radicalisation in North Africa: Politics and Process*, edited by George Joffé (Routledge, London, 2011).

7. Conversation between the primary author and Saif al-Islam Qadhafi, July 2008. Also confirmed by Saif al-Islam Qadhafi in a televised speech the same month.

8. For more on the history of the Sanussi family, consult the following monarchist Arabic website entitled, *24 December 1951*. http://24dec1951 .com/2010–12–14–11–41–46/2011–03–03–14–08–20.html.

9. For background on Hizb al-Tahrir, see Suha Taji-Farouki, *A Fundamental Quest: Hizb al-Tahrir and the Search for the Islamic Caliphate* (London: Grey Seal Books,1996).

10. An English translation of Hizb al-Tahrir's communiqué to Qadhafi can be found at Hizb al-Tahrir's website http://www.khilafah.com/images /images/PDF/Books/gadaffi_extract.pdf.

11. Ibid.

12. The relevant information on the Hizb al-Tahrir's website can be found at http://www.khilafah.com/index.php/activism/africa/11323-list-of -hizb-ut-tahrir-activists-martyred-by-gaddafi.

13. Amany Maged, "Presidential Candidate Mohamed Morsi Speaks to Ahram Online," *Al Ahram*, May 2, 2012, http://english.ahram.org.eg /NewsContent/36/122/40693/Presidential-elections-/Presidential-elections-news/Presidential-candidate-Mohamed-Mursi-speaks-to-Ahr .aspx.

14. Alison Pargeter, *The Muslim Brotherhood: The Burden of Tradition* (London: Saqi, 2010), 110–13.

15. On Qatar's relationship with the Muslim Brotherhood and its promotion of Al Jazeera, see Hugh Miles, *Al Jazeera: How Arab TV News Challenged the World* (London: Grove Atlantic, 2006).

16. Susan Tarkowski Tempelhoff and Manal Omar, "Stakeholders of Libya's February 17 Revolution," United States Institute of Peace, January 2012, 7.

17. Conversation between primary author and Saif al-Islam Qadhafi, January 2007.

18. Evidence of Ali Sallabi's connection with the Qadhafis can be found here: "Ali al-Sallabi: al-Islamiyun fi Libya Yu'ayyidun Manh Mansib Rasmiyy li-Saif al-Islam al-Qadhafi," *Agence France Press*, November 2, 2009, http://tinyurl.com/br4pa7p, and more specific information on his position on the constitution committee here: "Masadar Mutla: Juhat Tas'iy li-Ib'ad al-Tayyar al-Islamiyy 'an Lajna al-Dustur" *Lahona*, http://www

.lahona.com/show_news.aspx?nid=209622&pg=21, and his relationship with Saif al-Islam: Marwa Abdul-Aziz and 'Ilaa Sa'id, "Hal Yanjah al-Sallabi fi Iqsa' Jibril?" *Muhit,* October 26, 2011, http://www.masress.com/moheet/220659.

19. Ayoub, *Islam and the Third Universal Theory;* David Commins, *The Wahhabi Mission and Saudi Arabia* (London: I. B. Tauris, 2006).

20. For more on the relation between Wahhabism and Salafism and their joint evolution through the twentieth century, consult Kepel, *Jihad.*

21. Alison Pargeter, *Libya: the Rise and Fall of Qaddafi* (New Haven: Yale University Press, 2012), 115–16.

22. See Brahimi, "Islamic Radicalisation."

23. Primary author's observations.

24. Stéphane Lacroix, *Awakening Islam: The Politics of Religious Dissent in Contemporary Saudi Arabia* (Boston: Harvard University Press, 2011).

25. Pargeter, *Libya,* 166.

26. Primary author's personal observations while living in Libya.

27. Pargeter, *Libya,* 71. Compare with Lisa Anderson's assessment of Qadhafi's Islamic ideology as a reaction to the Sanussi Monarchy in Lisa Anderson, "Religion and State in Libya: The Politics of Identity," *The Annals of American Academy of Politics and Social Sciences* 483 (January 1986): 71.

28. Personal experience of primary author and Camille al-Tawil, *Brother in Arms: Al-Qai'da and the Arab Jihadist* (London: Saqi Press, 2010).

29. Pargeter, *Libya,* 167.

30. Ibid., 169.

31. Several conversations in the 1990s between primary author and leading jihadists in his previous capacity as LIFG commander.

32. *Al-Fajr* 3, no. 25 (1997).

33. *Al-Fajr* 5, no. 58 (1999).

34. Primary author conversations with Osama Bin Laden, as documented by Peter Bergenand and Paul Cruikshank, http://www.highbeam.com/doc/1G1–181021686.html.

35. One mid-level LIFG member initially planned to send his family and children back to Libya via the Qadhafi Foundation but was overruled by the group, but junior LIFG members availed themselves of the opportunity to return to Libya. Primary author's observations.

36. *Libya since 1969: Qadhafi's Revolution Revisited,* edited by Dirk Vandewalle (New York: Palgrave Macmillan, 2008).

37. al-Tawil, *Brother in Arms.*

38. Dr. Alia Brahimi of LSE deserves credit for influencing our understanding of Saif's personal motivations in leading the reconciliation with Libya's jihadists.

39. Jason Pack, "Gaddafi's Right-Hand Man Should Not Be Underestimated," *Guardian,* February 24, 2011, http://www.guardian.co.uk/commentis

free/2011/feb/24/gaddafi-successor-abdullah-senussi, Accessed October, 4, 2012.

40. Charles Dunne, "Terrorist Rehabilitation and Succession Politics in Libya: Opportunities for the United States?" in *Middle East Institute Website,* March 31, 2010, http://www.mei.edu/content/terrorist-rehabilitation-and-succession-politics-libya-opportunities-united-states. Accessed October, 4, 2012.

41. Primary author's observations.

42. "Abdul-Hakim Bilhajj 'Amir al-Jama'a al-Libiya al-Muqatila," Abdul-Hakim Bilhajj interviewed by *Al-Jazeera,* Youtube video http://www.youtube.com/watch?v=ygi3T7w2oWo&feature=related, http://alhadathnews.com/tube/ – z7d!zblsuNdsqbs.html.

43. Primary author, conversations and personal experience.

44. Ibid.

45. Ronald Bruce St John, *Libya from Colony to Revolution* (New York: One World Press, 2012).

46. "Ahali al-Dhahaya…Istimrar al-Waqfat…waTarbil Yutalib al-Dawla bi-l-Tawaqquf 'an al-Ibtizaz," *Libia al-Yawm,* September 19, 2010, http://www.libya-alyoum.com/news/index.php?id=21&textid=422.

47. Martin Van Creveld and Jason Pack, "Upheaval in Qaddafi's Libya Isn't Just Another Arab Uprising," *Christian Science Monitor,* February 23, 2011. "Historically in Libya [and elsewhere in the Middle East], firing into crowds of protesters has caused them to disperse; this time the revolutionary successes of Egypt and Tunisia have given average Libyans the belief that change was within their grasp. The regime missed the meaning of this unique historical moment and employed outdated tactics."

48. "Ishtibakat bi-Binghazi Tawaqqa'u Jurha," *Al Jazeera* February 16, 2011, http://www.aljazeera.net/news/pages/d1458993-1aae-4e04-a9f1–758239c23841.

49. Primary author's observation.

50. Thanks to Alison Pargeter for her insights on this matter.

51. One of the most flagrant cases is Webster G. Tarpley "The CIA's Libya Rebels: The Same Terrorists Who Killed US, NATO Troops in Iraq," *Tarpley.net* March 24, 2011, http://tarpley.net/2011/03/24/the-cia%E2%80%99s-libya-rebels-the-same-terrorists-who-killed-us-nato-troops-in-iraq/. Tarpley attempts to summarize the importance of Darna in world jihadism and then draws erroneous conclusions about the role of jihadists in the early rebel movement. Consider his section heading: "Rebel Leaders Jalil and Younis, Plus Most of Rebel Council Are Members of the al Qaeda-Linked Harabi Tribe."

52. See Alia Brahimi, "Libya's Revolution," *Journal of North African Studies* 16, no. 4 (December 2011).

53. Joseph Felter and Brian Fishman, *Al-Qaeda's Foreign Fighters in Iraq: A First Look at the Sinjar Records,* Combating Terrorism Centre, West Point, January 2, 2007, http://www.ctc.usma.edu/harmony/pdf/CTC ForeignFighter.19.Dec07.pdf.

54. Alison Pargeter, "Localism and Radicalization in North Africa: Local Factors and the Development of Political Islam in Morocco, Tunisia, and Libya," *International Affairs* 85, no. 5 (2009): 1031–44.
55. Charles Levinson, "Ex-Mujahedeen Help Lead Libyan Rebels," *Wall Street Journal*, April 2, 2011, http://online.wsj.com/article/SB100014 24052748703712504576237042432212406.html.
56. Primary author, phone conversations with LIFG members.
57. "Can the African Union Bring Relief to Libya?" Riz Khan Show with guest speakers Dirk Vandewalle and Jason Pack, *Al-Jazeera English*, April 12, 2011.
58. Abdul-Ghaffar was an author of the "Refutations" and was released from prison on 16 February 2011.
59. For information on Qatar's provision of funds, see: "Abdul Jalil Yata'arruf: Qatar Tadiss al-Amwal fi Jiyubina," *Middle East Online* August 3, 2012, http://www.middle-east-online.com/?id=136393; "Shalqam: Qatar Tasnua' Milishiyatiha al-Islamiyya fi Libya," *Algeria Times*, November 18, 2011, http://www.algeriatimes.net/print.php?print=18751.
60. French Documentary re-aired by the Norwegian Broadcasting Corporation (NRK2) entitled "The Truth about the Qatari Support of Abdul Hakim Bilhajj." This video includes footage of Mahmoud Jibril, Ambassador Gene Cretz, and many others explaining the connection between Qatar and Bilhajj as well as their competition for influence with the NTC, http://www.youtube.com/watch?v=LQGZtSRi2wY.
61. Abdul-Mun'im al-Madhuni was killed on 16 April 2011 in Ajdabiya.
62. Primary author's conversation with jihadist source in Benghazi.
63. "The Storm Surrounding the Killing of Abdul Fateh Younis," *Al-Sharq al-Awsat* November 30, 2011, http://aawsat.com/details.asp?section=4&issueno=12055&article=652195&feature=.
64. Ruth Sherlock, "Leading Libyan Islamist Met Free Syian Army Opposition Group," *Daily Telegraph*, November 27, 2011, http://www.telegraph.co.uk/news/worldnews/africaandindianocean/libya/8919057/Leading-Libyan-Islamist-met-Free-Syrian-Army-opposition-group.html#.
65. Author conversation with Muslim Brotherhood source, April 2012.
66. Ibid.
67. Susan Tarkowski Tempelhoff and Manal Omar, "Stakeholders of Libya's February 17 Revolution," United States Institutes of Peace, January 2012, 7.
68. Ramadan al-Masuri, "mas'ul jama'at al-ikwan al-muslimin," *Libia al-Yawm* February 14, 2012, http://www.libya-alyoum.com/news/index.php?id=21&textid=8980.
69. Lorenzo Vidino, *The New Muslim Brotherhood in the West* (New York: Columbia University Press, 2010).
70. Information on the Muslim Brotherhood's refusal to take part in the Libyan Opposition meeting in London can be found here: "Milf al-Taghtiya al-I'alamiya li-Mu'tamr al-Mu'arida al-Libiya fi London," *Libya Forum* June 26, 2005, http://tinyurl.com/bpcwn24.

71. "Quryna New: Is the First Media Outlet to Discover the Truth about the Assassination of General Younis," *Quryna New,* January 15, 2012, http://www.qurynanew.com/27375.
72. Authors' observation of regular talk shows discussing this issue.
73. There are various YouTube clips of Shaykh al-Haydan declaring Qadhafi's rule Islamically illegitimate. Here are some of the most informative: http://www.youtube.com/watch?v=KZ-ov0glP7k&feature=related; http://www.youtube.com/watch?v=G-2gK4xe6w0 ; http://www.youtube.com/watch?v=7K3RDZdAg-0&feature=related; http://www.youtube.com/watch?v=poPYDwiPtjE&feature=related.
74. Primary Author's conversations with Salafis.
75. "Libya Sufi Shrines Attacked by 'Islamist Hardliners,'" *BBC News* August 25, 2012, http://www.bbc.co.uk/news/world-africa-19380083.
76. Primary Author's conversations with ex-jihadists in Benghazi and security officials in Tripoli, November 2011.
77. Mary Fitzgerald, "Introducing the Libyan Muslim Brotherhood," *Foreign Policy,* November 2, 2012, http://mideast.foreignpolicy.com/posts/2012/11/02/introducing_the_libyan_muslim_brotherhood.
78. Jason Pack and Andrea Khalil, "Amid Chants of 'Free Libya, Terrorists Out,' a Nation at a Crossroads," *Wall Street Journal,* September 16, 2012, http://online.wsj.com/article/SB10000872396390443524904577651530322231506.html

Afterword

LIBYA: A JOURNEY FROM EXTRAORDINARY TO ORDINARY

Lisa Anderson

The images of Muammar Qadhafi's final day—as caught by cell phone camera and uploaded to YouTube—were definitely ugly; captured alive, his stringy hair caked in blood, he was manhandled briefly by his captors before gunshots rang out. The next pictures of the fallen tyrant seem to show a bullet hole in his head; he was definitively dead. But for those who wanted to see for themselves, his body was washed, his hair neatly trimmed, and he was laid out for four days in a meat locker in Misrata.

Why did so many families line up to see the decomposing body? Certainly, Libyans have grown inured to political violence. A century ago, on 3 October 1911, Italy invaded the Ottoman provinces of Tripolitania and Cyrenaica, ushering in a hundred years of almost unrelieved cruelty, incompetence, and corruption in government. Decades of arrogant and brutal fascist rule, negligent and self-seeking international influence under the auspices of the British Military Administration and the Sanussi Monarchy, and more than forty years of increasingly absurd and merciless tyranny had left the country shattered. By the time Qadhafi had been captured and killed on 20 October 2011, the country seemed broken, divided, and exhausted. Libya after Qadhafi seemed to be inauspicious material for the state-building and democratic transition promised by its new leaders.

Yet there was more in the fascination with Qadhafi's corpse than casualness about brutality. Certainly many in the international community—and even some in the new Libyan political circles—argued that building the rule of law should start with figures of the ancien régime receiving fair trials before being made to pay for their crimes.

There should be neither impunity nor summary justice. In rebuilding their society, Libyans now confront the difficult task of distinguishing the irredeemably guilty from the only somewhat blameworthy. They face painful choices in condemning the first, while showing compassion to the second. Certainly, no one should be above—or beneath—the law.

Nonetheless, perhaps a special measure of forgiveness should be accorded to the actions of the young Misratan militiamen on 20 October: for many Libyans, Qadhafi really *was* extraordinary. He had grown into a larger-than-life demon-like figure—terrifying even to his followers. It was inevitable that someone would need to vanquish the monster and that everyone would be called to witness it.

The deed is now done, and remarkably, as the chapters in this volume suggest, in many ways the country is moving surprisingly quickly to becoming a place where there may be pride in law and honor in mercy. Libya's collective memory of devastation must be recognized without fortifying the thousands of individual grievances and sorrows. Years of artificially induced scarcity produced widespread corruption, and decades of capricious cruelty led to generalized and deep-seated suspicion of government. In the absence of any serviceable public sector bureaucracy, family ties provided access to goods and services, and it was along tribal lines that the society fractured when the regime's capacity to divide and rule began to unravel. Under Qadhafi, the state's military capacity had been distributed across a deliberately confusing and uncoordinated array of police, army, revolutionary guards, and other special services. Unsurprisingly, there are a lot of scores to settle in post-Qadhafi Libya, plenty of weapons, and much temptation to exact revenge.

For these reasons and others, the restoration of order, the reestablishment of daily commerce, the rebuilding of ordinary public life, and the establishment of predictable quotidian rhythms is the primary project for the post-Qadhafi era. And, despite the enormity of these challenges, in the first year after the uprisings, Libya moved quite far towards that most precious of circumstances: ordinariness.

Obviously, the first challenge has been the restoration of security, the introduction of law, and the creation of bodies strong enough to enforce them. From there the revival of trust across clan and provincial cleavages, the reconstruction of a public administration, the building of organizations—political parties, media outlets, NGOs—for civic and civil public debate will not be simple, nor will these nascent institutions necessarily be entirely democratic at the outset. Accomplishing any of this, thus far, has been a struggle.

Indeed, as we have seen, for many Libyans, politics after Qadhafi is played out not in the institutionalized competition of the democratic political process, but in local, tribal, ethnic, and religious struggles. Politics in the new Libya encompasses regional strife, local tensions between old-school Islamists like the increasingly pragmatic Muslim Brotherhood and the newer more uncompromising Salafi and jihadi movements, and overt competition between returned exiles and long-time insiders—anything, in other words, but the conventional ideologically based political parties of Western democratic political practice. Moreover, the years of isolation during international sanctions have meant that the generation now in their thirties and forties is not particularly knowledgeable about the world outside Libya or these practices. Among the many cleavages in Libya, a generational divide looms large and the generation that should be coming into positions of authority is, as yet, poorly prepared to assume the responsibility that awaits them.

In this context, the reintroduction of predictability—of law and order, and accountability—has been exceptionally difficult. Of the tens of thousands of jail guards, favor seekers, government informants, and self-serving bureaucrats, who wheedled special access to schools and medicines for their children, turned a blind eye to smuggled books, and authorized informal exit visas to visit relatives, none are proud of these expedients, but even fewer escaped resorting to them. It was a way to make a livable life in a paradoxical place where money was not scarce, but nearly everything else was. Rebuilding trust, confidence, and pride will require conscious and determined effort.

*   *   *

Yet, as Jason Pack suggests at the end of the Introduction, right below the surface, nestled in the exhaustion, shame, weariness, and pain, is astonishing hope and determination. The remarkable campaign to get out the vote in the first contested elections in nearly sixty years in July 2012—the radio advertisements and billboards that blanketed the country asking people to redeem the sacrifice of the martyrs of the revolution by casting their ballot—conveyed a deep and abiding commitment to making the losses of the last decades into concrete lessons learned. If the new spheres of fairly harmonious public debate implied by the creation of consensus political parties and independent news outlets with a broad appeal come to reflect a measure of shared values and reinforce countrywide identities, then there is reason to think that the General National Congress might be able to manage the task with which it has been entrusted—transition to constitutional democratic governance that instills renewed trust, hope, and confidence in a population that today is still angry, aggrieved, and fearful. It is a tall order, of course, particularly since 40 years of turmoil have led Libyans not only to distrust their government, but also each other.

But many, many Libyans know all too well the costs of sacrificing means to achieve ends and of surrendering rights to acquire privileges, only to later have no recourse when those ends are not realized and those privileges withdrawn. The appetite for new approaches to political debate and contestation is enormous and there is little patience for cosmetic reform. The self-reliance and community bonds of local identities that were strengthened by the statelessness of the Qadhafi era and further fortified during the uprisings may yet prove to be building blocks for a novel experiment in the Arab world: government that is genuinely decentralized but still functional. Revulsion against the arrogance and vanity of charismatic leadership gone sour may encourage respect for rule—not by the alluring or the entitled—but by the qualified. As Jason Pack suggests at the end of his Introduction, if the right balance is struck between forming a "center" capable of governing while devolving enough authority to harness the energy of the "periphery" and counter its centrifugal tendencies, then there is no reason that Libya should not become the envy of the Arab World—a successful postauthoritarian state.

For all of us who would like to see a Libya in which Libyans are pleased and proud to live, not only as members of their local communities, but as participants in a nation and citizens of a state, there is ample cause for concern. But there are equally abundant reasons for optimism, in the slowly accumulating recognition of the satisfactions of ordinary life lived with dignity, freedom, and social justice.

Cairo, November 2012

INDEX

Printed in the United States of America